Economic Thought and Ideology
in Seventeenth-Century England

THE
ADVANCEMENT
OF
MERCHANDIZE:
OR,
CERTAIN PROPOSITIONS
For the Improvment of the Trade of this
Common-wealth, humbly prefented
to the Right Honorable the
Council of State.

AND ALSO,
Againſt the Tranſporting of GOLD and SILVER.

By Tho. VIOLET of *London* Goldſmith.

LONDON,
Printed by *William Du-Gard*, Printer to the *Council*
of State. Anno Dom. 1651.

ECONOMIC THOUGHT

AND

IDEOLOGY

IN

SEVENTEENTH-CENTURY

ENGLAND

By Joyce Oldham Appleby

Princeton
Princeton University Press
1 9 7 8

Copyright © 1978 by Princeton University Press
Published by Princeton University Press, Princeton, New Jersey
In the United Kingdom: Princeton University Press, Guildford, Surrey
All Rights Reserved
Library of Congress Cataloging in Publication Data will
be found on the last printed page of this book
Publication of this book has been aided by a grant from
The Andrew W. Mellon Foundation
This book has been composed in Linotype Baskerville
Printed in the United States of America
by Princeton University Press
Princeton, New Jersey

To
Andrew
for listening and approving

Contents

Preface
ix

One
The Models of Economic Development
3

Two
The Intellectual Response to Economic Crisis
24

Three
The Moral Economy in Retreat
52

Four
The Dutch as a Source of Evidence
73

Five
Contending Views of the Role of the State
99

Six
The Poor as a Productive Resource
129

Seven
A New Argument for Economic Freedom
158

Eight
A Crisis Over Money
199

Nine
An Ideological Triumph
242

Index
281

Preface

This study began with a puzzle and a persuasion. The puzzle was how Adam Smith was able to assume that human beings possessed an innate commercial mentality; the persuasion was that the modern concept of political freedom grew out of a prior reorganization of economic life which gave ordinary men and women a chance to demonstrate the compatibility of free choice and public order and thereby turn the traditional liberties of personal privilege into the natural liberty of a birthright. Both the puzzle and the persuasion carried me back from eighteenth-century America to seventeenth-century England when men initially came to grips with the challenge of explaining the new market forces in their lives. While I found much that I sought in the first public writings on trade, money, and market behavior, the capacity of the past to surprise the present was reaffirmed as well. For instance, the straightforward elaboration of economic theories which I traced from the 1620s came to a halt at the end of the century when the balance-of-trade theory was reasserted in its crudest form. This unexpected development forced me to reconsider economic reasoning as a tension point in the construction of a new social reality. Thus, I started out to explore an intellectual response and have ended with the discovery of an ideological crisis.

The three great collections of seventeenth-century English economic publications are at the British Museum, the Goldsmiths' Library of Economic Literature at the University of London, and the Kress Library of Business and Economics at the Harvard Graduate School of Business. Although the major part of the research for this study was done at the British Museum, I have included references to the numbered entries of the Kress Library Catalogue *of 1950 and the* Supplement *of 1967. These two volumes contain full titles and pertinent bibliographical information and are readily available in American research libraries. At present the Kress and Goldsmiths' Library collections are being filmed for a joint microform edition. Since with few exceptions the English works were published in London, I have included only those names of the cities of publication outside London. Wherever it was possible to establish that a publication date conformed to the old style, I have changed it to the new style date.*

September 1977

Joyce Appleby
San Diego, California

Economic Thought and Ideology
in Seventeenth-Century England

One

The Models of Economic Development

IN THE SIXTEENTH CENTURY NEW PATTERNS of trade linked Europe, Asia, and the Western Hemisphere into a world economy. This development marked the beginning of the end of the old European order.[1] Instead of the rhythmic expansion and contraction of people and their products that had taken place over the past millennium, the gains of the sixteenth century became the departure point for that sustained growth which has characterized the modern world. The moving force behind this change was economic, but the principal effects were social and intellectual. The steady commercialization of grain growing, grazing, fishing, and mining and the increase in cloth making, metalworking, and shipbuilding opened up gainful enterprise to farmers, artisans, clothiers, and landlords. New networks of buyers and sellers replaced the isolated economies of local consumption. Disruptions in the most basic relations made the past an uncertain guide to the future. As the social foundations of work and wealth changed, the forces causing these changes became objects of investigation.

By the beginning of the seventeenth century the persistence of change had brought an end to that equilibrium between people and land, labor and repose, peasant and lord, king and kingdom, production and consumption, custom and circumstance, that had made even the turbulent late Middle Ages appear a part of a timeless order. The distribution of food through the expanding European market

[1] Two very different but important studies of this development are Immanuel Wallerstein, *The Modern World-System*, New York, 1974, and Perry Anderson, *Lineages of the Absolute State*, London, 1974. Subtle implications of their theses are developed by Keith Thomas, *New York Review of Books* 22 (April 17, 1975). See also Ralph Davis, *The Rise of the Atlantic Economies*, Ithaca, New York, 1973.

helped support an upward spiral of people and prices. Specialization, new farming techniques, and more efficient ways of using labor made higher levels of productivity possible, but they were accompanied by overpopulation and inflation. Expanding markets created new interdependent economic units, which proved fragile. When demand for certain goods collapsed, those who lived by that trade suffered. When population outstripped food production, people died of starvation. When those invested with power were unable to maintain order in the face of change, their authority was undermined. To respond positively to the opportunities for further economic development meant to abandon customary ways of holding and working the land. It required the endorsement of new values, the acknowledgement of new occupations and the reassessment of the obligations of the individual to the society. Before these responses could be made, however, people had to perceive the changes and incorporate them into an intelligible account of their meaning. Before there could be new modes of behavior, there had to be ideas to explain them.

This study deals with the way in which the English first described their commercial economy. It traces the intellectual origins of capitalism through some 1,500 treatises, tracts, pamphlets, handbills, and broadsides written by Englishmen during the course of the seventeenth century. This body of economic literature owes its existence, in all probability, to the outpouring of writings on religion and politics. Because much of the conflict among the contending parties during England's century of revolution was waged through the printed word, there developed in England a vigorous public press and an equally novel phenomenon, a reading public. London, which has been praised as a place for conspicuous consumption and a lever under the kingdom's latent productive powers, should also be celebrated as a publishing center. Here were gathered the presses, the bookstores, the writers, and the readers to sustain a rapid acceleration of printed communication. Pamphlets and books streamed from the city's presses, in runs between 500 and 2,000.[2] A dozen titles appeared in the 1620s; by the 1670s hundreds were published each decade. Debates that were once argued exclusively in face-to-face encounters began to take shape through written words addressed to unseen audiences. Alongside the public discourse conducted in the Houses of Parliament, in churches, in corporation meetings, and in the banquet halls of great men, there grew up a new kind of forum where the absence of the immediate presence of speaker or listener made possible a freer, more impersonal kind of exchange. Compared to the number of religious and political tracts, the corpus of seventeenth-century economic writings is small. Its eventual impact, however, was profound for, in the effort to understand and control the new commercial system, the writers created interpretive models that shaped the consciousness of their contemporaries and proved decisive for all subsequent thinking about economic relations. The modern restructuring of England involved thousands of discrete acts, sorted through half-obscure processes of adaptation and reformation. Writings on trade, credit, agricultural improvements, and employment schemes offer a window on one of these—the way Englishmen used their imagination to explain the new market forces in their lives. Because commercial changes were so central to the reshaping of society, the ideas about them were necessarily ideological. Observations, recommendations, and assertions about reality were intertwined, making facts the most powerful carriers of value.

Ideology, as I will use the term, refers to a system of meaning shared by members of a society. Infused into every social act, the common system of meaning supplies information, gives direction, and provides justifications for behavior. Answering what one scholar has called "the human

[2] Philip Gaskell, *A New Introduction to Bibliography*, Oxford, 1972, p. 161. See also Frederick Seaton Siebert, *Freedom of the Press in England 1476-1776*, Urbana, Illinois, 1965.

craving for meaning," ideology forms a bridge between the individual and society. This definition differs from the familiar notion of ideology as a set of ideas adopted to mask special interests. Instead, it draws its inspiration from those sociologists and anthropologists who have emphasized the constructive role of shared beliefs.[3] From these scholars has come also the exploration of the world of consciousness as an ordered one, where ideas organize the perception of members of society and mediate between their experiences and reflections. Like the computer to which the brain is frequently compared, the human being is inert without a plan. Society provides the plan in an elaborate code of symbols. For literate societies an articulated theory undergirds shared beliefs about what is and what ought to be. While every ideological assertion may carry with it an implication about the distribution of power, ideas gain currency only when they serve purposes more comprehensive than those of self-interest. Implicit in this description of ideology is the conviction that a consensus of values makes coherent social action possible by providing, as David Apter has detailed, that solidarity essential to the exercise of authority.[4] Less obvious is the fact that once a satisfactory set of shared explanations has been accepted it acquires an objective reality for those it informs, and only under the most persistent examination does the content of ideology reveal itself as a social product rather than as a reflection of universal truth.[5]

[3] The writings that have influenced my conception of ideology have been Karl Mannheim, *Man and Society in an Age of Reconstruction*, New York, 1940; Peter L. Berger and Thomas Luckmann, *The Social Construction of Reality*, New York, 1966; George Lichtheim, "The Concept of Ideology," *History and Theory* 4 (1965); Norman Birnbaum, "The Sociological Study of Ideology," *Current Sociology* 9 (1960); David E. Apter, "Introduction," and Clifford Geertz, "Ideology as a Cultural System," in Apter, ed., *Ideology and Discontent*, Glencoe, Illinois, 1964.

[4] *Ibid.*, pp. 18-19.

[5] On this point see Peter Berger and Stanley Pullberg, "Reification and the Sociological Critique of Consciousness," *History and Theory* 4 (1965).

Scholarship on the emergence of capitalism has been dominated by two schools of thought: those of classical economics and Marx's dialectical materialism. Because the classical economists took it for granted that human beings would make economically rational choices, they were able to explain the transition from a feudal order to a modern one in terms of impersonal processes. Society as a force that shaped the behavior of its members did not figure in their explanations of change. Instead, the classical economists focused their attention upon the individual in relation to material objects—his or her propensity to truck and barter, to seek gain, to compete for limited resources. "The principal which prompts to save," Smith wrote, "is the desire of bettering our condition, a desire which, though generally calm and dispassionate, comes with us from the womb, and never leaves us till we go into the grave." In the whole interval which separates those two moments, Smith went on to say, "there is scarce perhaps a single instant in which any man is so perfectly and completely satisfied with his situation, as to be without any wish of alteration or improvement of any kind."[6] Subsumed in this description of human motivation is the restless energy and material orientation of Smith's own age. With such a model, one could safely ignore the mores and mentality that might obstruct the natural progress toward productivity and attend to purely technical questions about the accumulation of capital, the extension of the market, and the increase in the division of labor.

The hypotheses of classical economics do more than explain relations; they contain a theory about the causes of economic development. The historian who accepts the general validity of classical economy theory will, therefore, concentrate upon certain factual areas.[7] Events that put capital in the hands of entrepreneurs will receive more attention than shifts in social priorities that encourage free

[6] *An inquiry into the nature and causes of the wealth of nations*, New York, 1937 (originally published in 1776), pp. 324-25.

[7] On this point, see T. S. Ashton, "The Relation of Economic History to Economic Theory," *Economica* 13 (1946), 93.

enterprise. Changes in the terms of trade will appear more important than changes in the personal values and the rewarding system of the society. The microeconomic model of economic relations adopted by Smith and his successors dispensed with the indeterminacy of cultural perceptions by defining them out of existence. In the 1930s the collapse of the western economies undermined the credibility of the market's self-regulating harmony. John Maynard Keynes then shifted attention away from individual economic agents and marginal determinants, and the economy as a whole reappeared as an analytical concept.[8] Yet the Keynesian revolution has not produced a redrawing of the economic person. There persists in the English-speaking world a widely shared presumption that political and economic liberalism so adequately meets the basic needs of human beings that its acceptance in the early modern period may be taken as a natural response.[9]

In this, continental European attitudes differ. As R. H. Tawney pointed out long ago, the modern transformation of the English economy took place over so long a period of time that the categories of thought associated with capitalism appeared to the English as timeless forms imprinted on the very stuff of the human brain.[10] While two centuries of agricultural and commercial change preceded England's industrialization, Germans, French, and Italians saw their economies wrenched from an age-old structure within a

[8] John Maynard Keynes, *The General Theory of Employment, Interest, and Money*, New York, 1967 (originally published in 1935), pp. 333-71; Joseph A. Schumpeter, *History of Economic Analysis*, Oxford, 1954, pp. 335-76; Mark Blaug, "Economic Theory and Economic History in Great Britain, 1650-1776," *Past and Present* 28 (July 1964); and Alexander Gerschenkron, "History of Economic Doctrines and Economic History," *American Economic Review* 59 (1969), 1-17.

[9] Joan Robinson, "What has become of the Keynesian Revolution?" *Challenge* 16 (1974); and Ronald Meek, *Economics and Ideology*, London, 1967, pp. 210-15

[10] "Essays in Bibliography and Criticism: XIII. A History of Capitalism," *Economic History Review* 2nd ser. 2 (1950), 307.

single generation.[11] This dimension of time powerfully affected the perception of the change. For those on the continent, industrialization was a radical force that required explanation; for the English, the final stages of advanced capitalism appeared as the end product of what seemed a predictable and wholly natural progression. Modes of behavior shaped by a commercial society were viewed as characteristics of human nature in general. Relationships in a modern economy appeared as laws of nature, applicable to all societies and discoverable through empirical investigations. It is not then surprising that much of the early scholarship on the social nature of reality came from the continent. European scholars—especially Germans working within the folds of the nineteenth-century historical school —could not accept the self-evident association of modern behavior and human nature. Modernization appeared to them as an historical force rather than a natural process. Through their analyses, the shaping fingers of society replaced the invisible hand of the market.

From Karl Marx came the central contention that it is not the consciousness of men that determines existence, but, on the contrary, their social being that determines their consciousness.[12] This observation gave birth to the sociology of knowledge and the redirection of epistemology from the mind of human beings to the social context in which people think. For Marx, however, there was nothing open-ended about this connection. Consciousness was joined to a fixed chain of causal links: societies of human beings must produce to survive, individual members are forced to assume particular roles in production, the different roles create

[11] This difference is explored in Bert F. Hoselitz, *Sociological Aspects of Economic Growth*, Glencoe, Illinois, 1960, pp. 20ff; Norman Birnbaum, "Conflicting Interpretations of the Rise of Capitalism," *British Journal of Sociology* 4 (1953); and Erskine McKinley, "Mankind in the History of Economic Thought," in Hoselitz, ed., *Economics and the Idea of Mankind*, New York, 1965.

[12] As cited in Erich Fromm, ed., *Marx's Concept of Man*, New York, 1961, p. 19.

classes that are external to the individual member, the class that benefits most from the prevailing mode of production controls the terms of social existence for others, which precipitates conflicts between the classes. Therefore all social consciousness reflects the ideals, modes of thought, and rationalizations of the dominant class.

Marx thus directed historians to the actions of the culture-forming class. Where the classical economists ascribed economic growth to a series of interlocking mechanisms supported by the nature of man and the geographic juxtaposition of nation states, the Marxist interpretation relied on an inexorable dialectic of social forces set in motion by the material conditions of life and the relationships of different groups to them. In Marx's analysis, novelty enters human experience through representatives of an antagonistic system of production who form the values, techniques, and political instruments necessary to destroy the old ways and institutionalize the new. Historical investigators need only to locate the agents of the new class—in the case of early modern England, the bourgeoisie—in order to lay bare the origins of change.[13]

Marx's concept of a vanguard class creating the coherent structure of ideas that forms the modern world view is more a description of, than an explanation for, the innovating forces of seventeenth-century England. The rise to power of a new class is very persuasive, as is the whole notion of a fresh class consciousness arising from new social tasks, but there is no conclusive evidence that the socially innovative ideas came from members of a new class. More serious still is the lack of proof that a bourgeoisie or middle class came to power in England during the early modern period when the market became the dominant economic institution.[14] Despite the frequency with which the "rising middle class"

[13] Birnbaum, "Conflicting Interpretations," 130-32; Lichtheim, "Concept of Ideology," pp. 180ff.

[14] J. H. Hexter, "The Myth of the Middle Class in Tudor England," *Reappraisals in History*, London, 1961.

is invoked, events in England indicate that the most important change was the reorientation of goals and ideals of England's hereditary leaders. If a middle class did in fact emerge and improve its social standing, it coalesced with, rather than displaced, the existing ruling class.[15] The process through which both landlords and merchants were able to reshape social thought is not disclosed by the assertion that it happened.

Although it is plausible that interests inform our opinions, subtly predisposing us to believe those things that it benefits us to believe, it is equally obvious that interests do not have the field of belief to themselves. Where new ideas must make way in the face of entrenched belief, their reception depends in part upon their attractions for others besides those who benefit directly. Certainly, to attract support, ideas must be capable of serving more interests than their authors', which is another way of saying that the ideas must facilitate the attainment of widely shared goals. Equally troublesome from a theoretical point of view is Marx's insistence that people holding similar ideas must have formed alliances prior to the acceptance of the ideas rather than subsequently. Marx's explanation for the formation of classes and ideology is grounded on his contention that group loyalties grow out of economic relations, that people joined by a common interest in a system of production adopt similar beliefs, which further cements solidarity. Such a developmental sequence rests on Marx's belief that it is in and through action that thought arises. However, since ideas are more often selected than created, it could well be that men coalesce into a new ruling class in recognition of commonly held opinions. In this case, the origins of the agents of historical change would be less important than the shared attitude to material changes from people of differing backgrounds. While a new ideology is required to rationalize new forms of social organization, there is no necessity for

15 Lawrence Stone, *The Causes of the English Revolution, 1529-1642*, London, 1972, pp. 54ff.

new men—in the sense of parvenus—to be the innovators. Social change through economic development requires not a new class but a modern class, however formed. In all probability this new elite achieved dominance because its members saw and articulated the social possibilities implicit in the new situation.[16] If this is so, we are once more thrown back upon the fundamental task of explaining the intellectual response that permitted the development of modern society.

Both Marxist and classical economic theories about change have forced historical inquiry along lines laid out by their *a priori* assumptions. In neither case have the theories been entirely satisfying on the empirical level, although the stimulus to scholarship could hardly be exaggerated. Classical economic theory directed attention to uniformities that connected certain economic phenomena, making it possible for historians to see how thousands of discrete acts of buying and selling could be studied as parts of a self-sustaining mechanism. Classical economists showed how the market would perform in a social environment favorable to the spread of commerce.[17] Marx, on the other hand, returned historical inquiry to questions about the class determinants of that favorable environment. He recaptured the sense that capitalism was an historical development. Despite the determinism of his own theory, he liberated investigators from the tyranny of an empiricism based on a universal human nature.

Into the interstices of Marx's generalizations about the class origins of ideology moved Max Weber. Where Marx had assumed that the dominant class created and popularized its world view, Weber explored what was involved in

[16] On this point see George Lukács, *History and Class Consciousness*, trans. by Rodney Livingstone, Cambridge, 1971 (originally published in 1923), pp. 52ff.

[17] For an assessment of how continuities and discontinuities in market developments have influenced economic theory see Meek, *Economics and Ideology*, pp. 179-95.

belief in general, imputing to human psychology "an inner necessity to comprehend the world as a meaningful cosmos."[18] For Weber, the capitalist revolution did not require a new class so much as a new ethic. "Man does not by nature wish to earn more and more money," he wrote, "but simply to live as he is accustomed to live and to earn as much as is necessary for that purpose."[19] Against that ingrained and socially formed predisposition toward stable economic patterns, Weber saw Evangelical Protestantism, especially Calvinism, thrusting a new man of exalted spiritual ambition. A worldly ascetic bound to work, self-discipline, and the rationalization of daily habits, Calvin's new man carried his religious attitudes into the marketplace. With this radical reordering of the human personality, the qualities originally dedicated to God became available for demanding new economic tasks. In vivid contrast to classical economic theory, which assumed a human nature inherently geared to ceaseless economic striving, Weber viewed the emergence of this behavior as the key development to be explained. The dimension of the historian's task stood forth sharply in Weber's presentation: modernization requires a radical transformation of human habits in the interest of purposes as yet unperceived. If material achievements were valued only at the end of a train of advances, what prompted the redirection of social effort toward market production in the first place? How could a society reject an order hallowed by custom and reinforced by habituation for another social organization as yet unimagined? Small wonder that he turned to religion as the initiator of a change that called

[18] *Wirtschaft und Gesellschaft*, vol. 1, Tubingen, 1947, as trans. and cited in Birnbaum, "Conflicting Interpretations," p. 126. For a fine analysis of the assumptions that led Weber to concentrate upon formal religion, see David Little, *Religion, Order, and Law*, New York, 1969.

[19] *The Protestant Ethic and the Spirit of Capitalism*, trans. by Talcott Parsons, New York, 1958 (originally published in 1904-06), p. 60. For a recent assessment of Weber's purposes see Ehud Sprinzak, "Weber's Thesis as an Historical Explanation," *History and Theory* 11 (1972).

forth supreme sacrifices for goals as yet uncherished. Weber speculated that, for God, men might be able to do what, as social beings, they could never do for themselves.

There are lacunae, however, in the association of Calvinism and capitalism. The unrevolutionary pace of English economic change required persisting influences effective through many generations, but religion had spent its force in England before the modern restructuring was half complete. If part of the Puritan legacy found permanence in new patterns of behavior and other parts were jettisoned, then historical attention must fall upon the sorting process itself. What forces determined which characteristics endured? There is the additional problem of explaining those Puritan attitudes that were antithetical to the development of the market economy. The very powerful religious character of all Calvinist ideas inhibited the freeing of economic activities from social control. Yet this secularization of economic life was basic to the triumph of a capitalistic organization grounded upon the right and efficacy of private, economic decision making. The ideology that made possible the material orientation of modern society had to facilitate a shift of loyalties from the sacred to the profane without a disruptive demoralization of society.[20] Weber's famous thesis tells only part of the story. Like Marx's theory of the class-based formation of ideology, Weber's analysis of the spirit of capitalism rests upon the assumption that, having established one vital link, the rest of the chain can be taken for granted.

In another elaboration of Marx's insights, the market mechanism has been named the force behind sustained social change.[21] Once economic power is redistributed to

[20] On this point see Neil Smelzer, "Mechanisms of Change and Adjustment to Change," in Bert F. Hoselitz and Wilbert E. Moore, eds., *Industrialization and Society*, The Hague, 1968, p. 38.

[21] C. B. Macpherson, *The Political Theory of Possessive Individualism*, Oxford, 1962, pp. 48ff; George Dalton, "Economic Theory and Primitive Society," *American Anthropologist* 63 (1961); and Eric

those who embrace the productive ideal, their leverage as buyers, investors, and employers is seen as moving the rest of society. The critical step in establishing a market momentum is the alienation of land and labor. When these fundamental components of social existence come under the influence of the price mechanism, social direction itself passes to economic determinants. Where labor has become a commodity, C. B. Macpherson has written, "market relations so shape or permeate all social relations that it may properly be called a market society, not merely a market economy."[22] The market, in this view, exerts pressures in many ways: as a persistent force for the efficient allocation of resources; as a depersonalizing mechanism using men and women as things; as a promoter of economic liberties; as à purveyor of new attitudes about utility; as an all-pervasive pedagogue teaching people to plan, economize, calculate. In the social criticism of Karl Polanyi, the market becomes the source of a new utopian vision of freedom in which society is conceived of as functioning without power and compulsion. The self-regulating features of the market suggested this vision, Polanyi said, the dream itself being "the result of a market-view of society which equated economics with contractural relationships, and contractural relations with freedom."[23]

The influence of so central an institution as the market cannot be denied, but the real question is how the market becomes central in a given society. The countless examples of markets confined to the modest activity of exchanging commodities indicate that the critical precondition for the spread of the market's influence lies in the social acceptability of buying and selling land and labor. Clearly, only human beings are capable of making decisions, and the

---

Hobsbawm, "The Seventeenth Century in the Development of Capitalism," *Science and Society* 24 (1960).

22 *Political Theory of Possessive Individualism*, p. 48.

23 *The Great Transformation*, New York, 1944, p. 258.

acceptance of a market in land and labor represents a crucial cultural change rather than an automatic response to the existence of a mechanism for exchanging goods. Moreover, as Polanyi's comparative studies have shown, the extent of the market is limited by the social purposes expressed through the market; only if the pursuit of unlimited profit becomes a socially acceptable goal can the market exercise the pervasive influence attributed to it.[24] Once properly tuned to a new social ethic, however, the market can become a powerful instrument for change.

In none of these interpretations of the emergence of capitalism has there been an attempt to examine the exact way in which the reconceptualization of economic life took place or to explore the ideas first used to understand the workings of the market. It has been assumed that the process of modernization is comprehended by its causes, that once the formation of a new class or the accumulation of capital or the articulation of a new ethic is detected, the means by which this new historical force imposes itself upon actual events is unimportant. The modern transformation of European society has been viewed as a process rather than a series of developments capable of leading to conclusions other than the one actually realized. The means to change are thus subordinated to the initial cause or causes. Means become important, however, if one assumes that there is not an overarching determinant in human affairs but rather a constant flow of events where the consequences of each historical moment become an influence upon the next, each sequence carrying with it possibilities that may not be realized, but are nonetheless realizable. If human events are the results of actions by persons or groups coping selectively with the problems and opportunities in their lives, then it is

[24] *The Great Transformation*, pp. 43-67. For a discussion of Polanyi's work, see S. C. Humphreys, "History, Economics and Anthropology: The Work of Karl Polanyi," *History and Theory* 8 (1969). For one of the earliest discussions of this point, see Charles Horton Cooley, *Social Process*, New York, 1918, pp. 295ff.

to those acts and the ideas that prompted them that we must look for the clues about the restructuring of English society.

During the last twenty years social historians have conducted the kind of research that makes it difficult to believe in single, all-powerful forces in human affairs. Through investigations of the multifarious details of everyday life in the early modern centuries, they have been able to reveal the extraordinary complexity of developments that touch at the same time the family, the local community, the national economy, and the body politic.[25] As sweeping generalizations about enclosure movements and price revolutions have been replaced by detailed studies of changes in land-ownership, population growth, agricultural technology, labor mobility, and shifts in capital investments, the historian has come to appreciate how erratic the momentum behind change was. The crucial element of timing—that is the necessity for a synchronization of developments before a major shift in population or production could take place—has drawn attention to the uncertainty of the line of progress that leads away from reliance upon tradition.

Easier to describe than explain, the creation of the first modern society continues to provoke analysis because the career of modernization has yet to run its course. In the past two decades, events in the economically backward nations of the world have posed fresh questions for the historian of early modern England. Changes that could once be accepted as natural, if not automatic, no longer appear so. Where even twenty years ago problems of growth and

[25] E.g. Robert Brenner, "Agrarian Class Structure and Economic Development in Pre-Industrial Europe," *Past and Present* 70 (1976) 30-74; J. D. Chambers, *Population, Economy, and Society in Pre-Industrial England*, Oxford, 1972; J. P. Cooper, "The Social Distribution of Land and Men in England, 1436-1700," *Economic History Review* 2nd ser. 20 (1967); D.E.C. Eversley, "Population, Economy and Society," in D. V. Glass and Eversley, eds., *Population in History*, London, 1965; and E. L. Jones, "Agriculture and Economic Growth in England, 1660-1750," *Journal of Economic History* 25 (1965), 1-18.

development were treated in terms of the material resources of a country, the indeterminate response of members of traditional societies to the pressure to modernize has focused attention upon the intangible aspects of social change: attitudes, imaginative responses, moral codes, adaptability, casts of mind. Writing about the social resistance to change, Robert Solo has remarked that anything that "relates to that incapacity must be opened to inquiry."[26] If this holds true for developing nations today, then the reverse can be said of the first modern transformation: anything that relates to that capacity must be opened to inquiry.

The ability to invest the new market relations with an accessible logic should not be taken for granted. Material changes in England prompted a sustained effort to explain them. Through published writings a conception of a commercial economy took shape. Awareness of this intellectual achievement has been obscured by the classical economists' assumption that the economy was a natural phenomenon and by the Marxists' belief that the benefits accruing to a capitalist class accounted for the ideas that were formed about the economy. Neither school of thought has approached the intellectual response to capitalism as a creative social act. Yet a close examination of the writings on economic topics in seventeenth-century England reveals distinctly radical reworkings of the meaning of wealth, money,

[26] *Economic Organization and Social Systems*, Indianapolis, 1967, p. 358. Solo goes on to say, "the economist needs a conceptual framework that will encompass the whole of a society, enabling him to take into systematic account the diverse elements relevant to the organization of coherent, effective social action and (hence) fundamental change." A new group of scholars, effectively represented by Immanuel Wallerstein, "The Rise and Future Demise of the World Capitalist System: Concepts for Comparative Analysis," *Comparative Studies in Society and History* 16 (1974), 392ff, has criticized the concept of underdeveloped nations because of the implication that there are no discernible forces preventing the nations' development. The differing responses of these nations, however, would indicate that there are factors in their own culture relevant to their development, the actions of western nations notwithstanding.

private initiative, economic growth, and the motive of gain. The writers whose purpose was to persuade readers to support such things as statutory limits on interest rates or prohibitions on wool exports created an abstract model of the economy in order to make their points. Seeking to illuminate specific activities, they adopted a way of analyzing human behavior that was easily transferred to discussions in the political domain. Indeed, since the men and women who in their tracts figured as workers, lenders, investors, and consumers were also society's parents, subjects, and communicants, the containment of economic reasoning was impossible. It is in this sense that the initial effort to explain the wide-ranging influence of the free market became a part of the secular ideology that replaced traditional social assumptions in England by the end of the century.

Peter Laslett has reminded us that "the world we have lost" is so irretrievably lost that we have made up a myth to fill the gap in our memory. In that mythic preindustrial era we imagine people joined in communities where work and play, obligation and reward, habit and precedent, composed a way of life accepted unquestionably as man's lot under God's dispensation.[27] Confirmatory evidence for such a world is disconcertingly hard to find. Each cut of the historian's axe backward into the layers of the past proves that the roots of modern society are very deep, and the ordered world against which to project the disruptive forces of modernity retreats. Yet the seventeenth century brought fundamental changes to England, and contemporaries were aware of them. New phenomena challenged people's capacity for comprehension and mastery. New sources of authority emerged; new explanations took shape; new sensibilities entered into social life to redirect energies and redistribute emotional attachments.

By the beginning of the seventeenth century, English

[27] *The World We Have Lost*, London, 1965, pp. 3-8. See also William J. Goode, *The Family*, Englewood Cliffs, New Jersey, 1964, pp. 238-39, 251.

statesmen had ceased to think of turning back to a more contained economy in order to prevent the social disruptions produced by the acceleration of commerce.[28] Changes brought about by a century-long inflation, by overpopulation, by a redistribution of incomes unrelated to the traditional allocation by privilege or prescriptive right, had persisted long enough to be taken for permanent elements in the social situation. The dislocations unmistakably associated with the producing and marketing of agricultural and industrial goods in the 1620s prompted wide-ranging discussions focusing on relevant economic factors. There was enough disruption in social life over a long enough period to make new assessments both possible and necessary. Traditional expectations lost their credibility, and the increasing invisibility of buyers and sellers prompted men to treat them as impersonal economic agents. Harvest-destroying rains could be seen, felt, smelled. Gluts in foreign markets had to be imagined, and persistent gluts could be explained only through a more elaborate concept of commercial relations. The removal of key links in production and consumption from the range of tactile experience promoted the creation of symbolic representations. Price, rate, and credit began to stand in place of the bargain, the payment, the contract they represented.

Precept and habituation channel our perceptions of the external world. Imagination and memory transform individual experiences into a private mental world. Expectations are a kind of prediction that human beings make in order to mediate between their past and their future. Novelty acts like a wedge between the social and the private world, for it is thrust in between what has been learned and what must be coped with spontaneously by the single person. It undermines confidence in habits. It frustrates anticipations. It forces the imagination to rearrange remembered experience. Because men and women think about what they

[28] B. E. Supple, *Commercial Crisis and Change in England, 1600-1642*, Cambridge, 1959, pp. 231ff.

do, there is a constant interaction between the real and the objectification of the real. Any divergences between the two must provoke thought about the gap. For historians, the question is to discover what form reflections took and how certain concepts succeeded in satisfying the need to understand. The extension of the market in England throughout the seventeenth century is not in doubt. Nor is the fact that economic acts fell more and more within the ambit of private transactions. What needs to be detailed is the process through which men and women changed their ideas about the production and distribution of goods.

For over a century hundreds of new relationships had appeared in production and trade, in the mobilization of labor, and the exchange of coins. Initially, the men who wrote on economic life had no analytical framework for discussing the shaping force of the market. Nor, indeed, at the beginning of the period had the single abstract market yet emerged in men's minds as an appropriate representation for the hundreds of formal and informal exchanges that regularly took place. These speculative thinkers enjoyed a freedom from a consensus on the meaning of the evidence. They lacked a paradigm and the unambiguous identification of specific theories with their social implications. In fact, the recording of observations on the new economic phenomena went on simultaneously with the construction of a framework for analysis. However, by the time the merchants and policy makers who adumbrated the new science of economics turned over their field to Scottish philosophers, the foundations for classical economic thought had already been laid. The choice had been made between a macro- and a microeconomic model. The centrifugal forces had been legitimized; the idea of inexorable economic laws had been accepted. The quantitative properties of people, land, and movable goods had found a common denominator in price. Abstractions describing commercial transactions had become more real in men's discourse than the tactile and concrete context in which they happened. Economic life had been· successfully differentiated from the society it served. There was still tension between the interests of the whole and the individual, but the concept of a social goal greater than the sum of private ones appeared less as an eternal verity and more as a vestigial notion.

Historians have criticized seventeenth-century pamphleteers for their obvious self-interest in the issues they attempted to clarify. Such charges are irrelevant to this inquiry, which asks instead why certain explanations satisfied and others did not? Why did analogies to beehives illuminate economic truths while comparisons to the heavenly hierarchy or the elements of a biblical parable did not? Assuming that every writer seeks to establish a vital connection with his or her audience, the means chosen to accomplish this connection are significant. The material conditions of English life changed in the seventeenth century and prompted some participants to explain and justify, others to attack, the innovations introduced. The modes of argument also changed during the course of the century. To what resources of logic, evidence, and moral values did these pamphleteers resort? What impact did particular lines of reasoning have on subsequent intellectual trends? How did observations on economic activities influence the emerging modern world view? These are the questions this study will address.

The advent of the market, and the reorganization of social life through it, made men reconsider the terms of their lives. Like the simultaneous effort to reimagine the mechanical relationships of the physical universe, the process of conceiving the market economy became an intellectual influence of paramount importance to the developments it investigated. The imaginative reconstruction of economic relations by seventeenth-century thinkers created new truths, suggested possible activities, imposed moral lessons, and contributed analogies to the other areas of social thinking. As men studied the market, they in turn were changed by their studies. The order they discerned became an object and was given a power in the minds of its creators and their contemporaries. The selection of analytical tools became social determinants because the new economic concepts influenced policies. They also contributed to the ideology that produced a socially cohesive movement toward the modern restructuring of their society. It is this intellectual development that will be traced in the following chapters.

Two

The Intellectual Response to Economic Crisis

THE WEIGHT OF ENGLISH SOCIAL THOUGHT
shifted to its modern foundations during the course of the
seventeenth century. In politics the movement was abrupt
and jarring, brought to a head in the Civil War and accompanied by a body of great literature. The break with
the past was unmistakable. Never again could a mindless
traditionalism take the place of an articulated theory of
government. Even as the personnel of the losing side re-
assumed positions of power in the 1660s, the silent memory
of heroic civil disobedience marked the breach between the
old monarchy and the new. The terms of obedience were
different. The collective consciousness had changed. The
elaborate rationale for legitimate rule set forth in the works
of Filmer, Hobbes, Harrington, Sydney, and Locke paid
tribute to the unspoken demand for an explanation of the
power which men once justified through myth and ceremony. A conservatism that earlier could be assumed was
pushed to explicit justification. Political thought no longer
appeared in a religious context, and religion itself became
differentiated from the social activities it had once mediated.
As the state disentangled its authority from God's, Englishmen in the course of the century separated their religious
lives from their secular ones, restricting worship to a new
sphere of relevance.

Economic thought, which played so large a part in the
modern world-view being formed in the seventeenth century, did not have behind it the long intellectual traditions
of theology or political philosophy. It had no place as a
separate field of inquiry. When Aristotle talked of economies he spoke of the types of households, that is, of the
units in the social structure. In the writings of the church
fathers, economic ideas were embedded in texts on vice and

virtue. There was little in the contained, face-to-face direct consumption economies of the late Middle Ages to stimulate speculation on economic topics. The organization of agricultural duties was simple. Even with the introduction of new crops there were few alternatives to the way things were done, and continued reliance upon local food supplies made the basic farm tasks critically important. Low-level crop yields placed population in constant jeopardy. The propriety of political control went unquestioned. In the law economic relationships appeared enmeshed in a social context where duties and rights were closely tied to the needs of security and survival. As long as the principal elements in the economic structure remained visible and tangible, the understanding of the system was the possession of the whole society.

All of this changed with the expansion of trade in the sixteenth and seventeenth centuries. Commercialism, with its free-floating price and profit system, spread from the cities to the countryside. A new network of communications superimposed itself upon the kingdom, breaking down the barriers of local markets. Incentives for increased production went hand in hand with the cost advantages of specialization and economies of size. Production for an expandable market presented Englishmen with more choices, more options, more decisions. An economy contained within the limits of supply slowly became attuned to the peculiarities of demand. Individual tastes registered anonymously in unseen transactions acquired a new power. Central to the creation of a kingdomwide market was a new level of food production, which released labor for other commercial activities and helped put famine out of mind. In the commercially integrated economy, consumer preferences, the size of markets, transportation efficiencies, and the medium of payments became more important than the quantity of any particular harvest. No less vulnerable than the economy of direct consumption, the seventeenth-century commercial order of England was exposed to a new battery of dislocating forces: international competition, monetary fluctuations, and discontinuities in the levels of supply and demand. No longer visible and tangible, the economy became generally incomprehensible.

Mastery of the details of the new market economy was an intellectual task. Without it there could be no effective planning or control. The first men to engage in a sustained analysis of economic relations were the writers of the seventeenth century whom Adam Smith described as the authors of the mercantile system. Smith and most nineteenth-century economists and historians have given special attention to the mercantilists' support of governmental regulation of the economy. Indeed, confronted with increased knowledge about the diversity of their opinions, historians have concluded that the only common thread among these writings is a tolerance of state intervention in economic matters.[1] This judgment is an anachronism that tells more about the period in which it was made than the object under observation. To define mercantilists by their reliance upon the political control of economic life separates them from the nineteenth century but certainly does not divide them from the preceding period. The minute details of economic activity had always been controlled by society through custom and law. It is the differentiation of things economic from their social context that truly distinguishes the writings of the so-called mercantilist period, not their infusion of social and political goals into economic policy. This requires no historical explanation; it is as old as the first social organization of human beings.

The traditional interpenetration of economic and social concerns can best be seen in the policies and statutes of the Tudors. It was to this intellectual world, not that of their successors, that the seventeenth-century writers addressed themselves. The growth of the intra-European market in

---

[1] Eli Heckscher, "Revisions in Economic History: Mercantilism," *Economic History Review* 1st ser. 7 (1936); Herbert Heaton, "Heckscher on Mercantilism," *Journal of Political Economy* 45 (1937).

cloth, timber, fish, coal, and metals brought wealth to many Englishmen, but the focus of royal policy and the over-whelming concern of those charged with executing the laws lay with maintaining social order. For the Tudor monarchs this was made difficult by a substantial increase in population, rising prices, and a growing number of families dependent upon the cloth trade for their support.[2] The sustained increase of births over deaths pushed cultivation to the famine-postponing margins of arable land and turned sons and daughters of poor families into vagabonds and beggars—the masterless men and women that clogged the roads during the late Elizabethan period. The expansion of English woolen exports created jobs for an increasing number of families in East Anglia, the West Country, and Yorkshire, but simultaneously created a new category of industrial workers whose survival was intimately connected with international trade factors outside the control of English rulers. The influx of gold and silver from the mines of Spain's New World empire made European trade relations extremely volatile, exacerbating the inflation caused by high food prices and redistributing incomes in unexpected ways.[3] These disruptive forces led to the enunciation of policies that made explicit the Tudor commitment to stability through the subordination of economic life to social and political considerations.

The fundamental importance of food production stands out in the Tudor codification of laws against forestalling, regrating, and engrossing.[4] In these explicit denials of the

[2] Karl Helleiner, "The Population of Europe from the Black Death to the Eve of the Vital Revolution," *Cambridge Economic History of Europe*, vol. 4, Cambridge, 1967; and Barry Emmanuel Supple, *Commercial Crisis and Change in England, 1600-1642*, Cambridge, 1959, pp. 2ff.

[3] J. D. Gould, *The Great Debasement*, Oxford, 1970, pp. 114ff; Peter Ramsey, *Tudor Economic Problems*, London, 1963.

[4] E. P. Thompson, "The Moral Economy of the English Crowd in the Eighteenth Century," *Past and Present* 50 (1971), 83ff; Margaret Gay Davies, *The Enforcement of English Apprenticeship*, Cambridge,

food producers' freedom to manipulate the market for personal gain, the Tudors, like their predecessors, were affirming their conviction that the growing and marketing of corn, the milling of flour, and the baking of bread were principally social rather than economic activities. Grain was not seen as a commodity to be moved through the countryside in search of the best price, nor was it ever absolutely possessed by the producer. The farmer who grew it—be he tenant or landlord—did not really own the corn; he attended it during its passage from the field to the market. He could not store it in order to wait for a more propitious moment of sale; he could not move it to a distant market; he could not sell it to a middleman, a regrater, while it stood in the field. Rather, he must load up his carts with his grain, proceed to the nearest market, and offer his year's harvest to his traditional customers. Similarly, the miller and the baker were constrained to push the grain processing along in an orderly fashion to its final form as a loaf of bread selling at a price set by the local assize court. If people died from hunger, as they did in the last decade of Elizabeth's reign,[5] they did so blaming the harvest not the harvester. In a later age the regrating and engrossing that figured so large in statute law would be innocuously described as waiting for a better market, but their clear interference with feeding the people put these activities in a different light in the Tudor era. At a time when the tiller of the soil had God to thank for the weather and the king to thank for his land, manipulating the fruits of the two could easily be viewed as wicked and ungrateful.

The selling of wares in towns and cities was as closely guarded by the company of craftsmen as the justices of the peace watched grain sales. Again, the social purpose of labor

1956, pp. 10ff; and Edgar Augustus Johnson, *Some Origins of the Modern Economic World*, New York, 1936, pp. 96-97.

[5] Andrew B. Appleby, "Disease or Famine? Mortality in Cumberland and Westmorland, 1580-1640," *Economic History Review* 2nd ser. 26 (1973).

predominated. A body of craftsmen was first of all a body of household heads whose families and apprentices depended upon a regular and regularized trade. The pitting of skilled workman against skilled workman would neither promote the practice of their craft nor the well-being of their households. Restrictions drawn up by companies of craftsmen and honored by the law supplied the direction sure to be lost if every one looked out for himself. Trading companies followed a similar organizational plan. Cities might compete with cities and nations with nations but, within a town or an agricultural community, order was imposed.

The Statute of Artificers and the famous Elizabethan Poor Laws attempted to deal with the disordering population growth. Alarmed by the roving bands of beggars and vagabonds, which at the time were perceived not as extra sons and daughters but as the displaced poor, the government sought valiantly to replant its people in their native soil.[6] The Statute of Artificers, prescribing the standards for all contracted services in the country, wrote into law the ideal of a settled population where each laborer had his superior. Employers were bound to keep their wage servants for at least a year, to observe the statutory limit in wages, and determine when a laborer might responsibly move to another area. Equally concerned with reknitting the old social fabric, the Poor Laws reaffirmed society's commitment to feed its members and look to their need for work. Both statutes looked backward to the time when one's birth cast a shadow as long as life itself; both sought to reestablish through national authority the local responsibility that was so clearly being disrupted by forces beyond local control.

The social order reflected in these statutes is the traditional one where each person's status and location is prescribed, duties and responsibilities are fixed, purposes clear, and commitments arranged hierarchically: to God, to king,

---

[6] Davies, *Enforcement of English Apprenticeship*, pp. 2-10.

to overlord, to one's superiors, to one's dependents. There was no truly economic Tudor legislation, for statesmen did not then distinguish the grain trade from the social cycle of harvesting, marketing, and feeding. The capacity of a weavers' loom to support four families predominated over considerations of the woolen industry as a discrete economic unit. Setting the price of bread required information about the household expenses of the baker rather than the methods of baking.[7] When disruptions menaced the ability of English society to feed its members and keep them firmly settled in an appropriate station in life, royal authority moved in to give direction, fix responsibilities, and apply old wisdom to the new situation.

The Tudor legacy to their Stuart successors of the seventeenth century was a style of government that has been called patrimonial. As Max Weber defined the term, it represented a significant variation of a traditional exercise of power.[8] Patrimonialism offers a responsiveness to new circumstances that is expressed through the personal authority of the king but does not involve structural changes in society. Under the aegis of the king, new industries may be started, new trades may be licensed, even new forms of legal action opened up. The power and prestige of the king make acceptable breaches in tradition that would otherwise be unthinkable. The king's approval justifies the novelty; the king's disapproval signals its discontinuance. A measure of flexibility is thus added to the rigidity of a traditional order but, since the means of change is the personal will of the monarch, an element of capriciousness is introduced as well. This was the Tudor legacy, but when Stuart kings attempted to take possession of their ideological inheritance,

[7] Peter Laslett, *The World We Have Lost*, New York, 1965, p. 1; Supple, *Commercial Crisis*, p. 2; Stone, "Social Mobility in England, 1500-1700," *Past and Present* 33 (1966), 52.

[8] For an interesting assessment of the Puritan opposition to patrimonialism, see David Little, *Religion, Order, and Law*, New York, 1969, pp. 16-18.

royal prerogatives became the targets of organized opposition.

The social underpinnings of the old Tudor order were badly shaken by the economic developments that turned England's peripheral location in a Mediterranean-dominated Europe into the center of an expanding Atlantic trade. James I arrived on the English throne with the expectation that the traditional subordination of subjects to royal authority would prevail. Instead, he and the members of England's landed class quickly became adversaries. King, nobles, and commoners were forced to adjust to a complicated, if crude, new set of interdependent relations. The intrusion of royal will in the economic domain sent reverberations far beyond the immediate act. James's money problems forced him to summon Parliament and, once summoned, the members formed the kinds of alliances that turned local issues into national concerns. Outside Parliament's doors in London were also the great merchants, their bankers, and suppliers whose enterprise and capital had laid the foundation for England's globe-girdling trades. In this great administrative and commercial capital were the elements for a new political nation joined by a common exposure to the vicissitudes of a primitive commercial organization and a shared interest in those decisions Parliament and the Court made in response to changing circumstances. Here, too, sprang up the public press, which permitted a new vehicle for discussion, interpretation, and persuasion.

Unlike other European countries, in England the nobility and gentry became deeply involved in the commercial restructuring of their country's economy. Through this involvement, England's traditional leaders identified themselves with the innovating forces of their times. During the inflation that reached England in the second half of the sixteenth century, the members of the landed class had been hard hit. The terms of customary tenantry that had previously contributed to their stable social position caused the instability of fixed incomes in a time of rising prices. However, the deteriorating position of the nobility turned out to be temporary. Continued population growth and widening European markets in foodstuffs, minerals, and fibers offered exceptional opportunities for profitable enterprise to those with access to the resources of the land. Through renegotiated leases, efficient methods of estate management, and new mining ventures, many decayed estates were repaired and put on modern footings.[9] Between 1608 and 1620, when Europe enjoyed a respite from war, the nobility and gentry began buying joint stock trading shares. True to their social moorings, the genteel investors favored those commercial enterprises that turned England into a colonizing power.[10] Thus, as members of England's landed class shed their traditional economic attitudes, they transformed the social meaning of economic decisions. Identifying themselves with national ambitions, they carried concern for England's progressive economic development into Parliament.

The king was also a landlord, and the inflation that pushed prices well ahead of returns from rents affected him most of all. Elizabeth had left her successor a depleted treasury, and James's extravagance increased the gap between expenditures and revenues. The ill-defined scope of royal prerogatives offered the means for the king to tap the prosperity that followed the expansion of peacetime trade. A judgment from the Court of the Exchequer confirmed the king's right to levy additional custom duties without the consent of Parliament.[11] In addition, the king had long had

[9] Lawrence Stone, *The Crisis of the Aristocracy, 1558-1641*, Oxford, 1965, pp. 188-89.

[10] Theodore K. Rabb, *Enterprise and Empire*, Cambridge, Massachusetts, 1967, pp. 39-42. See also Robert Ashton, "The Parliamentary Agitation for Free Trade in the Opening Years of the Reign of James I," *Past and Present* 38 (1967), and "Jacobean Free Trade Again," *ibid.* 43 (1969).

[11] E. R. Foster, ed., *Proceedings in Parliament 1610*, vol. 1, New Haven, 1966, pp. xv-xvi. See also Robert Ashton, "Deficit Finance in the Reign of James I," *Economic History Review* 2nd ser. 10 (1957).

the power to grant monopolies, which took the form of issuing licenses for the exclusive public control of a product, a trade, or even a government service like the inspection of tobacco. James found the granting of monopolies a particularly facile way of increasing his income. A typical Englishman, as Christopher Hill noted, lived "in a house built with monopoly bricks . . . heated by monopoly coal. . . . His clothes were held up by monopoly belts, monopoly buttons, monopoly pins. . . . He ate monopoly butter, monopoly currants, monopoly red herrings, monopoly salmon, monopoly lobsters."[12] Such lavish sale of royal privilege would have been a burden at any time but, with the growth of both the internal and external markets, monopolies distorted the whole pattern of trade.

Thus, the fiscal problems of the monarchy evoked the anxieties of England's upper class—the nobles, gentry, and merchants who mingled their own ambitions with plans for the nation's commercial prowess. When James turned to Parliament to levy taxes to make good the shortfall in royal finances, he simultaneously provided the means for his critics to form a consensus on his fiscal innovations. The last session of Elizabeth's Parliaments had given a foretaste of what was to come. Then the question of monopolies had led to an unusually acrimonious debate, and efforts to put statutory limits on the monopoly power had provoked the charge that the queen's prerogative was being invaded. When the House of Commons in James's first Parliament attacked impositions and began an exhaustive canvassing of authorities, the king forbade his critics to proceed.[13] But the economic issues could no more be contained than the religious and diplomatic differences that brought the king and his successive Parliaments into open conflict. Attuned to the critical importance of estate management, members of Par-

[12] *The Century of Revolution, 1603-1714*, Edinburgh, 1961, p. 32.
[13] William Cobbett, ed., *The Parliamentary History of England*, vol. 1, London, 1806, pp. 923-31; Foster, ed., *Parliament in 1610*, vol. 1, p. xvi.

liament attempted to unmask the economic cost of feudalism in negotiations over the Great Contract. The airing of
grievances advertised the growing complexity of English economic life. Royal patents were said to create artificial scarcities and company privileges were charged with raising
prices.[14] Traditional rhetorical themes mixed with pungent
descriptions of commercial realities in James's Parliaments.
Sir Francis Bacon evoked morality and the Council of Nice
to condemn usury, but he also explained that high interest
rates inhibited agricultural improvements for men would
not "labor upon drayning of Marshes, or in any other good
or ingenious device, but imploy their Money to more cer-
taine Profitt at use."[15] When the Lord Treasurer spoke to a
joint conference he called money "a base creature whearof
never any wise man spake without contempt" but such
asides did not prevent the House of Commons from ap-
proaching James's cherished union with Scotland as a business prospect that might lead "to the decay of English
shipping."[16]

There were as yet no well-articulated theories to help
disentangle the economic aspects of royal policy from the
political context in which they appeared. Nor indeed was
there any incentive to do so, for the opposition that formed
in James's Parliaments was not bent upon violent obstruction, but rather upon persuasion, or what one might call
negotiation in a field of commonly shared affirmations.[17]
The concept of England's ancient usages permitted a deferential opposition to insinuate new meanings into old forms
and to disguise obstruction as the preservation of the law
that was recognized by all. The market economy, however,

[14] David Harris Willson, *The Parliamentary Diary of Robert Bowyer*,
Minneapolis, 1931, pp. 141-42, 81-82. See also T. L. Moir, *The Addled
Parliament of 1614*, Oxford, 1958, pp. 95-110.

[15] Willson, ed., *Parliamentary Diary of Robert Bowyer*, p. 151.

[16] S. R. Gardiner, ed., *Parliamentary Debates in 1610*, London, 1862,
p. 2; Willson, ed., *Parliamentary Diary of Robert Bowyer*, p. 204.

[17] On this point see J.G.A. Pocock, *The Ancient Constitution and the
Feudal Law*, Cambridge, 1957.

was more than a nexus of private profit. It was a complicated, new social organization, which could not be understood without attention being paid to its particularities.
Unlike the great public institutions of church and state, it
had not been shaped by central authority but rather
through informal initiative. The commercial animation of
Englishmen in the second decade of the century had extended the range and power of purely economic forces. A
sudden, severe, and prolonged depression in 1620 made this
abundantly clear. Both Privy Council and Parliament responded to the abrupt interruption of prosperity. A wide
canvassing of expert opinions produced the usual reports
and furnished the material for parliamentary debates. More
important to the effort to understand the market economy,
the expert opinions were published in a series of tracts that
opened the official investigations to the public and created
a new forum different, if not independent, from the politics
of opposition.

The third decade of the seventeenth century brought
many of the strands of economic development into a knot,
tied together by a common crisis.[18] A decline in demand for
England's principal export, woolen cloths, worked its way
back through the chain of production to bring financial
distress to merchant, clothier, the families of weavers, spinners, carders, and sorters as well as the landlords who raised
the sheep. European monarchs had found temporary relief
from inflation by lowering either the nominal or actual
silver content of their coins, which wreaked havoc with the
international mechanisms for settling accounts. In addition
to these commercial problems, two years of bad harvests led
to a greater imbalance between exports and imports as the
government rushed to buy grain from abroad. This crisis

[18] J. D. Gould, "The Trade Depression of the Early 1620's," *Economic History Review* 2nd ser. 7 (1954); Charles Wilson, "Cloth Production and International Competition in the Seventeenth Century,"
Economic History Review 2nd ser. 13 (1960); Supple, *Commercial
Crisis*, pp. 15ff.

of the early 1620s touched every aspect of productivity in England: sheep raising, grain growing, the cottage industries, the import–export trade, as well as the hundreds of jobs servicing these activities. The Privy Council sought the advice of merchants, and at the beginning of the parliamentary session of 1621 an ad hoc committee in the Commons undertook a report on the causes for the decay of trade. Growing distrust of the arbitrary governing of James I encouraged the opposition in the House to conduct a vigorous inquiry into the state of English commerce. The Court's distaste for parliamentary initiative in turn prompted greater efforts from the Privy Council.

The timing of the crisis affected the quality of the analysis coming as it did after a decade and a half of prosperity and genuine economic development. Despite competition, English merchants had successfully merchandized a new line of fabrics in the Mediterranean and southern Europe. The growth of London, with its steady attraction of goods and people, called into being a large regional market that within fifty years encompassed the nation. Joint stock trading companies had brought together the capital necessary to open up far-flung foreign markets. In these early years of the century, adequate harvests and profitable new enterprises had dispelled much of the gloom of the last years of Elizabeth's reign.[19] Commercial expansion created jobs for many of the masterless men of the 1590s and the sharp price rise of England's inflation had begun to flatten out. The abrupt drop in European demand for English cloth brought this promising period to a halt. Woefully inadequate harvests sent grain prices soaring again, and the money that in good times would have been available for the English to buy clothing and other household items went for food. Clothiers stopped bringing wool to the cottages for spinning and weaving. Unemployment rose swiftly. Since for-

[19] William Robert Scott, *The Constitution and Finance of English, Scottish and Irish Joint-Stock Companies to 1720*, Cambridge, 1912, p. xiv.

eign grain purchases had to be paid in specie, coin—already in short supply because of the drop in foreign cloth purchases—became even rarer. The clothiers whose investments employed spinning and weaving families had dead stocks of cloth on their hands or in the storehouses of their customers, the merchants.[20] Unemployment in the major clothing centers followed swiftly on the heels of commercial retrenchment, and bad harvests reevoked the menace of starvation.

The extent of the depression discouraged the normal search for local bogies or simple causes. Moreover, the economic forces presented themselves as artificial and manipulatable, a quality clearly lacking in the economic disaster of a crop failure. The indisputable impact of declining cloth purchases, coin shortages, erratic exchange rates, and widespread unemployment forced contemporaries to focus on the purely economic factors disrupting the society.[21] The diversification of English enterprise, which had taken place since the closing years of the sixteenth century, presented too sophisticated a phenomenon for monocausal explanations. Parliament came up with a list of ten reasons for the trade glut, but Thomas Mun, the most astute economic analyst to emerge, went beyond mere cataloging and created a conceptual model of the market, the powerful new intruder.

Mun wrote three pieces during the 1620s: *A discourse of trade, from England unto the East Indies* in 1621; *England's treasure by forraign trade*, written in 1623 but not published until 1664; and *The petition and remonstrance of the governor and company of merchants of London trading to the East-Indies*, an elaborate company defense published in 1628. A magnate in the East India Company, Mun also served on the Privy Council's subcommittee commissioned to gather evidence on "the true causes of the

20 Supple, *Commercial Crisis*, p. 66.

21 See, for instance, Joan Thirsk and J. P. Cooper, eds., *Seventeenth-Century Economic Documents*, Oxford, 1972, pp. 1-6, 12-15.

decay of trade and scarcity of coin within this kingdom."[22] Mun is best known for articulating the balance of trade idea. A fourteenth-century writer had given simple expression to the truism that if you buy more than you sell, you must make up the difference in payments. The sixteenth-century pamphlet, *A discourse of the common weal of this realm of England*, had given fuller treatment to the notion of achieving a favorable balance of trade, but Mun's analysis focused attention upon certain key variables in such a way as to exclude others.

The balance of trade is a very inappropriate title for the model of commerce that Mun constructed. It was not the poise of perfectly balanced weights that he evoked in his writings but rather the persistent, complementary, and orderly flow of goods and money. Without examining the propelling force for this movement of purchases and payments, Mun laid out the grand design that linked country to country and knit together the interest of merchants, landlords, and servants. The consumer remains a shadowy figure who appeared to enjoy cheap East Indian goods or to be reproved for a taste for foreign luxuries, but more often than not the merchant stood as the surrogate for the consumer, buying things when prices were right and sales likely.

In Mun's view, the trading universe was essentially a coherent and mutually supporting community. Too much frugality at home would restrict foreign purchases of English goods, he warned, for, if the English did not use foreign goods, foreigners would not have the wherewithal to buy English ones and there would be no sale abroad. In a similar fashion, Mun cautioned that any restrictions introduced by English authorities would inevitably lead to similar restrictions being laid upon the English by foreign princes. The flow was better left untampered with, for "by

---

[22] Charles Wilson, *England's Apprenticeship, 1603-1763*, New York, 1965, pp. 58ff; Bruno Suviranta, *The Theory of the Balance of Trade in England*, Helsingfors, 1923, p. 22; Supple, *Commercial Crisis*, p. 96, n. 4.

a course of trafficke (which changeth according to the ac-currents of time) the particular members do accommodate each other, and all accomplish the whole body of the trade, which will ever languish if the harmony of her health be distempered by the diseases of excess at home, violence abroad, charges and restrictions at home or abroad."[23]

In reference to this flow, Mun made money the passive servant of commodities, following in the wake of com-merce to settle up the accounts of merchants. Money fol-lowed goods and the exchange rate followed money. Viewed from this perspective, it was not treasure that nations should seek, but earnings, the residual credits that remain as a kind of sedimentary deposit from the flow of trade. Mun was at great pains to insist that plentifulness or scarcity of money did not bring prosperity. A mere shortage of money might be rectified by melting down plate or over-valuing foreign currency to attract it to England, but these were artificial and temporary increases in money, which would disappear when called to settle accounts abroad. "Onely so much will remain and abide with us," he wrote, "as is gained and incorporated into the estate of the King-dom by the overballance of the trade."[24] Nothing but money called forth by the sale of English goods would remain in the country. These were earnings. Everything followed the flow of trade. Usury did not inhibit the expansion of trade by detracting money from investments, for interest rates responded to trade activity and had no independent motion of their own. When trade was poor there was plenty of money; when trading was brisk money was in demand. Trade and usury, he said "rise and fall together." Indeed, by means of usury "the moneys of Widows, Orphans, Law-yers, Gentlemen and others, are employed in the course of Forraign Trade, which themselves have no skill to per-form."[25] Interest rates and prices followed the movement of goods, and neither prince nor statute could restrain this

[23] *England's treasure by forraign trade*, 1664, p. 84, K 1139.
[24] *Ibid.*, p. 92.   [25] *Ibid.*, p. 145.

flow. Restraints upon the natural course were ineffective, he said, instancing the old Statute of Employment, which sought to force foreigners trading in England to take their credits from sales in England out in English goods for export. Similarly, restriction of the export of bullion by the East India Company were short-sighted because the money sent forth to the Orient fetched back goods for English consumption at low prices, and English merchants' profits from reexports created more wealth for England.[26]

Despite his interest in maintaining a favorable balance of trade, Mun was not a bullionist. It was money's command over goods that gave it value. "For what begot the Monies which we sent out, but our Wares?" he asked and, addressing himself to the role of treasure, he later said: "It is not therefore the keeping of our Money in the Kingdom which make a quick and ample Trade, but the necessity and use of our Wares in Forreign Countries, and our want of their Commodities which causeth the Vent and Consumption on all sides."[27] He rejected out of hand the idea that men prefer money to goods or that money could take the place of English cloth, lead, tin, iron, fish, or the like. However, in all these statements the merchant's blind spot was apparent, for it was the necessity and use of wares in foreign countries that moved trade and begot money, not domestic consumption. The goods of a country were its natural wealth yet they could only create money when sold abroad. The sterility of domestic consumption was presented as an assumed conclusion. The baleful effects of domestic consumption—whether in grain to feed more Englishmen or foreign luxuries for the rich—were sufficiently bad in his eyes to warrant statutory regulation of English buying habits. "Industry to encrease, and frugalitie to maintaine, are the true watchmen of a kingdomes treasury," Mun

[26] [Mun], *The petition and remonstrance of the governor and company of merchants of London trading to the East-Indies*, 1628, p. 6, K 454. Internal evidence points to Mun as the author.

[27] *Ibid.*, p. 21.

wrote in introducing his *Discourse of trade*.[28] The statement would appear as pure mercantilist rhetoric were it not connected with Mun's succinct and compelling explanation of the dynamics of growth through commercial expansion.

Collections of aphorisms and lists of causes did the work of economic analysis before Mun did his writing. Using Thomas Kuhn's description of scientific research, we can say that Mun created a paradigm. He abstracted England's trade relations from their real context and built in that place an intellectual model. The shipment of goods, the exchange of bills, the trading of commodities became parts of an overall, unseen commercial flow, which moved independently of the specific, the personal, and the concrete. For the first time economic factors were clearly differentiated from their social and political entanglements. Even the king appeared more often in Mun's works as the collector of customs receipts than as the ruler of England. In differentiating essential economic relations from contingent ones, Mun gave expression at the same time to the idea that the system of exchange was autonomous. The salience of the commercial causes of England's slump in the 1620s no doubt prepared his readers to accept an analysis that distinguished the buying, selling, and paying of goods from political and social issues. The intricate pattern of shipments and transshipments of East Indian and European commodities encouraged the isolation of the key variables of the transactions. Mun's mode of analysis helped separate purely economic factors. It also offered an explanation of the trade crisis that was particularly attractive to those critical of the patrimonial intrusions of the Stuarts.

The encounter between Gerald de Malynes, an Assay Master of the English mint, and Edward Misselden, a prominent merchant of Hackney, provides an excellent demonstration of the ideological stakes involved in explaining

28 [Mun], *A discourse of trade*, 1621, pp. 2, 55, K 382; *Petition*, pp. 9, 21-22.

the causes of the depression. In 1622 they both published tracts detailing the proper way to correct the shortage of coin.[29] The coin shortage attracted attention because many believed it had precipitated the severe depression in the cloth trade. The shortage itself was exacerbated by drastic currency debasements in England's two principal cloth-buying areas, Poland and Germany. Prices did not keep up with the intrinsic silver content of debased currency; English imports were therefore overpriced in these markets; sales dropped; and the settling of accounts created an outward flow of silver coin. Malynes and Misselden disagreed on the cause of the coin shortage, but in exploring the issue the two men indirectly touched upon the critical social implications involved in separating economic activities from assumptions about authority and order.

Malynes maintained that the reason gold and silver specie left England was because merchants, ill-informed and selfishly motivated, overvalued foreign coins and had the audacity to give up more English coins in exchange, thus causing an unnecessary loss. While Malynes conceded that English consumption of foreign goods had created an imbalance, the fault lay not with the quantity of goods imported, but the price in English coin that had been paid for the goods, that is, the amount of English coin being sent out to satisfy bills in a foreign coin. His solution to the problem was a revitalization of the Royal Exchange in London, to enforce published official rates of exchange between English and foreign coins. He further urged that regular checks be made of the weight and pureness of all coins to guard against debasement or clipping.[30]

The conceptual order behind Malynes' recommendation is worth examining. His is a mental terrain marked by fixed

[29] Gerald de Malynes, *The maintenance of free trade*, 1622, K 391; [Edward Misselden], *Free trade*, 1622, K 392; [Edward Misselden], *The circle of commerce*, 1623, K 403; and Malynes, *The center of the circle of commerce*, 1623, Ks 541.

[30] *The maintenance of free trade*, pp. 84-85.

points and real qualities. The weight and purity of coin determined values, and merchants would profit by attending to these substantial qualities rather than by making their own uneducated guesses of exchange value. His conception of pricing was both static and authoritarian. The value of goods was determined by their price, and the value of the money was determined by the amount and purity of precious metals in the circulating medium. All commercial calculations were denied by his assumption that sale prices depended upon intrinsic money value. Buyer and seller, consumer and merchant alike were unable to determine what they should pay for things without accurate information from the Royal Exchange. How else could people know the price of money except by knowing the value of coin? It became a self-evident truth: "The yard doth measure the Cloth, but the Cloth doth not measure the yard."[31]

Malynes' world was one of eternal values grounded in the nature of things. Merchants, when they pursued their own hunches about the exchange rate, were encroaching upon the king's sovereignty.[32] In pursuit of gain, merchants forgot the good of the commonwealth, which is why "Princes and Governors are to sit at the sterne of the course of Trade and Commerce." The point had to be driven home. Calling upon merchants' advice on correcting abuses in the exchange is like, he said, summoning vintners to the consultation of laws to be made against drunkards.[33] Given the validity of Malynes' assumptions, his remedies might have worked, but the observable phenomena of commercial life required another explanation, and merchants like Edward Misselden supplied it.

Rejecting out of hand Malynes' airy notions about royal fiat, Misselden explained that "Exchange is a kind of Commerce exercised in money, in merchandize, in both, in either; of one man with another, of one Country with an-

31 *Ibid.*, p. 62.
32 *The center of the circle of commerce*, pp. iii, 122.
33 *The maintenance of free trade*, p. 5.

other."[34] Innocuous as it may sound, the idea of a commerce in money was loaded with implications subversive to the concept of the world as containing an order of real things. A commerce in money suggested fluidity instead of fixed points and, even more insidiously, gave to common merchants a power that only princes enjoyed: to set the value of coin. Money exchanges had long been used to hide the taking of interest. But the prohibition against usury, which still occasionally surfaced in its Deuteronomic form, was not at issue between Malynes and Misselden in their dispute about the English coin drain. Rather they were arguing about two competing ideas of commerce. Malynes propounded the traditional one, an orderly buying and selling of useful items conforming to predictable exchanges of known value for known value. It is Platonic, with essences, forms, and a hierarchical structure requiring direction from the person at the top who appreciates its wholeness. Malynes' ideas are completely compatible with the patrimonialism of the Stuarts. In times of economic dislocation, the prince mediates between the disruptive forces and the needs of his kingdom. Through the prince's good offices, crises can be ameliorated. Neither his ability nor his right to direct the economic activities of his subjects is brought into question. Misselden's departure point is a recognition that everything pertaining to commerce is in flux, and that to operate in such a system requires the special talents and information of the man on the spot. Answering Malynes' moral indictment of men for making profit from the exchange of English coin, Misselden matter-of-factly observed that a natural exchange determined by weight and purity "exactly takes away all advantages in making the exchange and hence the reason for the exchange to be made." Rather, it is the presence of advantage that promotes exchange, and it is the merchant, not the king, who is in a position to calculate the factors affecting the advantage. Most note-

[34] *The circle of commerce*, p. 93.

(44)

worthy among the calculable factors is that of value: "the plenty or scarcitie of Commodities, their use or Non-use" for whose purchase money is required in the first place.[35]

Far more was at stake than the flow of coin in these debates. The commercial system Misselden described called forth different personal qualities, different attitudes toward authority, different perceptions of value. To operate in Malynes' world required submission not only to the coercive force of authority but to the order it represented. The good merchant was the good subject. The good exchange was the correct exchange. Scales, assays, and published rates supplied information, determined value, and exercised discipline.

Misselden disputed Malynes' concept of commerce in every particular. Reversing Malynes' reflection of value from the metallic worth of coin to the price of commodities, Misselden made the buying and selling of goods the basis of everything, pointing out that, far from the exchange rate being the spirit of trade, trade had and still did flourish without any money exchange at all. "Commodities and money, are the matter of trade: the manner of buying and selling, is the Forme of trade; He that tradeth the Efficient: gaine the End of trade. So that the Matter and Forme of trade, are the Essentiall parts of trade." Where Malynes had found a crime in the merchant's making a profit through the exchange of money, Misselden discovered an advantage. Exchange transactions enabled merchants to operate on credit, which enabled more people to enter trade. Take the profit out of exchange, and you have inhibited rather than enhanced trade. Carrying his attack upon Malynes' fundamental propositions still further, Misselden offered a definition of wealth that bypassed the prince and all he represented as a national symbol: "Is not gaine the end of trade? Is not the publique involved in the private, and the private in the publique? What else makes

[35] *Ibid.*, pp. 21, 104, 16-17.

a Common-wealth, but the private-wealth, if I may so say, of the members thereof in the exercise of Commerce amongst themselves, and with forraine Nations?"[36] There were no fixed points in Misselden's concept of economic values. Calculations, anticipations, expectations, possibilities of use or nonuse, alternations of plenty and scarcity—a sinuous course of things real, felt, imagined, and calculated had replaced the *terra firma* of weight, purity, and sovereign statement.

When Malynes chided merchants for robbing the sovereignty of the prince by exchanging coin according to their own ideas of relative values, he made no effort to defend the prince's right to this sovereign power; it was enough to indicate that merchants were doing something that impaired sovereign authority. Those like Malynes who moved in a conceptual world of fixed statuses and knowable substances could not foresee in 1623 that the social fabric of England was about to be roughly rent. What they did know was that the social order they perceived as immutable and unchallengeable had commanded respect for generations. Sovereignty was an end in itself, requiring no further justification. Not until the nineteenth century would there be another conceptual order capable of standing as its own justification and making claims to be a part of the natural order of things. This, of course, was the liberal world-view with its own unquestioned commitment to material progress and inexorable natural laws of society. In between the disintegration of the patrimonial order and the emergence of the liberal order a long period of reconceptualization took place in which diverging intellectual loyalties caused more disputes than conflicts over evidence and logical proof.

Misselden very explicitly challenged Malynes' fundamental assumptions. He even went so far as to pick up the gauntlet about vintners being consulted on laws about drunkenness.[37] But this direct and amusing retort is not

36 *Ibid.*, p. 17.   37 *Ibid.*

nearly so important as the powerful suggestion in *The circle of commerce* that there existed laws whose operation was beyond the power of the prince to control. Of course, there were other laws like this. No sane prince nor patrimonial philosopher expected royal edict to stay the stars, raise up the dead, or hasten the rainfall. Monarchs ruled men and God ruled nature. What Misselden's arguments threatened was the accepted dividing line between the natural and the social. The natural realm was clearly understood to comprehend the physical world of animate and inanimate things, including man's own involuntary bodily processes. However, man's voluntary activities of purpose, appetite, emotion, will, thought, reflection, imagining, desiring, obeying, defying, longing, revering, and understanding belonged to a social order directed by the appropriate institutions of church and state. To advance the idea that certain human responses possessed a uniformity and consistency that merited consideration as independent phenomena was to claim from the social world activities that had always been within the prince's domain. Misselden's hint that commerce had its own regularities, independent of edict or statute, also carried with it the interesting corollary that specific knowledge was required to understand its workings. The merchant, whom Malynes put down for his limited vision, could now be advanced as the specialist whose information and experience could unlock the secrets of this new field of learning.

Edward Misselden's answer to Malynes' appeal to sovereign authority to enforce the rate of exchange signaled the beginning of an effort to isolate commercial activity for purposes of analysis. The legacy of the economic writings of the 1620s was Mun's lucid model of international trade, the differentiation of economic relations from the society they served, and the planting of the insidious idea that there were laws affecting human activity that knew no royal sovereign. The arrogance of the sophisticated observer, which Misselden introduced into the exchange, is less easy to define, but an important addition. Malynes, although obviously competent to debate the issue of the exchange rate, was made to appear old-fashioned. In answering him, Misselden displayed a certain condescension, suggesting the superiority of one who had been liberated from conventional misconceptions. Without being irreverent, Misselden meted out his new truths with a matter-of-factness that belied the gravity of challenging the monarch's capacity to control the productive forces of his society. A part of his freedom from deferential address can be attributed to the impersonality of the printed word. Economic analysis in the future would go hand in hand with published writings.

In important ways Mun and Misselden complemented each other and marked a significant break with the past. By creating a comprehensive picture of trade, they tied each economic act to a series of consequences. What came to the fore in their model was the predominance of exchange over production in the "circle of commerce." Where previous commentators had provided lists of causes for economic malfunctioning, Mun and Misselden adumbrated an explanation that implicated each part in a conceptual whole. They separated economic activities from their social context, but they joined the discrete acts of buying and selling to a single commercial process. To a striking degree, they broke with the substantialists of their day. Rather than dwell on the attractiveness of treasure, they focused on the profitable movements of goods and money. They also drew attention to the difference between appearances and reality. Gold and silver leaving England for the East Indies was not what it appeared to be—an export of treasure—but rather a flow whose true consequences could only be gauged in reference to an explanation of the entire movement of trade. Similarly, if England should decide upon devaluation of its currency or enforce a melting down and minting of plate, the sudden plenty of coin jangling in men's pockets would be merely an illusion of prosperity. The money would not abide in England; no more English goods would be sold, nor English men and women put to productive work. By distinguishing appearance from reality, they were making way for the expert, the one who through mastery of the mechanics of trade can determine what men's eyes, and even their account books, cannot discover.

In the Mun model, the growth of the internal market was neglected, and the consequent emphasis upon the international aspects of England's economy led to a particular interpretation of the role of money. Contemporaries adduced two sources of value for money. Quoting Jean Bodin, Sir Robert Cotton distinguished between the "extrinsick Quality," which is at the king's pleasure, and the "intrinsick quantity of pure mettal, which is in the Merchant to value."[38] A much more astute observer, Rice Vaughn, recognized that there were a variety of forces to which the merchant responded. Vaughn, for instance, noted that price rises usually lagged behind changes in the intrinsic value of coin occasioned by devaluation or debasement, an observation that went behind coin to the behavior of the coin user. Nonetheless because the trade accounts Mun concerned himself with were international, the intrinsic value of coin predominated.[39] In foreign trade the silver content of coin—that is, the intrinsic value—acted as a kind of commercial lingua franca. This emphasis upon intrinsic value minimized the sovereign's role since it was his power to mint silver into legal tender that added the extrinsic value of coin. This emphasis also obscured the importance of the extrinsic value in domestic trade and created the impression that there could be no commerce independent of trade

[38] "A speech made by Sir Rob. Cotton," in *Cottoni posthuma*, 1651, p. 290, K 820. This was first published in 1641 and erroneously attributed to Sir Thomas Roe, K 598. A speech in Parliament, it was probably delivered in 1626.

[39] *A discourse of coin and coinage*, 1675, p. 62, K 1394. From internal evidence noted by Supple, *Commercial Crisis*, p. 219, n. 3, it appears that Vaughn wrote this in the mid-1620s.

in goods. From this perspective, the sovereign's power to stamp his mark upon minted bullion paled before the merchant and exchanger's skill in settling accounts. As the sovereign's power over trade declined, the force of innumerable commercial transactions—aggregated into market prices—increased. The exchange of goods became central to the new economic order, and money, consigned to move in the wake of commodity purchases, was denied a force of its own.

Despite the mercantilists' reputation for enlisting state support in the organization of economic life, Mun and Misselden's writings should rightly be celebrated for having invested the world of trade with its own self-sustaining momentum. They had rejected Malynes' ideas about royal authority as well as the power of particular bankers. Deductions based on either notion, Mun said, were fruitless and harmful. It was not the royal assayers who controlled the flow of coin, "For let no man doubt, but that money doth attend Merchandize, for money is the price of wares, and wares are the proper use of money; so that their coherence is unseparable."[40] The economic empire that knit kingdoms, principalities, republics, and colonies together in the seventeenth century had its apolitical features, which the critics of royal power did their best to emphasize when they were called upon to explain the depression of the 1620s. The secularization of economic life owed much to this fact for, if it was believed that commerce followed its own laws, then old standards became irrelevant. Or rather they were placed in a different perspective. They had to be strained through a new sieve, one that sorted for facts. The changing conceptualization of money that preoccupied English thinkers from the 1620s onward was largely an effort to determine what could be discovered about market relations in their actual operation. Malynes' views were obsolete not because he did not understand the causes of the depression—he did —but because he was unable to perceive the new terms of

[40] *A discourse*, p. 25.

commerce where the actions of self-serving merchants and exchangers would become the subject of legitimate investigation because they moved the flow of goods and money coursing through the markets of the world.[41] Mun captured the new reality very nicely when he declared emphatically, "Let the meer Exchanger do his worst; Let Princes oppress, Lawyers extort, Usurers bite, Prodigals wast . . . so much Treasure only will be brought in or carried out of a Commonwealth, as the Forraign Trade doth over or under ballance in value," adding with a boldness which the conviction of truth inspires, "And this must come to pass by a Necessity beyond all resistance."[42]

What was remarkable about the discussion of economic issues in the 1620s was that it moved outside the traditional arenas. Both members of Parliament and the men whose special knowledge warranted canvassing by Privy Counselors and parliamentary committees made public their ideas in printed tracts. Parliament and the Privy Council did not cease thereby to be the place where crucial decisions were made, but the creation of a new forum for assessing market relations strongly affected English political life because through it a new conception of the economy gained currency. In anonymous publications writers boldly pursued lines of reasoning unimpeded by procedures, personal confrontations, or the strategy of the king's opponents who turned all issues into constitutional contests. Thus, the challenge that the experts on trade laid down to authority was not political, but scientific. They did not debate the wisdom of sovereign power; they denied its efficacy. In the seventy years that followed, the stream of writings on interest rates, land values, trade regulations, and wage policies moved through the channels first cut in the debate on the crisis of the 1620s.

[41] On the strengths of Malynes' argument see Gould, "The Trade Depressions of the Early 1620s," pp. 87-89.

[42] *England's treasure by forraign trade*, pp. 218-19.

Three

The Moral Economy in Retreat

DISENTANGLING THE ECONOMY OF SALES AND exchanges from the moral economy of production and sustenance was not accomplished in a single decade. The sensibilities of contemporaries had not been formed in a commercial world; the ethos codified in the Tudor statutes regulating wages, poor relief, and the harvesting of grain rested upon powerful social assumptions undergirded by God's injunction to Adam to work by the sweat of his brow and Amos's direful warnings to those that "swallow up the needy." The salient features of the biblical economy were sufficiently congruent to the ordering of labor in the sixteenth century to invite belief: the world could be made fruitful through labor; labor came to man as both a punishment and a gift. As a gift it tied human society to God's charity. As a punishment it forever harnessed men and women in the common work of sustaining life and doing God's will. Biblical texts explained this social order, infusing the daily round of tasks with a divine rationale. If the poor tenant found himself ground down by a cruel lord, the pain of privation could be relieved by the Proverbial promise, "Rob not the poor, because he is poor: neither oppress the afflicted in the gate: For the Lord will plead their cause, and spoil the soul of those that spoiled them."

The imaginative world of Thomas Mun and Edward Misselden was a vastly different one. Without rejecting the moral economy of production and sustenance, they prepared the ground for its irrelevance. In order to grasp what caused the exchange fluctuations between guilders and pounds and pounds and reals, Mun and Misselden resorted to the calculation of individual decisions. The faceless relations of algebra moved to the fore. "If x number of merchants vent y number of cloths in Hamburg" became the initial proposition for gauging the consequences of a commercial economy. The individual had become subsumed in a depersonalized aggregation; the moral quality of his decisions was not only hidden from the examiner but, more important, the decisions were divorced from their consequences. The critical link between action and responsibility had been cut. Only an extraordinarily vigorous and knowledgeable government could have traced the moral connection between the acts of production and the fundamental social purposes they served through the labyrinth of commercial transactions.

Many profitable pursuits, like the colonial trades or the making of new draperies, escaped critical comment because they were not departures from traditional ways, but totally new endeavors.[1] This was not true of all aspects of the new commercial economy. Three areas critical to the development of a rational, profit-oriented market economy remained vulnerable to the scrutiny of moralists. These were the grain trade, the conversion of commonly held land to private property, and the lending of money for interest. Here social purposes and religious doctrines were so clearly defined that deviations could not escape notice. Tudor regulations controlling the sale of grain were codifications of ancient laws based upon the explicit assumption that, in matters affecting the feeding of the people, individual actions based on considerations of private gain were sufficiently detrimental to the common weal to be named crimes. In E. P. Thompson's view, popular notions of society's right to order the sale of grain had so thoroughly penetrated the collective consciousness that in times of dearth the

[1] Peter Clark and Paul Slack, eds., *Crisis and Order in English Towns 1500-1700*, London, 1972, pp. 30-37; G. D. Ramsay, "Industrial *laissez-Faire* and the Policy of Cromwell," *Economic History Review* 1st ser. 16 (1946); and Robert Brenner, "The Social Basis of English Commercial Expansion, 1550-1650," *Journal of Economic History* 32 (1972). For a contemporary lament on this score see John May, *A declaration of the estate of clothing*, 1613, p. 32, K 323.

vulnerable members of society expressed their moral claim to bread through riots for food that took on the aspects of a just assertion of rights.[2]

As long as a primitive agricultural technique prevailed, there was a coherence between law and religious sentiments and the economy. Low yields guaranteed repeated food shortages, which justified the strict control of food production. Fear of want secured the poor's support for laws that controlled the rich, and the rioting that often accompanied grain movements during times of scarcity made the laws acceptable to the gentry and nobility who had the responsibility for maintaining order in the countryside.[3] Moralists who were wont to look at actual conditions for clues about God's wishes saw the crises of subsistence as demonstrations of the mutual dependency of rich and poor. In times of distress acts of charity affirmed the Christians' submission to God's laws. The moral economy of Tudor England thus began with the likelihood of food shortages and worked its way through the necessities of the needy, the fears of social disorders, and the clergy's extrapolations of information about divine intentions.[4]

By the beginning of the seventeenth century, however, a significant number of landlords and husbandmen had begun changing their ways of farming, greatly enhancing England's agricultural productivity. Late sixteenth-century

[2] "The Moral Economy of the English Crowd in the Eighteenth Century," *Past and Present* 50 (1971).

[3] John Walter and Keith Wrightson, "Dearth and the Social Order in Early Modern England," *Past and Present* 71 (1976); and J. P. Cooper, "Social and Economic Policies under the Commonwealth," in G. E. Aylmer, ed., *The Interregnum*, London, 1972, pp. 126-28.

[4] The critical relation between the Tudor moral economy and food shortages is demonstrated by the reassertion of the old rationale for controlling the grain trade when population again presses upon food supplies in the eighteenth century. On this see Thompson, "The Moral Economy"; and some countervailing evidence in Dale Edward Williams, "Were 'Hunger' Rioters Really Hungry? Some Demographic Evidence," *Past and Present* 71 (1976).

population growth had pushed food prices above the already inflated price level and the well-established European market in foodstuffs had created an incentive for the adoption of new techniques: the enclosing, ditching, draining, irrigating, rotating, and planting of new crops, which contemporaries lumped together as "improvements."[5] The power of the English landlords to raise rents and force their tenants into competition for leases made it possible to dislodge the English peasantry from their old ways and sometimes from their old holdings.[6] If, as Lawrence Stone has suggested, the nobility of the sixteenth century chose ways of repairing their fortunes that did not upset the agrarian order, by the early seventeenth century these restraints had disappeared.[7] With their entrepreneurial outlook and social leverage, members of the English landed class had forged a crucial link between market incentives and farming practices, but in doing so they had dissolved the coherence between religion and economic life reflected in the laws regulating the grain trade. For a while both views existed in uneasy tension, and any disruption provided the occasion for attacking the new attitudes.

A typical appeal to the old order is Robert Powell's *Depopulation arraigned*, which charged that forestallers and engrossers rob "the people of their due means and maintenance, and thereby disables them both in body and state from performing their service." Mixing social needs and biblical injunctions, Powell described how the farmer and husbandman would use "any art or shift to inhaunce the price of his Corne, and rather than he will sell it at the ordinary price of the market, slide it into some private corner, to remaine for a dearer sale." Powell's detailing of

---

[5] Ralph Davis, *The Rise of the Atlantic Economies*, Ithaca, New York, 1973, pp. 19-25.

[6] Robert Brenner, "Agrarian Class Structure and Economic Development in Pre-Industrial Europe," *Past and Present* 70 (1976), 71-75.

[7] Lawrence Stone, *The Crisis of the Aristocracy, 1558-1641*, Oxford, 1965, p. 380.

the shifts and arts used to enhance prices indicates the scope of the problem. More telling still is his report that private grain sellers defended themselves by saying that contracts made in the market are legal or that after the poor are taken care of the farmer is free to dispose of his grain. The evil of such face-saving excuses "hath so long dwelt amongst us," he noted, "that the offendors are ready to prescribe use and custome."[8] Twelve years later John Cook, a barrister of Gary's Inn, evoked the same moral universe as Powell in his *Unum necessarium*. Cook was more explicit about the moral context in which economic activities must be judged. Society, he explained, was natural, by which he evidently meant that men cooperate and accept authority amongst themselves because of their natural needs. "Governours must of necessity and in all reason provide for the preservation and sustenance of the meanest members, he that is but as the little toe of the Bodie Politique."[9] Those who would profit from the scarcity of corn to the risk of other men's lives were no better than criminals, he maintained, retelling with approval the story of a Neapolitan merchant who was convicted of treason for charging high prices for corn. The case was clear to Cook. The freedom to set prices was a petty, pretentious assertion, incompatible with the laws of man and God:

> the rule of charity is, that one mans superfluity should give place to another mans conveniency, his conveniency to anothers necessity, his lesser necessities to anothers extreamer necessities, and so the mechanicall poore to relieve the mendicant poor in their extreamer need, and this is but the Dictate of the Law of Nature: and can any man question but that the Magistrate is

[8] [Powell], *Depopulation arraigned, convicted and condemned*, 1636, pp. 6, 114-15, 110, K 520.

[9] *Unum necessarium*, 1648, p. 12, K 731. For a discussion of Cook, who was the solicitor for the Rump in the King's trial, see Cooper, "Social and Economic Policies," p. 127.

impowred by God to command every man to live according to the rule of nature and right reason.[10]

Neither Powell nor Cook evoked a response from a defender of liberty and private property, and after 1662 abundant harvests brought about a new level of agricultural productivity in England that rendered moot the question of the poor man's right to bread in times of dearth.[11] When supply outstripped domestic demand, the grain dealers' activities escaped the purview of the moralists. The fear of famine ceased to haunt the English. Increasingly, grain appears in economic tracts as a commodity interchangeable with other commodities. Its peculiar life-supporting qualities—which provided the rationale for preventing the maltmaker from engaging the farmer's harvest while it rested "in mow or barne"—were ignored, while its capacity to find a ready market abroad assumed a new importance. This shift of emphasis affected more than the operations of grain dealers. Tempted by Powell's maltmaker in the countryside, farmers found in the "the freedome and liberty of the Subject" justification for extricating themselves from a corporate concept that fell particularly hard on them. Good harvests eroded memories of dearth and helped to disconnect the link between the survival of society and the need to restrain the economic freedom of the husbandman.

The mid-century balance between people and food also helps to explain why the enclosure of the common land, so vigorously opposed in the sixteenth century and again in the eighteenth century, provoked relatively little discussion during the seventeenth.[12] But an activity so packed with

[10] *Unum necessarium*, p. 13.

[11] See W. G. Hoskins, "Harvest Fluctuations and English Economic History, 1620-1759," *Agricultural History Review* (1968).

[12] Godfrey Davies, ed., *Bibliography of British History, Stuart Period, 1603-1714*, 2nd ed. by Mary Frear Keeler, Oxford, 1970, p. 277; and E.C.K. Gonner, "The Progress of Inclosure during the Seventeenth Century," *English History Review* 23 (1908), 478.

social consequence could not escape reassessment in the light of a changing economic ethic. From a legal point of view, enclosure meant to extinguish common rights to a particular piece of land. In practice, it involved fencing or hedging a piece of land in preparation for private use. Morally, it signified the individual's intention of pursuing his own activities independent of others. Economically, it permitted the individual to organize his own resources, usually for more effective exploitation of market possibilities. The expansion of the European cloth industry had encouraged sixteenth-century landlords to convert land to pasturage, and enclosing landlords were blamed both for robbing the poor of their rights in the village commons and for diminishing England's overall food-growing potential. The central government did not retard the enclosure movement, and enclosing and opposition to it continued into the seventeenth century.[13] Popular uprisings in the early decades prompted the creation of an investigating commission whose reports reveal that enclosing landlords were also responding to the new incentives to grow grain by converting pasturage to arable acreage and consolidating several farms into one.[14] Charles I's reluctance to summon Parliament checked the possibility of legislating in this area, and the interest in growing more food, spurred on by the market, removed the seventeenth-century enclosure movement from the most telling criticisms. The engrossing of farms facilitated the adoption of new farming techniques, and former tenants found work in new forms of agricultural labor.[15]

[13] E. F. Gay, "The Midland Revolt and the Inquisitions of Depopulation of 1607," Royal Historical Society *Transactions* n.s. 18 (1904), 219-27; and J. D. Gould, "The Inquisition of Depopulation of 1608 in Lincolnshire," *English History Review* 67 (1952), 394-95.

[14] Gay, "The Midland Revolt"; E. M. Leonard, "The Inclosure of Common Fields in the Seventeenth Century," Royal Historical Society *Transactions* n.s. 19 (1905); and D.G.C. Allan, "The Rising in the West, 1628-1631," *Economic History Review* 2nd ser. 5 (1952).

[15] Leonard, "The Inclosure of Common Fields," and Alan Everitt,

Much of the opprobrium attached to the depopulators faded. What remained to be worked out was an answer to the moralists' attack upon the changing attitudes toward individual economic initiative.

Like the commercialization of the grain trade, the enclosing of common fields altered the bond between subject and society. Consolidating strips of land into enclosed private farms led to a radical restructuring of village life. The persistent consciousness of a common fate faded when the principal director of agricultural production became an individual rather than a group of villagers coordinating their farming activities. Unlike so many other features of the market economy that were unobtrusively innovative, enclosures were visible departures from customary ways. The social consequences of turning open fields to private farms were starkly apparent. Born of necessity, the cooperative farming of the commons had created patterns of work, play, and ceremony that reinforced the corporate life of the village. The weak, the irresponsible, and the unlucky were knit into the same village responsibilities with the able. Enclosure disentangled each person from this web of community obligations. The customs and values affected by enclosures in many ways represented in microcosm the macrocosmic restructuring of English society. For the moralists who opposed enclosures, community farming was worth maintaining because of its pedagogical value: it taught men to appreciate their fraternal obligations and underscored Christ's injunctions to lay up their treasures in heaven. The pressure for efficient production promoted instead a sense of individual responsibility and encouraged a defense of those private ambitions frustrated in the common fields.

Two ministers, Joseph Lee and John Moore, wrote five separate pamphlets between 1653 and 1656 that epitomized

---

"Farm Labourers," in Joan Thirsk ed., *The Agrarian History of England and Wales, 1500-1640*, vol. 4, Cambridge, 1967, p. 462.

the opposing rationales for enclosures and common fields. Moore's *The crying sin of England*, started the exchange and made the case against enclosure in purely evangelical terms: enclosures turn husbandmen into cottagers, which undid them because they could not care for their families on tiny plots. Not to care for the poor, by treating them in this way, amounted to not loving Christ.[16] Lee, in his anonymous answer, *Considerations concerning common fields and inclosures*, readily conceded that not caring for the poor was a sin, but shifted the argument to utilitarian considerations of land usage. Since all were agreed that private farming yielded more than farming in common— whether the enclosure was for arable land or pasturage— Lee argued that tenants and freeholders would be better able, after enclosure, to make weekly contributions for relief of the impotent poor. Lee's flood of assertions answered more than Moore asked and amounted to a defense of change: "Suppose it . . . hath heretofore been so, is it therefore necessary that it must be so alwayes?" Why should men not "have liberty then to lay down their Arable land for grasse, when pasturage is more profitable than tillage," he asked. Vigorously endorsing economic efficiency, he claimed that "the monarch of one acre will make more profit thereof, then he that hath his share in forty in common."[17] In his second pamphlet, *A vindication of a regulated enclosure*, Lee identified himself as "A Minister of the Gospel" and a participating owner in the proposed enclosure of Catthorp in Leicestershire. Although he tried here to remove the stigma of depopulation and exploitation from the name of enclosure, he ended up disavowing the landlord's social responsibility altogether:

16 John Moore, *The crying sin of England, of not caring for the poor*, 1653, pp. 8-19, Ks 1089. The other pamphlets are [Joseph Lee], *Considerations concerning common fields and inclosures*, 1654, K 906; *A vindication of a regulated enclosure*, 1656, K 936; John Moore, *A scripture-word against inclosure*, 1656; and [Joseph Lee], *A vindication of the considerations concerning common-fields and inclosures*, 1656.

17 *Considerations*, pp. 18, 39.

Let it be granted that our land and businesse lying nearer together fewer servants will be kept; are any bound to keep more servants then are needful for their businesse; or may they not cast how to do the same businesse with least labour . . . Is a man bound to keep servants to pill strawes or labour in vain? by what Law? if this principle be good, that all are bound so to carry on their affairs in the world, as to imploy servants, although to their own disadvantage; I dare say, the much applauded plough must be cast into the ditch, and much admired manufacture of tillage . . . be exchanged for digging with spades and mattocks, which would imploy more men than tillage.[18]

Advantage, Lee asserted, would determine whether men put their enclosed land in tillage or pasturage, and he defended private choice on the grounds that only the increased yield of corn from enclosed fields could explain what made food currently cheap. With a boldness that suggests that his position had gained ground among contemporaries, he asked rhetorically: "By what Law of God or man is every man bound to plow his land at all times, whether there be need of corn or no, although he can make more advantage to himself by pasture?"[19] Clearly pushed to the fore in Lee's aggressive justification of his particular enclosure was the general affirmation of each man's right to take stock of his own resources and calculate how they might be deployed profitably. "May not every man lawfully put his commodity to the best advantage, provided he do it without prejudice to others?" The others, however, are not the body politic Moore evoked, or those affected by the laws of charity, which command every man to relieve the need of his less well-off fellow. The others are individuals equally free to seek their advantage, and the poor benefited when others pursued their gain, for, as Lee explained: "When-

18 *A vindication of a regulated enclosure*, p. 7.
19 *Ibid.*, p. 9.

soever there is the least want of corn, and mens Land is fit to bear corn, men will plow up their inclosed land for their own profit," underscoring this assertion with the "undeniable maxime, That every one by the light of nature and reason will do that which makes for his greatest advantage."[20] The nature and reason that Moore invoked to justify the magistrate's God-given power to control the economy for the good of the whole had become for Lee the mediator between self-interest and information from the market.[21]

When Lee detailed what men might do on private farms, he conveyed very explicitly the advanced techniques for enhancing agricultural production that the educated, "improving" landlords could bring about. "The advancement of private persons will be the advantage of the publick," he argued, "if men by good husbandry, trenching, manuring their Land, &c do better their Land, is not the Commonwealth inriched thereby?" Moore had charged that filthy lucre was the end of enclosures, to which Lee replied: "Why is not Gods glory our end? forsooth because we aim at our own gains and advancement of our estates. Are these two ends alwaies incompatible?"[22] The question had the ring of Cain's agonized "Am I My brother's keeper." Moore, in replying to Lee, scorned the justification of improvement. "We shall gaine by it," he mimicked the enclosers, "we shall treble our rents. Hence those Heathenish speeches of theirs, May I not make the best of mine own . . . Our estates are ours, Who is Lord over us?" Recognizing the wedge that Lee's concept of private property had driven between society and the land upon which it depended for survival, Moore recalled the older ethic: "although thou are a *civill Owner*, yet thou are a *spirituall Usurper*." Asserting again the wrong done by enclosing, he ignored economic concerns altogether. Moore took the position that the poor did

20 *Ibid.*
21 *A scripture-word against inclosure*, pp. 6ff.
22 *A vindication of a regulated inclosure*, pp. 22-23, 20.

not represent a needy group of people so much as the silent reminder of Christ's appeal for the brotherly love through which men might overcome their own selfishness. Like the evildoing described by Amos, Moore said the enclosers of Leicestershire buy "the poore for silver . . . make chaffer and merchandize of them for gain and profit: they use them as they doe their beasts, keep them or put them off for advantage: they buy them, and sell them, as may best serve their turns to get by them."[23]

There was no common ground for Lee and Moore to meet upon and resolve their differences. Two different codes, two different conceptions of the relation of the private to the public, two different social visions informed their values as well as their reading of the same biblical texts. "God is the God of order, and order is the soul of things, the life of a Common-wealth: but Common-fields are the seat of disorder, the seed-plot of contention, the nursery of beggery," Lee insisted, while Moore invoked Christ's injunction to cherish the poor.[24] That they both addressed the public as clergymen only strengthens the impression that a profound transformation of values was in the making, one in which the very source of order was being redefined.

In this exchange over enclosures there are similarities with the debate over usury as it was conducted in a cluster of pamphlets in the first half of the century. Here, too, specific laws supported by a deeply rooted religious rationale impeded the free use of one's property in money and projected social values inimicable to commercial expansion. The critics of commercial growth drew heavily on the social vision embedded in Jewish law and intensified by the Christian church's interpretation of Christ's ministry as the fulfillment of that law. Unable to criticize much in the new economic order that was novel or hidden from public scrutiny, they clung tenaciously to the tie of charity binding rich

[23] *A scripture-word against inclosure*, p. 6.

[24] *A vindication of the considerations concerning common-fields and inclosures*, p. 42.

to poor. Biblical assertions that men were properly each others' brothers were abundant, and the famous verses on usury in Deuteronomy explicitly denied legitimacy to the extension of credit for profit: "Thou shalt not lend upon usury to thy brother; usury of money, usury of victuals, usury of any thing that is lent upon usury; Unto a stranger thou mayest lend upon usury; but unto thy brother thou shalt not lend upon usury: that the Lord thy God may bless thee in all that thou settest thine hand to in the land whither thou goest to possess it."

For Jews the laws of the Pentateuch were both positive and normative.[25] Actual practices were proscribed or enjoined while the rationale behind the laws clearly evoked the goal of a Hebrew brotherhood. The Deuteronomic injunction against usury was thus a part of a moral code that sharply distinguished between acceptable behavior toward the members of one's community and acceptable behavior toward outsiders. The Catholic church had maintained that Christ's coming had erased the distinction between brother and other. The laws of the Hebrew brotherhood became a part of canonical law, and the taking of usury came to represent the church's stand against an unrestricted commercial economy. However, like any simple prohibition, prosecution depended upon the unambiguous nature of the crime; and commercial developments in the heart of Catholic Europe in the fourteenth and fifteenth centuries had eroded many of the distinctions that separated usurious from nonusurious practices. The imaginative evasions of merchants and the casuistry employed by clerical apologists had made a simple ban against charging interest difficult to enforce. The medium of exchange for international trade was not gold and silver, but gold and silver minted into the specific coinage of the sovereignty where it circulated. Accounts were settled in the specific area where goods were bought and sold.

25 Benjamin Nelson, *The Idea of Usury*, 2nd ed., Chicago, 1969 (originally published in 1949), pp. 229ff, 74ff.

Hence, as international trade increased, the coins from one sovereignty were regularly exchanged for those of another. The settling of accounts thus required monetary exchanges that involved several sequential transactions. Fees or charges could be added into this process by the exchangers. They were not totally unlike interest rates and could indeed cloak the charging of interest. Was the financing of a commercial enterprise by a passive man of wealth in concert with an entrepreneur without investment capital a loan? Did this putative partnership actually veil a usurious contract? For both silent partners and exchangers, mere possession of money yielded a return. Both cases escaped the application of canon law, but the presence of the usury ban clearly influenced the development of business practices.[26]

The broad trends of the Reformation prepared the ground for the nullification of the prohibition against usury. Efforts of sectarian radicals to reassert the egalitarianism of the Hebrew brotherhood made universal in Christ's coming were not successful.[27] Protestant theologians, from Luther to Calvin, moved away from a policy of enforcing Hebrew law as positive civil laws, invoking instead the Christian conscience. Usury was not to be condemned in all cases. Rather, charity and the equity of the golden rule were to guide the Christian. English law makers vacillated. In 1488 an anti-usury statute proclaimed that all usury was to be extirpated and that anyone lending money at interest should forfeit one half of the principal sum involved, but statutes during the subsequent reigns of Henry and Elizabeth established a 10 percent ceiling, which was dropped to 8 percent in James's reign. In 1652 the maximum allowable rate was reduced to 6 percent, where it stayed for the rest of the century.

[26] Raymond de Roover, "What is 'Dry Exchange'? A Contribution to the Study of English Mercantilism," *Journal of Political Economy* 52 (1944), 264-65; Edgar Augustus Johnson, *Some Origins of the Modern Economic World*, New York, 1939, p. 48.

[27] Nelson, *The Idea of Usury*, pp. 40-50.

Despite the common practice of charging interest, moralists made usury a symbol of all that was distasteful in the commercial world where private gain was sought, treasure tolled, hard bargains struck and unlucky competitors illused. In 1611 Roger Fenton published *A treatise of usury*, which covered the moral ground of the usury battle with a thoroughness that stood for the rest of the century. Leaning upon St. Ambrose's interpretation of Deuteronomy, Fenton showed how social and religious conservatives found in the usury issue the means to expose the dangers of an unregulated market economy. Taking the Catholic view, Fenton said that for Christians there can be no wall between brethren and stranger. Therefore, Christians must study what practices God permitted Jews among themselves. Moreover, he said, religion and piety teach Christian men, in all their affairs, to depend upon God's providence. "Of all men the Usurers thinke worst of God, and will least trust him: be it faire or foule, all is one; they will have their money." The rational pursuit of profit was thus not only against the law of charity, but it flouted Providentialism by its implicit reliance upon self. Not content with setting forth the rationale for usury, Fenton detailed with great care the arguments used in support of usury—including Calvin's—and answered them point by point. Beyond this logic chopping, he asserted the fundamental incompatibility of religion and the profit-oriented commercial activities that had become the salient features of the new economic order. Charity—in the sense of a vibrant tie binding human beings into one Christian body—was violated by usury, he said, and the imperatives of the Christian ethic were challenged by the new priorities of the efficient man of business. Contemptuously dismissing the argument that usury is a necessity of trade, Fenton charged that "Necessitie is lawlesse." He rejected the need for usury as peremptorily as he dismissed the new need for great gain. The two were only necessary, he snorted, to live in high style and drive a larger trade. God preferred that men "drinke of the waters of their owne well."[28]

John Blaxton, Robert Bolton, and Nathaniel Holmes pursued these same lines of criticism. Their pamphlets do not add to the great body of contemporary commentary on the Deuteronomic ban against usury, but they do reveal that in the seventeenth century, when the influence of the market became more pervasive, the issue of usury continued to draw fire from those representatives of a social order totally antagonistic to the self-centered, calculating spirit of the entrepreneur, be he merchant, tenant, or landlord. Where much of the fifteenth- and sixteenth-century literature on usury had centered on the barrenness of money, economic changes had weakened that line of attack. Money as capital had proved during the intervening years to be very fruitful, and the enhanced productivity that followed investments in agriculture or industry seemed to many to justify the taking of interest. For Dr. Nathaniel Holmes this rationalization only proved that the borrower enjoyed the fruits of the use of money, not the commonwealth. "Yet if the borrower upon Use, sels unconscionably dear, that he may make his customers to pay for the commodity, pay his Use, and finde him present maintenance, and an estate for time to come, what boast can there be made of the fruitfulnesse of this money to the Commonwealth?"[29] There remains in this analysis an inability to comprehend the productive possibilities of an underdeveloped economy, but there is also a resistance to the legitimization of individual gain even when it does not hurt the community. For the critics of the new commercial order, usury epitomized a depersonalized age against which they thrust God's command not to charge interest to the poor, asserting as a final logical proposition that in a loan the borrower by definition is poorer than the lender. "The biting worme of usury . . . hath corrupted all

[28] pp. 95, 121.
[29] *Usury is injury*, 1640, p. 16, K 551.

England," John Blaxton maintained, evoking in turn the neighborly ideal, the role of Christian charity, and the sin of storing up treasure, in an effort to awaken the conscience of those who deluded themselves that usury was acceptable in the eyes of God. Usury turned charity into an act of self-love, he said.[30] Bolton similarly condemned usury as a sin and summoned St. Ambrose and the three hundred divines at Nicea to help in his attack.[31]

The churchmen's attack on usury as an unmitigated sin evidently troubled some Englishmen, especially those members of the gentry whose conformity to Christian doctrine was all of a piece with loyalty to the traditional order. Sir Robert Filmer was such a man, and he wrote a response to Roger Fenton that circulated in manuscript among his Kentish neighbors in the 1630s.[32] Filmer took the line marked out by Calvin and stressed that it was the spirit of the act that counted. "If many men who are fit for Callings live idley on Usury, they sinne," he wrote, "but no otherwise than those that let their lands."[33] Idleness, not usury, was the evil, just as not acting charitably toward the poor, rather than charging interest, was what was condemned. This line of equivocation enabled the defenders of usury to fix upon idleness and ignore the more fundamental moral absolute at issue. The divisions within the clergy, moreover, permitted people to choose among the authorities. One clergyman surveying the literature in 1616 maintained that even ministers were taking usury.[34]

The Bible offered an absolute ethic on charity and a set of specific injunctions. Because the specific injunctions were mingled with narratives and laws drawn from experiences in a traditional agricultural economy, their application to a

30 *The English usurer*, 1634, pp. 9-10, 26, K 492.

31 *A short and private discourse*, 1627, pp. 4-6, K 523.

32 Peter Laslett, ed., *Patriarcha and Other Political Works of Sir Robert Filmer*, Oxford, 1949, p. 3.

33 [Filmer], *Quaestio quodlibetica*, 1653, p. 146, K 877.

34 [James Spottiswood], *The execution of Neschech*, Edinburgh, 1616, p. 41, Ks 454.

changing society required interpretations, and these interpretations could be reworked to favor economic innova-
tion. This was particularly so when critics condemned usury
for its effects. The anonymous author of *Usury araigned* and
Sir Francis Bacon, for instance, attacked the charging of
interest because it drew men from their callings and in-
duced a drug-like dependence upon money not earned.[35]
In this form, the argument can be changed and allowance of
interest presented as a way of stimulating economic investments, which would promote productivity rather than the
deadly sin of sloth.[36] The general consensus on the evil of
idleness could also be turned to account by the advocates of
enclosures. Defenders of the poor attacked agricultural improvements because the "racking and raising of rents," as
one writer put it, thrust people out, made their lives un-
comfortable and the commonwealth less charitable, but
proponents of the new farming techniques could answer this
by extolling the material benefits for all from enclosure.[37]
Silvanus Taylor emphasized this feature when he described
a new day for English tillage when "every man had all his
own ground at his own disposing to make choyce of those
grounds most fit for Corn, and then to employ with less
labor, less cost, and much more encrease."[38] Through such
logic the promotion of enclosures was joined to improving
the waste lands, all under the biblical ideal of making the
land fruitful. The problem that the superior productivity of
enclosed land posed to opponents of enclosures is mirrored
in Henry Halhead's vigorous attack. Although Halhead
clung to the biblical priority of caring for the poor, he
expressed genuine puzzlement that God would allow more
corn to grow on enclosed land. Despite the mixed signs of

---

[35] *Usury araigned*, 1625, p. 5, K 422; and J. M. McNeill, ed., *Bacon's Essays*, London, 1959 (original, last revised, ed. 1625), pp. 118-20.

[36] This is the tack taken by Thomas Mun, *England's treasure by forraign trade*, 1664, p. 178, K 1139; and Henry Robinson, *Englands safety*, 1641, p. 42, K 597.

[37] Joseph Bentham, *The Christian conflict*, 1635, p. 318, Ks 647.

[38] [Taylor], *Common good*, 1652, p. 13, K 860.

providence, Halhead concluded that greater yields with fewer people represented a violation of God's command to multiply and replenish the earth with people.[39]

The most significant development in the seventeenth-century writings on the charging of interest, however, did not come from the ministers and moralists who used the traditional proscription against usury as a means of stigmatizing the new market mentality. Their ideas about brotherly love and the commonwealth knit together with bonds of personal obligation were rarely mentioned after the 1650s. What did emerge as a fully debated issue was whether or not interest rates should be forced down by statutes to prevent usury from having an inhibiting effect upon the economy. In this debate, which surfaced first in the 1620s, the participants were not disputing the nature of the social order nor the relation of Christian ethics to business; instead they were addressing the problem of the effect of usury (by which they actually meant high interest rates) upon commercial development. Like the debate among Mun, Misselden, and Malynes on the role of the Royal Exchange, the modern recasting of the usury issue led the participants into a theoretical examination of market forces as relations separable from social norms and political decisions.

After mid-century, economic writers continued to present their arguments in terms of right and wrong, but the affirmation of a moral order where economic activities were means to social ends—God's and man's—fell from public view. Biblical quotations illuminated minor debating points, but the Bible as a source of information about God's intentions rarely obtruded. With this loss of a social vision to inform specific economic laws, political intrusion required justification on utilitarian grounds. The individual's right to look after his own, moreover, acquired a moral base through the value placed upon personal freedom. Without the underlying assumptions of traditional Christianity, the

[39] *Inclosure thrown open*, 1650, pp. 13-18.

burden of defending legislative interference shifted, and the proponents of economic regulation had to make good their case.

Published writings cannot explain why the moralists were unable to stay the course of commerce and the practices and values its expansion carried throughout the kingdom. They do, however, indicate how contemporaries interpreted the issues they confronted, and they record what views men were willing to circulate publicly. The positions staked out by Roger Fenton and Joseph Lee, both clergymen, are instructive on these points. Fenton, writing in 1611, directed his passion toward the hubris of the usurer, the man who least trusts God:

> The husbandman lookes up to the cloudes, and prayeth for the seasonable weather: The Merchant observes the windes, and prayeth God to deliver him from tempest and wreck: The tradesman wisheth the people may have money . . . The labouring man prayeth for worke and health . . . only the usurer of all others hath least need to say his prayers: be it wet or drie; be it tempt or calme; blow the wind East, West, North or South; be he well, or be he sicke; bee hee goutie and lame, or be he sound of body; let him be what he will, or doe what he list; he will be sure of his money.[40]

The Reverend Joseph Lee, writing in 1656, exuded a totally different spirit. Not only did he admire the control of natural forces and the motive of self-interest represented by the improving farmer, he boldly ascribed it to the sacred heroes of the Bible. "Did not Moses in all his afflictions with the children of God, aime at his own advantage?" Lee asked, adding in confirmation, "He by whom God did all those mighty things for his Israel, without controversie did glorifie God: yet had an eye also to the recompence of reward."[41]

[40] *A treatise of usurie*, pp. 95-96.
[41] *A vindication of a regulated inclosure*, pp. 20-21.

Between these two concepts of good there lies a generation of revolutionary events. Not one, but many social visions found expression in published works. While Christian radicals again reaffirmed the brotherhood of man, others saw in the liberated individual a powerful source for new values. The communal ethic of the Bible mixes poorly with the insistence of Fenton's usurer to control his own destiny, but it is not for all that an ideal without virtue. Recurring food shortages throughout history had created a dependency that acted as the invisible support to religious and political solidarity. As economic development began to remove this dependency, it was possible to question the validity of restraining individuals and to conceive of human independence as a goal worth extolling.

Four

The Dutch as a Source of Evidence

ENVY AND WONDER STIMULATED A GREAT DEAL of economic thinking in England during the middle decades of the seventeenth century. Across the channel, on land wrested from the tidal incursions of the North Sea, the citizens of the United Provinces of the Dutch Republic were growing wealthy. They extracted tons of herring from waters that washed on English shores, had the largest merchant fleet in Europe, magnetized Spanish gold, could borrow at the lowest interest rate, and bested all comers in the commerce of the Baltic, the Mediterranean, and the West Indies. The Dutch represented, in fact, a kind of anti-fairy tale. The rags-to-riches heroes of medieval folklore invariably discovered their fortunes or earned them through acts of valor or virtue. Elfin magicians, fairy godmothers, and subdued giants were the bestowers of great wealth. Spanish exploits in the New World had been entirely in keeping with this legendary tradition. The conquistadors had won the fabled mines of the Incas and Aztecs with their military victories. Even the less glamorous triumphs of the Portuguese conformed to the "treasure" image of wealth. Venturing into uncharted oceans, they had found their way to the riches of the Orient. The Dutch, on the other hand, had made their money in a most mundane fashion. No aura of gold and silver, perfumed woods, rare stones, aromatic spices, or luxurious fabrics attended their initial successes. Instead, broad-bottomed Dutch fluyboats had plied the waters of the North Sea in a seemingly endless circulation of European staples. From this inglorious beginning the industrious people of the Low Countries had turned their cities into the emporiums of the world. The sustained demonstration of this Dutch commercial prowess acted more forcefully upon the English imagination than any other economic development of the seventeenth century.

If it can be said that the first step in economic reasoning was the isolation of the key variables of the subject—value, profit, interest rates, markets, production processes—from the social context in which they were enmeshed, then the Dutch can be held responsible for pushing English thinkers in this direction. Goaded by a curious mixture of jealousy and admiration, commentators from the first to the last decade of the century turned to Dutch examples to pose and resolve problems. The Dutch example provided a means of observing buying, selling, producing, lending, and exchanging, independent of the social and political considerations that had often veiled the purely economic aspect of these activities. The inevitable contrast with Spain, the possessor of legendary treasure teetering on the verge of bankruptcy for nearly a century, only underscored the novelty of the Dutch success. The Dutch were the ones to emulate, but to emulate was not easy, for the market economy was not a single thing, but a complex of human activities which appeared as a self-sustaining process.

English observers consistently focused on three elements in Dutch prosperity: the exploitation of the herring fisheries, low interest rates, and their command over the products of other nations. Dutch success obviously puzzled Englishmen. Their innovative methods often involved a denial of conventional wisdom; their departures from traditional expectations compelled analysis. Dutch prosperity, like Dutch land, seemed to have been created out of nothing. Clearly there was something at work, but it was hard to define. Most English writers from the beginning to the end of the century pointed to the herring fishery and tried to stir their countrymen to imitation. Tobias Gentlemen reported that Hollanders called fishing their "onely rich Treasury," and detailed for his readers the techniques for catching and salting herring.[1] John Keymer, whose tracts in

---

[1] *Englands way to win wealth* [1614], p. 7, K 330. For a full treatment of the Anglo-Dutch rivalry, see Charles Wilson, *Profit and Power*, London, 1957.

support of an English fishing industry were reprinted in various guises, stressed the value of the fishing industry for "making imployment for all people, both young and old."[2] Robert Kayll also attributed the Hollanders' great prosperity to the herring fishery, which had not only bred its sailors and increased its shipping but, most importantly, profitably filled the need for employment.[3] At the end of the century, James Puckle goaded his English readers with a dialogue wherein a Dutchman detailed for his English listener the delightful foreign goods that his countrymen bought with fish taken from English waters.[4]

The absence of a natural base for its wealth clearly made the Dutch a thought-provoking phenomenon for seventeenth-century Englishmen. They considered themselves well endowed with resources—grain, tin, wool; the French were also richly endowed, but the Dutch were giving the laws of trade to them both. Sir William Temple, whose *Observations upon the United Provinces of the Netherlands* represented the wisdom distilled from long years of diplomatic service in the Low Countries, pronounced the Dutch truly remarkable because they possessed no natural commodities to explain their success.[5] In *A cleare and evident way*, John Keymer laid out the wizardry of Dutch commerce:

> The abundance of Corne groweth in the East Kingdoms: but the great Store-houses for Grain, to serve Christendome, and the Heathen Countries (in time of Dearth) is in the Low-Countries . . . The mighty Vineyards, and store of Salt, is in France and Spain: But

---

[2] *John Keymer's observation made upon the Dutch fishing about the year 1601*, 1664, p. 33, K 1137. For a discussion of the provenance of Keymer's many publications, see the introduction to M. F. Lloyd Prichard, ed., *Original Papers Regarding Trade in England and Abroad Drawn Up by John Keymer*, New York, 1967.

[3] [Kayll], *The trades increase*, 1615, pp. 48-50, K 347.

[4] *England's way to wealth and honour*, 1699, p. 11, K 2129.

[5] *Observations upon the United Provinces*, 1673, pp. 185-87, K 1349.

> the great Vintage, and Staple of Salt, is in the Low-Countries . . . The exceeding Groves of Wood are in the East-Kingdomes: But the huge Piles of Wainscot, Clapboards, Fir-deale, Masts, and Timber, is in the Low-Countries . . .

adding pointedly, "where none groweth."[6] No wonder trade flagged for the English, William Goffe exclaimed, when they exported raw materials and imported manufactured ones. "The Dutch buy their Hemp at Riga, and other places where we buy ours; but they employ their People to manufacture the same into Sail-cloth, and they import it on us, and we, to encourage them, use it for our Royal Navy, and all our Merchants Ships."[7] Henry Robinson lamented that the Dutch could outstrip English shipbuilding efforts, despite their lack of timber.[8]

If the Dutch were able to produce ships without natural resources in timber and naval stores, they also seemed able to draw from their people a level of output that surpassed all earlier calculations of human capacities. Thomas Mun paid tribute to Dutch enterprise and frugality in his *England's treasure by forraign trade*.[9] Even the Dutch who settled in Colchester, Canterbury, and Sandwich in the 1560s retained the legendary Dutch work habits, according to Thomas Manley, who compared them to the "lazy, wastfull, and disorderly" English.[10] The marvels of Dutch industry prompted John Evelyn to a little apotheosis on man's economic virtues: "the Lillies which spin not, and are yet so splendidly clad, are not in this respect, so happy as an In-

[6] [Keymer], *A cleare and evident way*, 1650, p. 8, K 808.

[7] *How to advance the trade of the nation and employ the poor*, 1641, in *Harleian Miscellany* vol. 4, London, 1745, p. 367.

[8] *Englands safety in trades encrease*, 1641, p. 1, K 597.

[9] *England's treasure by forraign trade*, 1664, pp. 182ff, K 1139. See also [William Aglionby], *The present state of the United Provinces* vol. 1, 1669, p. 366, K 1229.

[10] *Usury at six per cent. examined*, 1669, p. 25, K 1241.

dustrious and prudent man; because they have neither knowledge, or sense of their Being and Perfections."[11]

The ingenuity of the Dutch, however, was not considered in isolation. English writers worked to connect the elements in Dutch prosperity. William Petty, reviewing the advantages of secure title to land, the use of banks, and the reduction in shipbuilding costs through the division of labor, finally decided that Dutch prosperity rested on their shipping. The Dutch fishing had led to shipbuilding, the shipbuilding to the carrying trade and the carrying trade to the extension of commercial relations.[12] Benjamin Worsley wanted England to adopt the Dutch policy of free ports which, he claimed, would "conduce to the Quickening of Trade; to the Imploiment of the poor . . . to the preventing of Famine, and scarcitie of Corn."[13] Henry Robinson suggested that the English could promote trade if they copied the Dutch by cutting ditches, building interconnected cities, regulating the draining of fens, and prohibiting the slaughtering of lambs to increase the amount of wool for industrial purposes.[14] Why do the Dutch "manage trade better than the English," Roger Coke asked, and supplied eighteen reasons, among which were their accessibility to timber and naval stores, the richness of the German hinterland, the training of the youth of both sexes in geometry and numbers, their lower customs duties and interest rates, and finally the fact that merchants and their wives were more conversant in trade.[15]

What Dutch success suggested more strongly than any-

[11] *Navigation and commerce, their original and progress*, 1674, p. 5, K 1358.

[12] *Political arithmetick*, 1690, pp. 19-23, K 1741. According to Charles Henry Hull, ed., *The Economic Writings of Sir William Petty* vol. 1, New York, 1899, pp. 235-38, Petty completed this manuscript in 1676 and circulated it among his friends.

[13] [Worsley], *Free ports*, 1651, p. 4, K 840.

[14] *Certain proposalls*, 1652, p. 11, K 858.

[15] *A discourse of trade*, 1670, pp. 49-51, K 1260.

thing else was the productive possibilities of well-organized human efforts. To the men who wrote in the years following the trade depression of the 1620s it was clear that trade needed encouragement. The management mentality found its fullest expression in the writings of Henry Robinson, who proposed everything from compulsory swimming lessons for the poor to the concentration of people in cities to cut transportation costs. Industrious foreigners should be encouraged to emigrate to England to teach Englishmen lessons by putting them out of business. Felons should be sent to the plantations to promote colonial growth. The poor should be forced to work a full week. Land purchases should be promoted by the publication of encumbrances. English goods should be sold cheaply and ways found to make this possible. Pawn shops for the poor, speedy justice for merchants, workhouses, embargo threats to secure lower customs abroad, biweekly fish days—all found their way into Robinson's pamphlets. Nor was he unaware of where he stood, having announced in *Certain proposalls* that "even the worst kinde of Government is capable of being so managed, so ordered, as that a People might enjoy better dayes under it, than ever any yet did under the very best of Governments from the beginning of the world."[16]

In the Dutch success story there was not only the lesson of superior organization but a demonstration of the possibility of human ingenuity triumphing over the limits nature seemed to have set upon productivity. The marvel of the Dutch was that they foiled each competitor at his own game. Dutch superiority, Worsley explained, came from the greatness of the stock employed, which was further increased by their method of shipping, which "did enable them the more to give the Laws of Trade to us, both in the Government of the Exchange, and of the Markets abroad for Forreign Commodities."[17] It was, as R.W.K. Hinton has pointed out, an

[16] p. 2. See also Robinson's *Englands safety* and *Briefe considerations*, 1649, K 797.
[17] [Worsley], *The advocate*, 1651, p. 7, K 837.

inescapable idea of the period that improvement and national strength went together and the Dutch taught the world that private profit led to "national strength and back to private profit."[18]

If Dutch accomplishments inspired some Englishmen with a zeal for the right ordering of trade, it prompted those with a more speculative bent to search for the secret spring of the new market economy. Analyzing the Dutch economy of necessity required the creation of an abstract model and hastened an appreciation of the unseen forces at work in the market. With the widening of the market, uniform and known prices replaced the face-to-face bargaining of the local market. Like gravity, aggregate demand represented power exercised from a distance, motion through a void. As the ultimate consumers moved further and further from the producer, the process linking production and consumption became the focus of attention. The predominance of foreign commerce in the Dutch economy made these links accessible for investigation. In the Dutch example there were, moreover, challenging contradictions between appearances and reality, and puzzling divergences between expectations based upon established truths and the actual developments. Without mines, how did the Dutch come to have plenty of coin? With few natural resources for export, how could the Dutch engross the production of other countries? How did the Dutch have low interest rates and high land values? How were high wages maintained with a burgeoning population? How could high prices and widespread prosperity exist simultaneously in the Low Countries? Pet theories, which could be indulged in private conversations, were exposed to critical analysis through publications on the Dutch example. Throughout the middle decades of the century when the Dutch were such formidable rivals to English merchants, writers systematically investigated the interconnections of their commercial economy. By the end

[18] "The Mercantile System in the Time of Thomas Mun," *Economic History Review* 2nd ser. 7 (1955), p. 287.

of the period, key assumptions about market relations had entered the public discourse in a way that decisively influenced all subsequent social thought. The discrete facts of buying and paying, employing and earning, producing and selling were woven into a single economic paradigm susceptible to sustained inquiry.

Central to the efforts to analyze market relations was the conviction that there existed a determinable order. When Edward Misselden and Thomas Mun challenged Gerald de Malynes' belief that a properly run economy required the wisdom and authority of the monarch, they redirected attention from the council chamber to the activity in the market. In denying the central place to sovereignty, however, they did not suggest that individual market decisions determining the flow of coin were random or idiosyncratic. Rather they assumed a uniformity operating at all economic levels. This assumption led to the idea of economic laws and the conviction that anarchy was not the inevitable alternative to external control. It laid the scientific foundation for individual economic freedom. Mun's famous explanation of the coin shortage of the 1620s exemplified this new intellectual orientation. Not only was he at pains to reveal the actual workings of commerce but he also chose to focus upon the uniformities he saw and to ignore the deviations. Implicit in Mun's analysis was the autonomy of commercial relations. Money, he explained, was not an independent force in the economy. Rather it followed trade. Only by selling more goods to a country than one bought from it could coin be permanently attracted to England. Without a favorable balance of trade, every statutory gimmick to attract coin would be unavailing.[19] Experience tended to confirm Mun's explanation, and the balance of trade theory prompted the demand for accurate trade figures.[20] In time it was used to defend proposals for encouraging manufactur-

[19] *Englands treasure by forraign trade*, pp. 11-14, 217-20.
[20] G. N. Clark, *Guide to English Commercial Statistics, 1696-1782*, London, 1938, p. xiii.

ing, restricting consumption and disencumbering foreign trade, but the more enduring contribution of Mun's economic reasoning was to fix attention upon the process behind the acquisition of wealth.

The assumption that predictable cause-and-effect relationships operated in the world of commerce made the economic analysis of the seventeenth century a search for order. However self-serving a writer might be, he embedded his pet program in an explanatory context of antecedent conditions and consequent effects. Slowly the novelty and diversity of market relations assumed a pattern. Benjamin Worsley, publicizing "certain general Canons or Rules belonging to Manufactures" reflects very accurately this cast of mind:

> . . . all manufactures . . . if they are of a certain goodness, They are (like Coin) of a certain value and price also . . .

> . . . two persons selling or making Commodities of a like goodness hee shall have the preference of the Market, that will sell them the cheapest: And so two Nations likewise.

> . . . the Cheapness of Manufactures, and artificial commodities, doth altogether depend upon the plentie and cheapness of the matter, and upon the like cheapness of price, for Handie-labour.[21]

An indefatigable analyzer, Sir William Petty, tried to calculate the intrinsic value of all things. The creation of value in the market tantalized him. Trying to cut into the circle of prices that bound land rent, corn prices, and money, he hypothesized that the value of corn determined the value of rent and the value of silver determined the value of—that is, the amount paid for—corn. Hence, if you figured the production during a ten-year period between

[21] *The advocate*, pp. 7-8.

one hundred men growing corn and one hundred men mining silver, you could compute the price of land.[22] In other works over a thirty-year period of grappling with the same problems, Petty came to appreciate that events made "Silver rise and fall, and consequently take from the perfect Aptitude for being an uniform steady Rule and Measure of all things."[23] Labor, he believed, created value, and a day's work was tied to the price of a day's food. Caught in the puzzle between accepting market prices as evidence of value—sailors being three times more valuable than husbandmen because they were paid three times more—and determining what influenced market prices—the division of labor lowered prices and events influenced the change in the value of silver—Petty never resolved the basic question of value, but his systematic inquiries lead him through voluminous calculations and hypotheses. "I . . . who Profess no Politicks," he announced, "have for my curiosity at large attempted the first essay of political anatomy." Petty assumed that economic relationships were amenable to scientific investigation. He was mindful of the overwhelming difficulty of achieving precision, but driven on by the conviction that without the effort to discover basic laws "Trade will be too conjectural a work for any man to imploy his thoughts about."[24]

John Graunt, another cultivator of the spirit of analysis, raised the question at the end of his *Natural and political observations* of why one should study the kinds of facts he had assembled about the hay yields of different sorts of meadows and the man hours of work required for particular jobs, and he answered that the art of governing is how to preserve the subject in peace and plenty. Men have generally studied how to supplant and overreach one another, he explained, anticipating the benign trade notion by characterizing his as "This honest, harmless Policy" of providing

---

[22] [Petty] *A treatise of taxes and contributions*, 1662, pp. 30-31, K 1098.
[23] *Political anatomy of Ireland*, 1691, pp. 68-69, K 1769.
[24] *Ibid.*, pp. 65-69; *A treatise of taxes*, p. 33.

for peace and plenty.[25] For Graunt, like William Petty, the close study of the actual details of economic life was going to enhance the capacity of man to make accurate predictions. Writers who did not stress the peacefulness of trade like Samuel Fortrey nonetheless reinforced the notion of the importance of collecting and analyzing data.[26] In the works of these men, almost every observable social fact became a dependent variable of an economic cause. Trade restrictions only invited retaliation, Henry Robinson argued, and farmers who raised prices prompted nonfarmers to import food.[27] Thomas Culpeper, Jr., inferred a thriving commerce for France by observing the safety of her cities, for he believed that prosperity, and not severe laws, inhibited crime.[28] The Dutch were industrious, Sir William Temple decided, not because of their natural disposition but because the dearness of prices in the Low Countries forced them to effort, ingenuity, and parsimony.[29] England's underemployment produced more murderers and more emigrants, John Keymer maintained, and Sir William Petty confirmed the low market value of soldiers and husbandmen by noting their scarcity in wealthy Holland.[30] From fact to fact these writers worked themselves back to the economic starting point as they slowly created a new reality for their society.

The intrusiveness of the market became a subtle and persistent force. The market offered an opportunity for exchange—originally at a designated spot—but with increasing commercialization the market represented an area laced by a communication–transportation network within which uniform prices prevailed. Prices expressed the coalescence of

[25] *Natural and political observations*, 1662, pp. 67-68, K 1094.

[26] *Englands interest*, 1663, K. 1337.

[27] *Englands safety*, pp. 51, 8.

[28] [Culpeper, Jr.], *A discourse, shewing the many advantages which will accrue to this kingdom by the abatement of usury*, 1668, pp. 11-12, K 1215.

[29] *An essay upon the advancement of trade in Ireland*, Dublin, 1673; [Temple], *Miscellanea*, 1680, pp. 90-100, K 1522.

[30] *Political arithmetick*, p. 30.

human demands and capacities in relation to desired objects. The diversity of goods for sale suggested the possibility of committing time and energy to the production of surpluses to be exchanged for other goods. The market mechanism thus became a regulator of human activity: dispensing rewards, providing valuable information, and encouraging long-range planning through rational calculations. It turned individuals and their communities outward toward the assessment of the economic demands and productive possibilities of others.

The market also prompted the reordering of social values, placing a premium upon utility and efficiency. Unchecked, this propensity to value things by their utility extended to the valuing of people and land. The involvement of people and land in the logic of the market was a critical stage in the transformation of modern society. When the calculations originally appropriate for products became an acceptable way for evaluating the principal components of a society— the men, women and children and the ground which sustained life—then social relations were directed by economic processes rather than tradition, authority, or moral precepts. The development of economic reasoning in seventeenth-century England indicates that the extension of market analysis from commodities to people and land was undertaken as an intellectual problem rather than a moral decision. As Sir William Petty expressed it, what remained to be done was to reduce market activities to a comprehensible formula. The most important consideration in political economy, he announced, was "how to make a Par and Equation between Lands and Labour, so as to express the Value of any thing be either alone."[31]

The very success of food production in England and the Netherlands in the seventeenth century broke the vital connection between social needs and individual responsibility which had so long kept work and profit subordinated to

[31] *Political anatomy of Ireland,* pp. 63-64.

the subsistence needs of society. With food surpluses visible to strangers in the great storehouses of Holland, and impressed upon Englishmen after the 1650s by the depressed price of grain, there emerged the possibility of treating food like any other commodity. Once liberated from the restrictions justified by scarcity, food could assume its place in a rational economic scheme as an interchangeable commodity equalized by a price tag. The recognition of this fact found its way into economic literature by the 1640s. "Amsterdam is never without 700,000 Quarters of Corn, besides the plenty they daily vent, and none of this groweth in their own Country," John Keymer informed his readers.[32] Henry Robinson noted that: "Spaine, Portugal and Holland, have very little Corne of their owne sowing, and yet eate as much bread as we doe." The international flow of food suggested to Robinson that no one was dependent upon any particular set of farmers. In fact, he wrote that if farmers raised their prices instead of productivity, nonfarmers would import their food from foreign countries.[33] Food surpluses had created a regular market in food products, which in turn affected the market in land. The price of land, the author of *The decay of trade* announced, was determined by the balance of trade. If there were plenty of trade, land prices would be high, but if land prices "be too much raised, then the proprieties of monies (or many of them) will indeavour to deliver it for more profit at Interest, to supply the occasions of those who will imploy it in forraigne Trade or otherwise . . ."[34] Another writer drew attention to the importance of the inland trade in making improvements profitable. "If Land be made fruitful or fertile, and the fruit of it have no vent, or prove unprofitable," he hypothesized, "where is the improvement? It rather causes a great plenty, and as great waste, where a Domestick Trade is wanting."[35]

[32] *A clear and evident way*, p. 5.   [33] *Englands safety*, p. 8.
[34] *The decay of trade*, 1641, p. 2.
[35] *The use and abuses of money*, 1671, pp. 14-15, K 1303.

This awareness of the marketing problem of agricultural surpluses dawned in the latter part of the century when higher yields had led to depressed prices, but earlier pamphleteers had written as though greater yields required no justification. The possibility of enhancing productivity led to a rash of pamphlets. Sir Richard Weston detailed his experiences in Flanders where Dutch "bores" turned heathland into arable acreage in flax, turnips, and clover grass. He computed the profit by years from these crops and produced a formula for converting 500 acres of barren land in five years to an income of £7,000 a year.[36] William Blith's *English improver* and *The improver improved*, James Lambert's *The countryman's treasure*, Gervaise Markham's frequently reissued pamphlets, Moses Cook's *The manner of raising, ordering, and improving forrest-trees*, John Houghton's periodical publications, Captain John Smith's *England's improvement reviv'd*, Arthur Standish's *New directions*, Rowland Vaughan's *Most approved, and long experienced water-workes*, and Samuel Hartlib's many tracts take up and elaborate the refrain of turning mercury into gold through the modern alchemy of agricultural improvements. The new cult of productivity is epitomized by the utopia of Macaria where anyone who persisted in holding land without improvement would be banished by the Council of Husbandry.[37]

From the market came the cues for proper crops. Samuel Fortrey advanced the theory that since other nations sell corn cheap, England should import it and turn the land to cattle, which could be exported more profitably: "our care should therefore be to increase chiefly those things which

36 [Weston], *A discourse of husbandry*, 1605 [i.e. 1650], p. 20, K 905. For a discussion of Samuel Hartlib's association with this publication sometimes attributed to him, see Charles Webster, "The Authorship and Significance of 'Macaria," in *idem*, ed., *The Intellectual Revolution of the Seventeenth Century*, London, 1974, p. 383, n. 44.

37 *Ibid.*, pp. 370-80; [Hartlib?], *A description of the famous kingdome of Macaria*, 1641, p. 4, K 579.

are of least charge at home, and greatest value abroad." He went on to explain that as long as neighboring countries had cheap corn, anything Englishmen could raise that was more expensive would fetch not only corn but the difference in "plenty of money to boot."[38] What Fortrey generalized for the nation, the Reverend Joseph Lee had earlier personalized when he asked, "By what Law of God or man is every man bound to plow his land at all times, whether there be need of corn or no, although he can make more advantage to himself by pasture?"[39] The experience with abundance made it possible to contemplate a freer economic life.

Increasingly, questions of productivity for profit turned to the role of interest rates, and here again the Dutch example stimulated a wide-ranging discussion in the 1660s and 1670s. The long shadow of the Deuteronomic injunction against the charging of interest had been totally eclipsed by the analytic spirit, and those who wrapped themselves in biblical quotations did so not to evoke the Mosaic law against profiting from one's brother's need but rather to urge the lowering of rates so that more people might become enterprising. The dispute over statutory limitations of interest rates forced a precision upon the economic writings, for interest rates affected the most conspicuous market nexus when demand for credit for economic expansion pressed hard against available capital resources. Observers clearly perceived that the competition for money among landlords, tenants, merchants, manufacturers, and spenders created a situation in which the behavior of the one necessarily influenced the options open to the other. As Henry Robinson put it, "Interest is the rule by which wee buy, sell, and governe our selves when wee are to imploy our moneys both in building, planting, trading, &c."[40]

[38] *Englands interest*, p. 14. See also [Richard Haines], *The prevention of poverty*, 1674, p. 7, K 1361.
[39] *A vindication of a regulated enclosure*, 1956, p. 8, K 936.
[40] *Englands safety*, pp. 6-7.

As with so many other contemporary issues, both the Dutch example and the painful necessity of competing with the Dutch in foreign markets stimulated economic reasoning. The Dutch enjoyed a burgeoning trade, a remarkable prosperity, had plenty of money, high land values, high prices, and the lowest interest rate in Europe. A group of English writers were convinced that Dutch success stemmed from their low rate of interest. In the late 1660s Thomas Culpeper, Jr., republished his father's pamphlet against usury and added several new tracts arguing the same points. Wrestling with the problem of gauging the impact of interest rates upon the price of land, Culpeper came close to a marginal utility conception as the basis of rent. Some land, he explained, was so poor that no one could afford to put stock into it: "Nay, if the Land be naturally very poor, no man can afford it ordinary Culture or Stock, but to his present undoing." But Culpeper's goal was not to arrive at a method for calculating rents but rather to demonstrate what reduced interest rates would do to stimulate agricultural improvements. The results, he foresaw, would be dramatic: "no Commons undivided, nor common fields un-inclosed."[41] Sir Josiah Child joined the Culpeper cause, adding his own pamphlets advocating a statutory reduction of the legal interest rate from 8 to 6 percent.[42] They said that usurers, without contributing to the economy, raised the cost of investment for those who did; high interest rates kept men from entering trade and prevented farmers from improving their land, because the cost of borrowing money to finance commercial or agricultural investments was greater than the likely profit. In all endeavors in which Englishmen had to compete with the Dutch, according to their argument, Englishmen were placed at a disadvantage because the Dutch could get money as low as 4 percent.

Evoking the universal disapproval of "mere consump-

---

[41] [Culpeper, Jr.,], *A discourse*, 1668, pp. 6-7, K 1217.

[42] [Child], *A short addition to the observations*, 1668, pp. 12-14, K 1213; and *Brief observations*, 1668, K 1212.

tion," Culpeper labeled usury the worst form of consumption, as it was an excise on both land and trade. Child maintained that to permit the unproductive usurer to garner 8 percent for his money was to "suffer Idleness to Suck the Breasts of Industry."[43] For Culpeper, the basis of national wealth lay with the improvement of land. "Every Countrey is so far forth considerable as it is manured, and no farther." Were the costs of farming lessened by low interest rates, he theorized, then the value of hundreds of newly improved acres would be added to the kingdom's wealth. "Who would longer think of three per cent. when, by purchasing and improving Land, (he) might make above ten," he asked rhetorically.[44] Thus, behind Culpeper's theories about the pernicious effect of high interest rates there lay the assumption that agricultural improvements were being actively checked by the high cost of borrowing; the differential between the costs of investment and the returns of those investments in agriculture kept improvable land uncultivated.

Both Child and Culpeper used the image of two buckets, presumed to be balanced on the shoulders of a carrier. For Culpeper, the buckets represented the tenants' payments in rents and in stock—when the one went up the other went down. For Child the buckets were land prices and interest rates—when interest rates went down, land prices went up. Child also emphasized the avenues of trade that went unexplored because of high interest rates. Only those trades that rendered a profit large enough to cover the cost of borrowing were currently developed, he maintained, and only those merchants who feared an increase in traders benefited from this restriction. Society, however, would benefit richly from a low interest rate because it would "certainly and necessarily increase Industry and good Husbandry."[45] The terms of the usury debate had finally been limited to factors influential in a commercial economy.

[43] *Ibid.*, p. 14.   [44] *A discourse*, p. 6.
[45] *A short addition*, p. 13.

Critics who entered the field against Child and Culpeper accused them of confusing a symptom with a cause. The low interest rate in Holland had not prompted the productivity that produced the prosperity of the Dutch, they said, rather, it had been their prosperity that had caused the low interest rate. Disputing Child and Culpeper's contention that the Dutch economy offered evidence that lower interest rates produced high land values, their opponents asserted that land values had not risen earlier in the century when the statutory interest rate had been lowered and, further, that land values were high in Holland because land was scarce. They capped their argument by pointing out that the Dutch operated without a statutory interest rate limit, proof in their eyes that other economic factors determined the interest rate and the thriving state of Dutch trade.[46] The anonymous author of the *Interest of money mistaken* maintained that if England wished to enjoy a lower interest rate she must do those things that Holland does, "which will bring it naturally low, and not to think to do that by compulsion with us, which with them is done by nature." What he went on to define as "by nature" turned out to be a process of sustained commercial growth: "They have, by the means of Trade, much more people than land; their trade makes plenty of money and people; their plenty of money, with abundance of people, makes land dear, and the dearness of land, with plenty of money, makes Interest, naturally low."[47]

The author of *The brief observations of J. C.* also attacked Child's notion that the Hollanders' low interest rates had caused their thriving trade and high land prices. Instancing Scotland and other countries that were poor and had high interest rates, he pointed out that their poverty had caused their high interest rates, not their high interest rates their poverty. Ridiculing the idea that low interest

[46] *The brief observations of J. C. . . . briefly examined*, 1668; *Interest of money mistaken*, 1668, K 1222.
[47] *Ibid.*, pp. 21-23.

rates had raised land values in Holland, he attributed the land prices to the scarcity of land, the density of the population in the country, and the great wealth there. Turning Child's argument for low interest rates on its head, he went on to say that raising interest rates would be a better way of stimulating the economy, for it would attract coin and multiply the number of traders "who will work hard to learn commerce and beat the Dutch and will give every man credit in his private affairs and those that suffer by it, the blame will be their own."[48] Thomas Mun, writing forty years earlier, had pointed out the need to expand credit and lure money into borrowing capital through higher interest rates. It did not follow, Mun had written, that usury hurt trade for the rich-men-turned-usurers enabled young merchants "to rise in the world, and to enlarge their dealings . . . so that our money lies not dead, it is still traded."[49] Thomas Manley in *Usury at six per cent. examined* echoed the point, arguing that the hiring of money for the quickening of trade and commerce was as necessary to mankind as the hiring of land.[50]

Culpeper and Child evidently believed that legislation could redistribute earnings from the lender to the investor, commercial or agricultural, while their opponents emphasized the relationship between the money supply and interest rates. Again, the international scope of trade worked to limit the political control over the economy. Henry Robinson, for instance, stressed that no law could increase the stock of money even if it lowered the interest rate, and pointed to the possibility of England's losing foreign capital. "Wee had better pay twelve or thirteen in the hundred," he wrote, "as they doe in Turkey, if we cannot get it cheaper, then be quite without it."[51] Explaining the decrease in the volume of trade to a committee of Parliament in 1650,

---

[48] *Ibid.*, pp. 64-65, 37.
[49] *England's treasure by forraign trade*, p. 144.
[50] *Usury at six per cent. examined*, 1669, Preface, pp. 32-33, K 1241.
[51] *Certain proposalls*, p. 10.

Thomas Violet pointed to the withdrawal of foreign capital at the outbreak of the Civil War while others claimed more positively that England's high interest rates attracted Dutch money to the country, an advantage that capital-hungry Englishmen could not ignore.[52] As the importance of credit expansion in stimulating the productive activities surfaced, so the creditor or usurer himself appeared in a new, more constructive, light. Waxing eloquent on the subject, the author of *The brief observations* explained that "as credit is the sinew of conversation, and nourisher of correspondency, the great manager of affairs: So is the Usurer the *causa emanativa* of this Credit."[53] Commenting more dryly on the issue, Sir William Petty said that he could see no reason to want to limit the rate of interest "unless it be that those who make such Laws were rather Borrowers than Lenders."[54] For Manley the answer was clear: if people could make 15 percent by the use of money, the person who supplied the money should enjoy half of the profit, whereas 4 percent interest "will hardly reward the telling in and out."[55]

While much of this pamphlet debate turned on disputes over facts—whether land values had or had not risen when the statutory limit was lowered earlier or whether the laws had actually influenced the usury rate—there were significant theoretical differences. Both sides aimed to promote productivity, but the critics of lowering the statutory limits imputed Dutch prosperity to its naturalness. Culpeper and Child extracted one relationship, that between interest rates and the return on investments, and advanced the idea that the manipulation of this one relationship would stimulate productivity. Their proposal implicitly denied that commerce represented a complicated set of interactions. By

---

[52] "Thomas Violet's Report on the Decay of Trade, 1650," in Joan Thirsk and J. P. Cooper, eds., *Seventeenth-Century Economic Documents*, Oxford, 1972, pp. 58-59.

[53] p. 63.   [54] *A treatise of taxes*, p. 29.

[55] *Usury at six per cent. examined*, p. 3.

pointing this out, the other writers strengthened the view that trade possessed its own laws, thus making it inherently difficult to control the economy through political authority. They pointed to the fact that the system transcended the separate political sovereignties and therefore operated outside the control of any one nation. Thomas Manley chided Child for thinking that the French and the Dutch would sit back and let England outdo them in trade by the mere expedient of lowering the interest rate.[56] What was more important for the future development of economic thought —and eventually all social theorizing—was the deduction that the system was in some sense natural because it operated without political direction.

Working through the discussions on usury, as through those on exchange rates and market values, was the pervasive assumption of an underlying order beneath the diversity of discrete actions in the market. Since the exchanges of the market—money for land, land for stock, money for labor, labor for money—had become almost entirely a matter of individual choice rather than the fulfillment of social obligations, any concept of order in a market economy necessarily implied a uniformity of human response. Prices, interest rates, exchange rates—once they slipped the bond of political control—represented the sum of individual decisions aggregated at the point of exchange. Behind the sales nexus of commerce was a human nexus. If market relations were treated as predictable, this necessarily involved a conception of human behavior as being sufficiently consistent to support that predictability. Whether consciously or not, economic writers imputed to human nature a constancy that permitted them to treat it as a dependable factor in analysis. Men might be charitable; they might be foolhardy or absent-minded, but for purposes of economic reasoning men were handled as rational calculators animated by a drive for personal gain. The pressure

[56] *Ibid.*, p. 13.

to understand economic relationships encouraged an emphasis upon regularities and consistency. Moreover, the random responses of others in international commerce were hidden from view. Instead, only the conclusion of the bargain was transmitted, summarized in the impersonal price, the method of whose exact determination could not be retraced. This reality not only worked to minimize the importance of personal influence but also strengthened the idea that trade was an inexorable process beyond the reach of human interference—like nature itself. Included in this concept was the embryonic economic man whose natural propensities moved the whole.

When Adam Smith freighted the full burden of automatic, self-sustaining economic laws upon the basic human qualities of a love to "truck and barter" and a ceaseless urge to "self-improvement," he was standing in a long line of thinkers who had rested their theories upon these tendencies in human behavior. As early as 1601 John Wheeler had written that "there was nothing in the world so ordinarie, and naturall unto men, as to contract, truck, merchandize, and traffike one with an other," adding that it was almost impossible "for three persons to converse together two houres, but they wil fal into talk of one bargaine or another, chopping, changing, or some other kinde of contract."[57] Similarly, Misselden detailed the elements of trade: commodities and money the matter, buying and selling the form of trade: "He that tradeth the Efficient: gaine the End of trade."[58] Thomas Culpeper, Sr., declared that "private gaine is the compass men generally saile by," and Gerald de Malynes spoke of a policy being executed more by gain than by authority "because Gaine doth beare sway and command with most men."[59] "I must apply my Conceit to the Commonwealth as it is," Rice Vaughn announced, "not as a

---

[57] *A treatise of commerce*, 1601, p. 6, K 242.

[58] [Misselden], *The circle of commerce*, 1623, p. 7, K 403.

[59] [Culpeper], *A tract against usurie*, 1621, p. 9, K 380; and *The maintenance of free trade*, 1622, p. 85, K 391.

Philosopher may frame it," as he went on to speak of the world of the merchant "who seeketh his profit."[60] Sir John Gilbert was equally explicit on this point: "So longe as there is a gayne in the weight . . . of monies they will be still transported notwithstandinge any laws or prohibitions."[61] For gain to be so widely recognized as a prompter of human action is not surprising, but what needs to be considered more fully is the way that the reliance upon the motive of gain in explanations of economic activities permitted writers to construe the social patterns as orderly processes. In this way the natural law of medieval Christianity of "what ought to be" gradually was replaced by a natural law of regularities, which could be manipulated but not changed. Subtly, the acceptance of the personal drive for private gain as a legitimate and ineradicable human quality became integrated into new theories about the economy.

Writers frequently expressed the belief that public authority could not enforce laws that went against the strong and universal desire for gain. Considering that stealing is a gainful occupation, the special exemption that economic writers made for breaking laws controlling trade is significant. Henry Robinson frequently described high customs duties as a temptation to evade the customs, and impugned efforts to prohibit the export of bullion. Appealing to his reader's common sense, he wrote: "But put the case I had urgent occasion to use £100 in Paris, and find no body that will take it by Exchange . . . the danger or penalty not answerable to my expected profit, no doubt I may likely be moved to export it in specie."[62] His hypothetical case of the overriding lure of "expected profit" is all the more interesting for being presented in the first person. Thomas Violet similarly urged the reduction of customs on French wines

---

[60] *A discourse of coin and coinage*, 1675, p. 36, K 1394.

[61] Sir John Gilbert, "The Humble Remonstrance," 1626 in William A. Shaw, ed., *Select Tracts and Documents Illustrative of English Monetary History, 1626-1720*, London, 1896, p. 140.

[62] *Englands safety*, p. 58.

to remove the abuse of "falsely labeled Rhenish wine."[63] Sir William Petty also cautioned that "care must be had in laying impositions on luxuries to restrain the use of them that they not be so high that it be not better to smuckle than to pay."[64] Such statements hint at an attitudinal change of great importance. Laws were not seen as coming down from authority; rather they worked up from the propensities of the people. Policy makers could best realize their aims by working with the known nature of man, relying upon his tendency to seek profit instead of his disposition to obey authority and avoid punishment. Unwanted trade patterns were not prohibited; they were rendered expensive. Items that could be smuggled easily should not be heavily dutied. Magistrates and legislators no doubt had always appreciated the human incentives to break the law. What the commercial economy added to the situation was a tremendous increase in the number of occasions for violating the law in what might be called the normal course of business. The extension of the market was simultaneously the extension of the individual subject's access to the informal communication network represented by the market. The Dutch had been willing to nurture this complex social organization of the market by protecting the individual initiative on which it throve. Their success compelled attention, and their policies brought to light a system of uncoerced human activity. As one astute pamphleteer put it, the Dutch had "Triumphed over Nature" through a steady pursuit of policy, because in the United Provinces, concern with trade was interwoven with the "Original Scheme of Government."[65]

To borrow an explanation from the sociologists, we can say that the economic writings of the middle decades of the seventeenth century indicate the construction of a new social reality. Contemporaries were legitimizing the acquisitive

---

[63] *The advancement of merchandize*, 1651, p. 19, K 839.

[64] *A treatise of taxes*, p. 36.

[65] *Considerations requiring greater care for trade in England*, 1695, p. 6, K 1877.

instinct by incorporating it in economic theories that promised to unlock the secrets of success in the new market economy. Pressed to bring intellectual order to the world of trade, economic writers sought out the hidden relations in market operations. Slowly there grew up a concept of trade that emphasized the interrelatedness of the thousands of discrete acts of buying and selling. Implanted and propagated as a part of this concept of commerce was a new vision of man's essential nature. What began as an explanation became a rationale for market practices. The uniform propensity to seek gain was turned into a constant in human behavior that permitted calculation and prediction. Equally significant in theorizing on the economy were the unseen forces in the market. The Dutch created wealth out of nothing; they attracted goods with the new power of quick sales, easy exchanges, and ready cash. In terms of sensibilities, the Dutch displayed unheroic qualities; they popularized the value of commercial virtues. Searching for the origins of Dutch wealth, English writers found it in the mundane world of herring, efficient labor, low interest rates, and land registers. In the Dutch experience there was also the revelation of the dynamics of productivity. Steady work habits, increased expenditures of human energy, efficient integration of industrial and commercial activities—these suggested that wealth could be expanded through organization and effort. As we have seen, this management lesson was often used polemically to advance particular legislative schemes. In fact, throughout the century there ran a debate between those who sought a properly managed foreign trade and those who extolled the benefits of an unrestrained commercial life, but underlying both of these arguments was the assumption that economic phenomena could be understood. The claims of the scientific mode of investigation to deliver mastery through knowledge were advanced by both sides.

Another explicit assumption in the economic reasoning was that all goods were readily available through the market. Effective demand replaced production or possession as the critical variable. The seventeenth-century theorizing about the preferability of buying or growing corn indicates that the economy had moved beyond the overriding concern with just obtaining food. With this gone, the vital link between society and economy that justified political direction was cut. As long as food can be bought, it can be treated like any other commodity and the economic calculations based on the complete interchangeability of goods can emerge. The new scarcity is an abstraction—a hypothetical condition created when people's desires outdistance actual goods. The real scarcity of a subsistence economy with population pressing upon its productive resources had now been replaced by the psychological scarcities of imagined wants heightened by a commerce rapidly extending in size and diversity of goods.

No doubt market practices preceded published analyses of them, but the growing body of economic literature in mid-century England was more than a passive response to economic developments. The propagation of common assumptions converted shared observations into operating premises. It also directed attention to the critical links needing further analysis. Contemporaries now had a language for discussing the market force in their lives and, because the conceptualization of the commercial economy was carried out in pamphlets and tracts, the language was both public and impersonal, like the market it described.

Five

Contending Views of the Role of the State

DESPITE THE UNCHALLENGED ASSUMPTION that the English government had the right and the responsibility to regulate economic activities in the interest of the common good, the ambit of private initiative widened considerably during the middle decades of the seventeenth century. Circumstances—usually in the form of a political crisis—permitted men to pursue their private profit with little official interference. The only enduring policy decision in the economic domain came early in the century when, as Barry Supple has explained, "as far as official doctrine was concerned, all thoughts of unduly restraining the processes of industrialization had disappeared."[1] Once diversification and the exploitation of new markets were seen as preferable to the protection of a stable agrarian order, opportunities for enterprise grew at a much more rapid rate than the capacity of government to oversee them. Enclosures continued to provoke protests just as depressions prompted government inquiries, but relief from distress usually came from the economy itself. In the absence of political direction, the informal incentives of gain guided men toward new avenues of investment and new ways of mobilizing resources. Conventional convictions about the propriety of state intervention, however, enabled opponents of economic freedom to view this situation as anomalous while sensibilities formed in the past and attitudes preserved in the law stoked the fires of criticism.

In every aspect of economic life in the 1640s, 1650s and 1660s, practices violated the expectations framed in an earlier period. Cloth making was so venerable an occupation

[1] *Commercial Crisis and Change in England 1600-1642*, Cambridge, 1964, pp. 235-36.

that there were dozens of statutes specifying the proper procedures in the producing and selling of England's famous woolens. The strengthening of English commercial ties with the Mediterranean markets, however, had encouraged clothiers to organize the weaving of new fabrics. This meant that the elaborate industrial code of the Tudors became increasingly obsolete. Political distractions prevented the working out of new legislation. Enforcement of the old laws was generally neglected except in times of severe crisis. Renewed efforts to achieve some measure of political supervision over the cloth industry foundered with successive changes of government.[2] Although during the Restoration there was general agreement on the need to control the quality of cloth and to suppress the export of raw wool, neither goal was achieved. A final burst of enthusiasm for industrial regulation led to only one new law and that was for the compulsory wearing of woolens.[3] At the same time, municipal governments were losing their grip on urban industrial life. The conservatism of the city magistracies encouraged entrepreneurs to move to the suburbs where they were able to avoid yet another set of restraints.[4]

After mid-century abundant harvests contributed to economic freedom. The society's dependence upon the food supply provided, after all, the rock bottom reason for political control of economic activities. The terrible harvests of the late 1640s had prompted authorities to enforce the old Tudor Statutes. Alehouses were suppressed and the sale of grain to maltsters limited.[5] The vitality of the govern-

[2] J. P. Cooper, "Economic Regulation and the Cloth Industry in Seventeenth-Century England," Royal Historical Society *Transactions* 5th ser. 20 (1970), 76; and G. D. Ramsay, "Industrial *laissez-faire* and the policy of Cromwell," *Economic History Review* 1st ser. 16 (1946), 108.

[3] Cooper, "Economic Regulation and the Cloth Industry," pp. 92-93.

[4] Peter Clark and Paul Slack, eds., *Crisis and Order in English Towns 1500-1700*, London, 1972, pp. 33-36.

[5] John Walter and Keith Wrightson, "Dearth and the Social Order in Early Modern England," *Past and Present* 71 (1976); A. L. Beier,

ment's concern about famine indicated the perseverence of traditional attitudes, but when dearth disappeared in subsequent years so too did the urgency for government action. And as the fear of famine receded, food lost its special character and became a commodity like all others. Proposals to reform the Poor Laws expired with the Rump.[6] Thenceforth increasing employment appeared a better way to relieve the needy than controlling the grain trade. The ideal of government responsibility did not die altogether. Samuel Hartlib received a pension from Cromwell to promote agricultural improvements.[7] Many in Hartlib's circle hoped that the government would take the lead in reclaiming wastes, draining fens, and introducing new crops, but here, as elsewhere in the economy, private individuals initiated change.[8] The ordinance of 1645, which converted all land tenure by knight tenure into free and common socage not only lifted the burden of fuedal dues from the country's principal landlords but also strengthened the conviction that property was a private rather than a public resource. Seventeenth-century enclosures still called forth popular protests and official disapproval, but landowners could justify the extinguishing of common rights on the grounds that village control inhibited the adoption of advanced farming techniques. With abundant yields landlords extended the range of their private interests as exporters in the international grain trade.[9]

Opportunities in foreign commerce grew apace. England's

"Poor Relief in Warwickshire, 1630-1660," *ibid.* 35 (1966); and J. P. Cooper, "Social and Economic Policies under the Commonwealth," in G. E. Aylmer, ed., *The Interregnum*, London, 1972, pp. 140-41.

[6] *Ibid.*, p. 139.

[7] E. L. Jones, ed., *Agriculture and Economic Growth in England 1650-1815*, London, 1967, p. 7, n. 1.

[8] Charles Webster, "The Authorship and Significance of 'Macaria," in *idem*, ed., *The Intellectual Revolution of the Seventeenth Century*, London, 1974, pp. 378-79.

[9] Eric Kerridge, *The Agricultural Revolution*, New York, 1968, p. 332.

penetration of world markets in the late sixteenth and early seventeenth centuries had been carefully guided by the specifications of royal charters granting well-defined privileges to merchant groups. The right of free entrance into new trades received an unexpected boost from the political opposition to James I.[10] The association of the rights of Englishmen with economic liberties continued through the remainder of the century. Changing estimates of the value of the trading companies made it harder to retain the old charter privileges. Free access to markets became an issue. The new colonial trades grew up outside the restrictions of the chartered companies.[11] The Merchant Adventurers, who controlled the export of cloths to England's old markets in Germany and the Low Countries, found their monopoly repeatedly at risk.[12] The East India Company lost its charter during the Interregnum,[13] and the domestic traders whose collective enterprise created a single internal English market operated almost entirely outside the purview of government.

Englishmen enjoyed an increasingly free hand with their money as well. The East India Company secured the right to export bullion, a concession that was later extended to all. The Free Coinage Act of 1666 abolished mint charges and facilitated the conversion of silver into coin at the discretion of the individual.[14] The clipping of silver coins, a felonious but widely practiced act, could have been stopped, but laws to remint with an unclippable fluted edge were not passed, and clipping went on for the rest of the century.[15] The statu-

[10] Theodore K. Rabb, "Free Trade and the Gentry in the Parliament of 1604," *Past and Present* 40 (1968).

[11] Robert Brenner, "The Social Basis of English Commercial Expansion, 1550-1650," *Journal of Economic History* 32 (1972), 374-80.

[12] W. K. Jordan, *Men of Substance*, Chicago, 1942, pp. 207-09.

[13] Maurice Ashley, *Financial and Commercial Policy Under the Cromwellian Protectorate*, 2nd ed., London, 1962, p. 37; Cooper, "Social and Economic Policies," p. 124.

[14] Sir Albert Feavearyear, *The Pound Sterling*, Oxford, 1963 (originally published in 1931), p. 119.

[15] Cooper, "Social and Economic Policies," p. 139.

tory maximum on the interest rate was dropped to 6 percent in 1666, but contemporary evidence suggests that rates followed private bargains, not legal standards. Moreover, this private but vigorous money market relieved landlords of the necessity of bleeding capital from their tenants and thereby helped promote leasing arrangements attuned to the rhythms of the market.[16] The exigencies of opposition also encouraged Parliament to curtail the privileges of the king's creditors, thus cutting one more link between state authority and economic life.[17]

The Navigation Act of 1651 represented a genuine departure in public policy.[18] Its goal was economic and progressive rather than social and conservative. The provisions of the act were designed to eliminate the Dutch as the principal shippers of English imports, a purpose that had the merit of joining various economic and political interests.[19] In the Restoration a new Navigation Act confirmed the first and went on to lay the foundation for national trade monopolies within which individual English entrepreneurs might operate. The succession of Anglo–Dutch wars did more than the embryonic seventeenth-century navigation system to check Dutch commercial dominance, but the acts signified a new attitude toward government regulation. Traditionally, public authority had entered the economic domain to prevent social disturbances. Here the government was seizing the initiative to promote English enterprise and was placing the power of the state behind national economic development.

[16] Lawrence Stone, *The Crisis of the Aristocracy, 1558-1641*, Oxford, 1965, pp. 316-17.

[17] Robert Ashton, "Revenue Farming Under the Early Stuarts," *Economic History Review* 2nd ser. 8 (1955-56), 322.

[18] The historiography on the Navigation Acts is nicely recapitulated in the bibliography to Cooper, "Social and Economic Policies," p. 211.

[19] J. E. Farnell, "The Navigation Act of 1651, The First Dutch War and the London Merchant Community," *Economic History Review* 2nd ser. 16 (1964); and Charles Wilson, *Profit and Power*, London, 1957, pp. 56-57.

During the changes of government from monarchy to Parliament to Protectorate to restored monarchy there had been no clarion call for economic freedom. In the absence of control, market changes had produced the event without conscious intention. Throughout this period, men close to power continued to evoke the old ideal of subordinating economic activities in deference to social solidarity. The commercial buoyancy after mid-century, however, meant that individuals were responsible for starting up new manufacturing concerns, marketing colonial products, strengthening internal transportation systems, and building the great emporium of London. A complicated social organization took form, uncoerced but patterned, untraditional but not disordered, unrestrained but not without its own regulation. Contemporaries had to take stock of this complex market economy in order to protect their interests. The effort to understand economic relations compelled attention to the results of economic freedom even among those writers for whom a well-ordered trade was one that was strictly watched.

Most of the authors of economic tracts represented a particular facet of commercial life and drew upon the experience they gained in their specific dealings. As English commerce changed so did perspectives and consequently the richness of analysis. In the last half of the sixteenth century the export of cloth to Northern Europe had been the most important mercantile venture, closed to all but the Merchant Adventurers. At the end of the sixteenth century a second merchant group coalesced around the successive joint stock trading companies organized to open up markets in Russia, the Levant, and the East Indies. These merchants imported commodities that traders had formerly secured through middlemen in Spain, Portugal, and the Low Countries. Unable to find buyers for English goods in their far-flung ports, the merchants of the Levant, Turkey, Muscovy, and East India companies frequently exported specie, a practice sufficiently suspect in the early seventeenth century to require public justification. The conventional expectations about profits, markets, and ways of doing business inhibited established English merchants from pioneering the new avenues of trade that followed the English men and women who settled in the West Indies and along the Atlantic shelf of the North American continent. The colonial trade, unlike the great corporate structures of the older trades, involved both exports and imports, and it fell to a goodly number of small firms to make the connecting links for this new Atlantic network.[20] Thus, by the middle decades of the seventeenth century the merchant community itself represented strongly differentiated economic interests, which were sharply reflected in the analyses of economic relations that came from writers for the different groups.

The Merchant Adventurers had benefited greatly from the expansion of the English cloth trade to Northern Europe, an outcome of the accelerated tempo of international trade, but they retained, nonetheless, a traditional attitude toward society. The understood benefits of social stability and the assumption that there was just so much trade to go around provided the rationale for the company's trading privileges. The erratic fiscal policies of James I and Charles I disturbed the company's relations with the crown, but did not undermine the Adventurers' loyalty to the fixed, hierarchical arrangements of the kingdom. The real threat to the Merchant Adventurers came from interlopers and would-be interlopers, newcomers to foreign trade who chafed at the limited entry to lucrative markets and hoped to profit from the fact that an unpopular monarch's cavalier dispensation of favors had made monopolies a national issue.

Defenders of the Merchant Adventurers in public exchanges exuded the confidence of carriers of an old commercial tradition, appealing more to sensibilities than economic reasoning. John Wheeler set the tone for later

[20] Robert Brenner, "The Civil War Politics of London's Merchant Community," *Past and Present* 58 (1973), and *idem*, "The Social Basis of English Commercial Expansion."

apologies by comparing the advantages of the well-ordered Merchant Adventurers to "a dispersed, stragling, and promiscuous trade." Although he rehearsed the familiar claims that the Merchant Adventurers had succeeded in getting important privileges from princes and that private traders lowered the price of English wares by competing with one another, he built his case upon the antiquity of the Merchant Adventurers and the unseemliness of the new practices. Wheeler dismissed the argument for free trade with a pious statement that a trader who loses a little bit of his liberty will be better off "being restrained . . . in that estate, then if he were left to his owne greedy appetite." However, his concession that the right to trade was a proper liberty of the subject suggests that as early as 1601 lip-service was demanded for that position. His insistence that too many traders ruined any trade would also indicate that, despite the growth of the woolen trade, a sense of limited economic opportunity still dominated thinking about commerce.[21] When John Kayll publicly lamented the injustice of the company's monopoly "to keepe others out for ever," the company not only produced an answer from Sir Dudley Digges, a distinguished member of the enterprising gentry, but also secured the suppression of the pamphlet from the Archbishop of Canterbury and a stint in the Fleet for Kayll.[22]

By the 1640s the presumption that the established church, state, and trading corporations could not be challenged without damage to the social fabric no longer prevailed. Royal privileges shared in the opprobrium of all things royal. When attacks on company privileges reached a peak in the late 1640s, company defenders like Lewes

21 *A treatise of commerce,* 1601, pp. 54, 109-12. See also Jordan, *Men of Substance,* pp. 207-09.

22 [Kayll], *The trades increase,* 1615, p. 55, K 347. For the account of Kayll's imprisonment, see William Foster, "The Author of 'The Trades Increase,'" *Times Literary Supplement,* March 29, 1934; also [Digges], *The defence of trade,* 1615, K 341.

Roberts added a liberal program for the encouragement of trade to his recommendations for limiting participation to corporations and companies whose membership was restricted to the wealthy and the noble.[23] Under the deceptive title, *Of a free trade*, another company defender, Henry Parker, extolled the strengths of a rightly governed commerce. He emphasized both the need for quality control in the manufacturing of English woolens and the power the Merchant Adventurers could bring to bear in negotiating in foreign cities for trade privileges.[24] Henry Robinson explained to his readers that free trade might be beneficial at first but would run into disorder and the utter ruin of many "which must needs be the conclusion of all affaires managed by such as observe no good order, nor understand well what they goe about."[25] Critics of the great merchant companies wrote in the same moralistic vein. Thomas Johnson's *A plea for free-mens liberties* began with a little apostrophe to the "Machivilian empoysoned principles of king's cozening citizens of rights of liberty to which all civil government is subservient."[26] Referring to the standard of liberty raised by Lilburne, Johnson flailed away at all monopolies, but dealt with the subject exclusively in ethical and constitutional terms.

The merchant's profit remained suspect. When he facilitated the carrying off of English goods for foreign specie his worth was obvious, but he was frequently thought to desert his primary role in order to turn his hand at nefarious dealings in the exchange of monies. As a middle man in internal commerce, the retail trader was at best described as performing a sterile service; at worst he was a leech sucking from the commonwealth's agricultural and industrial producers. These attitudes precluded a constructive reevaluation of the role of self interest, and the widely accepted idea

[23] *The treasure of traffike*, 1641, p. 52, K 595.
[24] *Of a free trade*, 1648, passim, K 751.
[25] *Englands safety*, 1641, p. 46, K 597.
[26] *A plea for free-mens liberties*, 1646, prologue, K 694.

that those in trade were ruled by their pecuniary interests was used to combat the extension of freedoms. For Samuel Fortrey the recognition of the human tendency to seek personal gain was the strongest argument for central direction:

> private advantages are often impediments of publick profit; for in what any single person shall be a loser, there, endeavours will be made to hinder the publick gain, from whence proceeds the ill success that commonly attends the endeavours for publick good; for commonly it is but coldly prosecuted, because the benefit may possibly be something remote from them that promote it; but the mischief known and certain to them that oppose it: and Interest more than reason commonly sways most mens affections.

What is generally good for the public, he perceived, was too remote from the good of individuals to elicit any effort on their part, but those things that were immediately damaging to individuals would evoke their vigorous opposition. Hence, Fortrey concluded, the planning for public welfare should be placed in "a single power to direct, whose Interest is onely the benefit of the whole."[27] Writing forty years after Gerald de Malynes, Fortrey shared his belief in the need for central direction, but whereas Malynes advocated putting princes and statesmen at the helm of the ship of commerce because they understood commercial affairs better than mere merchants, Fortrey reflected the much more modern attitude that because merchants understood their interest too well they would act to protect it regardless of the effect upon the whole kingdom.

An articulate defender of merchants' interest, Robert Ferguson conceded that active traders were not always in the best position for judging trade "as it relates to the

[27] *Englands interest*, Cambridge, 1663, pp. 3-4, K 1337.

Profit or Power of a kingdom.''[28] Another pamphleteer explained that "the making of a great profit on a particular trade, may be fit for particular men to consider that trade, but was never yet thought a consideration worthy the legislators providing for," as he went on to explain, "the great profit which particular men may make, is for the most part directly opposite to the interest of the publick.''[29] Eager to check the English trade with France, Roger Coke referred his readers to Thomas Mun's observation that "the Kings Customs, and particular men, may grow rich by a Trade, whereby the Nation is impoverished: for Merchants, Vintners, Drawers, Exchange-people . . . grow Rich, and live higher than other men; but the Nation droops, and in a very short time will be beggared by them.''[30]

Initially, fears of merchants' shenanigans were not set forth with any clearly articulated theory of national wealth; rather they were baldly asserted as an appeal to the latent suspicions of the reader. This changed as writers attempted to define with some precision the basis for wealth. A new level of discourse was reached in the 1640s when advocates of free trade developed a theoretical argument for their demands for unrestricted entry to commercial endeavors. With the anonymous publication of *A discourse consisting of motives for the enlargement and freedom of trade*, the interlopers' cause was joined to the idea that economic growth could be stimulated by increasing the number of traders in the market. A very different notion of economic activity was projected from the one dominating the thinking of the members of the great trading companies. Reflecting the old closed circle mentality of the guilds, the older

[28] [Ferguson], *A treatise*, 1681, p. 1, K 1529. For the attribution to Ferguson, see William Letwin, *The Origins of Scientific Economics*, London, 1963, p. 234.

[29] *A discourse concerning the East-India trade*, in Walter Scott, ed., *Somers Tracts*, vol. 10, 1751, p. 642.

[30] *A treatise*, 1671, pp. 84-85, K 1287.

merchants had looked askance at competition among fellow traders and propagated the notion that such competition hurt England's trade as a whole—lowering the price of woolen exports and raising the price of foreign commodities purchased abroad.

The author of the *Discourse* conceded the point that opening the trade to all comers would beat down the price, but marked out a new ground for the dispute by asserting that lower prices could lead to higher total profits for the country because of the expansion of trade made possible by the price reductions. Attacking the Merchant Adventurers' contention that glutting would occur if merchants were allowed to go anywhere, he repudiated the notion that Englishmen should work to keep prices high. "As touching the esteeme and rates of our cloth, which they pretend would bee prejudiced, let them know, that it is not the high prices but plenty that propagates Trade," he wrote, adding that England's troubles began when the Dutch started making cloth. The only way England could compete, according to him, was to devise ways of making their own woolens cheaper. He compared trade to dung, which stinks when kept in a heap but, "being spread abroad, it doth fertilize the earth and make it fructifie." Merchants should beat down prices and carry English cloth to new markets throughout the world.[31] Thus the lowered profits of particular sales could be made up in volume if the restrictions of the Merchant Adventurers could be removed from the cloth export trade. Beginning with an attack on the Merchant Adventurers' dire warnings of glutted markets, this anonymous pamphleteer ended up advocating low costs, low prices, and aggressive marketing. His formula for prosperity through expansion achieved by "plenty of merchandize and multitude of Merchants" implied the inadequacy of the older concept of guarding markets like precious jewels.[32]

In *The poore mans advocate*, Peter Chamberlen elabo-

---

[31] *A discourse consisting of motives*, 1645, p. 25, K 678.
[32] *Ibid.*, p. 26.

rated the point: "The more Merchants, the more Trading, and the more flourishing of Merchants. All Rich places of the World, are Instances . . . as Merchants increase, so doe Gaines and Industrie . . ."[33] The indefatigable promoter of trade, John Keymer, speaking through a "discovered" manuscript of Sir Walter Raleigh's touted low customs in much the same spirit: "though the duties be but small, yet the customes for going out and comming in doth so abound, that they increase their Revenues greatly, and make profit, plenty, and imployment of all sorts by Sea and Land to serve themselves and other Nations, as is admirable to behold."[34] Thomas Violet, a London goldsmith and government consultant, charged that the Adventurers restricted shipments, which left cloths unsold and the poor without work, a situation that would be corrected, he said, only if all men were free to trade.[35] Defenses of the chartered company continued to appear through the rest of the century but, after the publication of this articulated rationale for lower prices, the argument for restrictions was hedged in with qualifications. The burden of proof had shifted. By the 1690s limited trades could be patronized as old-fashioned. The author of *The linnen and woollen manufactory discoursed* told his readers that it was very common to restrain trade in the early days "when Navigation was judged a Mystery next to that of the Black Art and such as would venture their Persons and Estates into the New World, as they termed new found Countries, Heroes equal to Alexander and Caesar" but, he continued, "as Trade and Commerce became familiar in the World, the Wisdome of Government made the Privileges of Trade universal to their Subjects." The idea that trading privileges could be justified because of the need for military protection in foreign parts, he concluded, was a demonstration of the deficiency of government, whose duty it was to protect its

[33] [Chamberlen], *The poore mans advocate*, 1649, p. 31, K 759.
[34] [Keymer], *Sir Walter Raleigh's observations*, 1653, p. 19, K 892.
[35] *The advancement of merchandize*, 1651, p. 12, K 839.

citizens, and should not be used as an excuse for companies.[36] The author of *Interest of money mistaken* cited the freeing of trade over the past century as the principal reason for its flourishing for, as he said, people make land high in value just as plenty of money makes interest low, and an expanded trade produces both results.[37]

At the heart of the argument that freeing trade would lead to prosperity, despite the beating down of prices through competition among England's merchants, was a new definition of wealth and wealth-producing activities. The very logic of commercial rivalry implied productivity advances, since all recognized that the winner was the cheapest producer. The idea of producing more involved the need for selling more and that of selling more supported the notion of allowing all comers into any given trade to scour the countryside for new markets. Although never explicitly stated in the 1660s and 1670s, the argument definitely implied that new markets could be created through lower prices. This expansion of consumption implied smaller returns to more people. Thus, the whole issue of freeing trade when once attached to a new concept of economic growth led back to the definition of wealth. The author of *An account of the French usurpation* spoke of the possibility of a nation's being rich in coin and yet the people poor when its money is in the hands of the few: "The Treasures of Princes are then greatest not when their own Coffers are full only, but their Subjects rich."[38] The idea of increasing wealth by increasing the number of traders strengthened the opinion that national wealth grew more surely from lowering profits and widening the market, contrary to the earlier commercial wisdom of carefully managing to ensure high prices. "The strength of a Kingdome consists in the riches of

36 *The linnen and woollen manufactory discoursed*, 1691, p. 3, Ks 1734.

37 *Interest of money mistaken*, 1668, pp. 20-21, K 1222.

38 *An account of the French usurpation*, 1679, p. 13, K 1477.

many Subjects, not of a few," announced the author of *A discourse consisting of motives* for "it is one of the maine reasons why there are fewer beggars seene in Commonwealths than in Kingdoms, because of community and freedome of trading, by which meanes the wealth of the Land is more equally distributed amongst the Natives."[39]

Whether the extension of trade called forth more goods or trade was promoted by increased production was never confronted in these works, but the social utility of increasing the incomes of ordinary people found repeated expression. Defending his proposal to admit foreigners freely into England, Roger Coke asserted that "scarce any man . . . but by industry might earn more than would supply his necessities; and so much as any man gets by being truly industrious above what supplies his necessities, is so much beneficial to himself & family & also an enriching to the place."[40] Another writer argued that it was "better for the nation to have 10 per cent gained on 300 employed in trade, than to have but 100 employed, by which the merchant shall get 30 per cent."[41] Carew Reynell, in *The true English interest*, advocated dividing land into smaller estates because "more People are maintained, and the Land better Husbanded."[42] The much-quoted Sir Josiah Child put the matter succinctly. Law makers, he wrote, must consider people in gross and not in particular because to have many in trade will make English manufacturers cheap abroad and foreign imports cheap in England and "our nation in general would have the advantage both ways." Elsewhere in the *Discourse* he explained that "if our Trade and shiping encrease, how small or low soever the profits are to private

[39] *A discourse consisting of motives*, pp. 22-23.
[40] *A treatise*, p. 3.
[41] *A discourse concerning the East-India trade*, p. 6.
[42] *The true English interest*, 1674, p. 20, K 1369. See Joan Thirsk and J. P. Cooper, eds., *Seventeenth-Century Economic Documents*, Oxford, 1972, p. 96, n. 1, for evidence that John Locke consulted this pamphlet in taking notes on trade.

men, it is an infallible Indication that the Nation in general thrives."[43]

Important implications flowed from this view that national wealth was an aggregate of the wealth of the nation's individual members. Not only did it promote the idea that lower prices and lower profits, enlarged by the volume of the trade, could bring prosperity but it also suggested that growth lay in releasing the economic energies of ordinary people. Commercial freedom, formerly defended on political grounds as part of the subjects' rightful liberties, found new support because it promoted general material well-being. Economic individualism acquired new legitimacy and free trade a practical justification. In their appreciation of the benefits of dispersing wealth, extending trade, and increasing production, these writers caught hold of a dynamic rhythm in economic growth. Pushing hard for the acceleration of commercial activities, they became apostles for change—change in the number and kinds of merchants, change in the tempo and patterns of marketing, change in the range and quantity of goods produced and sold. Eric Hobsbawm has argued that capitalism became a radical force with the move to maximize profits through an increase in the volume of sales rather than by the maintenance of high prices in a protected market.[44] The former economic wisdom dominated the thinking of those merchants who had occupied the interstices of a traditional society. Here power remained with hereditary groups whose taste for luxuries required the services of a commercial group. In the seventeenth century, through a fortuitous combination of the plantation production system and a latent market among people of moderate means, according to Hobsbawm, entrepreneurs foreclosed from the luxury trades discovered the possibility of mobilizing production in order to reduce prices and bring a whole range of desirable goods within the purchasing power of a significant number of new con-

[43] [Child], *A discourse about trade*, 1690, pp. 148-49, K 1725.
[44] "The Seventeenth Century in the Development of Capitalism," *Science and Society* 24 (1960).

sumers. The economic arguments of the middle of the century, although not addressed to the plantation trade, reflect this critical change. Writers touted the benefits of increasing profits from an expanded trade. They also publicized the idea that prosperity involved enlarging the incomes of those of middling fortune.

The idea that individuals when buying, selling, investing, and producing invariably sought to maximize their own profit appeared increasingly as a dependable theoretical element in these writings. The widespread acceptance of the naturalness of personal striving for private gain worked to legitimize and probably encourage this response. Acquisitiveness, long suffered as a barely repressible vice, shared in the respectability that naturalness acquired in seventeenth-century thought. Although many of the implications of this view of human nature remained undeveloped, writers began to reason that legislators and policy makers should accommodate normal human drives by relying less upon coercive authority and more upon the manipulation of economic incentives. Acceptance of private profit seeking as a kind of natural force also tended to redirect attention from the central authority and its comprehensive purposes to the market behavior of individuals seeking the satisfaction of personal goals. English economic commentators were articulating a new social reality in which the self-seeking drive appeared more powerful than institutional efforts to mold people's action.

This democratization of economic opportunity not only suggested a functional definition for economic status but also created a new distinction for discriminating among groups in society. As early as 1618 Bacon had advised that prosperity demanded that a nation not be overburdened by clergy or nobility "for they bring nothing to the stock."[45]

[45] J. M. McNeill, ed., *Bacon's Essays*, London, 1959, p. 41. According to R.W.K. Hinton, "The Mercantile System in the Time of Thomas Mun," *Economic History Review* 2nd ser. 7 (1955), 281, Bacon added this essay between 1618 and 1625.

By mid-century the division had become balder. John Keymer proclaimed that of the English population "two parts of them [of three] are mere Spenders and Consumers of a Commonwealth."[46] In the writings on trade a wedge of contempt had been slipped into the foundation of an aristocratic society. Approbation of productivity cast reflections of approval on the people and activities contributing to that productiveness. The old idea that Godliness, prosperity, and good order came from prescriptive status and assigned tasks was being challenged by what on the face of it was an apolitical discussion about mundane relations in commerce. The socially subversive aspects of economic analysis hovered behind the question of what constituted the wealth of a nation. Was it the totality of goods and specie at the disposal of the ruler? Was it the total producing capacity of the nation? Or the sum of the wealth of individual members of the commonwealth? In the inexorable travels of money behind the exchange of goods, which Mun had detailed, the only wealth that abided in a country was what came back and primed the pump of production. The additional notion that the wealth of England could grow by seeking out new markets carried with it the unsettling corollaries that competition among the nation's workers, manufacturers, and merchants led to the lower prices that captured markets, and that people should be free to define their economic goals. The "dispersed, stragling and promiscuous trade" that John Wheeler scorned in 1601 had been converted into the best way to exploit commercial possibilities. Roger Coke, perhaps reflecting the liberal notions of the Harrington circle, turned the new views into a maxim: "Any business which is more freely managed may be greatlier managed than if it were more restrained."[47]

The idea that there was a commercial process extending from the organization of production through the marketing of goods helped create a place for those pariahs—middle-

---

46 [Keymer], *A clear and evident way*, 1650, p. 17, K 808.
47 *A discourse of trade*, 1670, pp. 49-51, K 1260.

men and bankers. Conservatives such as John Bland continued to express the hope that trade might be so ordered that no man would follow two trades, no shopkeepers become merchants nor merchants become shopkeepers.[48] The clothiers drew on the same vestigial vision to describe "Broggers, Jobbers, Wool-drivers, Staple-wool buyers, Combsters, [and] Market-Spinsters" as a new breed of people drawn from all sorts of vocations who "though they deal with Most People, yet are they under no Regulation, either of Publique Laws, or Private Orders."[49] But the market created friends for them for, as J. P. Cooper has noted, the effort of clothiers to eliminate middlemen from the wool trade was resisted by landlords who saw that their removal would create a monopoly power to beat down the price of wool.[50] Similarly, economic development increased the importance of professional lenders, those bankers in London whose judgments influenced the returns enjoyed by landlords, farmers, manufacturers, and merchants. Earlier condemned as men who had made "a ware and merchandize of money," bankers in the second half of the century drew fire for the discriminations in the money market, in particular the fact that nonprofessional lenders could only get 6 or 8 percent for their money while bankers could earn 10 percent.[51] Answering an attack that implied the additional interest was feloniously acquired, the author of *Is not the hand of Joab in all this?* unfurled the sail of expertise and detailed for his readers the legal ways of getting 10 percent for money. More indicative of a new attitude toward business affairs, he proclaimed that bankers got more for their money simply because of their greater knowledge. "What gives the Knowledge of Men as Men," he demanded, "but

[48] [Bland], *Trade revived*, p. 1, 1660, K 1009.
[49] [W. Smith], *An essay for recovery of trade*, 1661, p. 4.
[50] "Social and Economic Policies," p. 124.
[51] [Thomas Milles], *The customers replie*, 1604, p. 5, Ks 344; and *The mystery of the new fashioned goldsmiths or bankers*, 1676, Ks 1442.

Converse?" What improves the knowledge of men's estates, he went on to ask, and answered: "frequent and ordinary Dealings with them in the Point of Money."[52] Although on a different theme, the banker's answer anticipated an attitude that John Briscoe made universal. "People," he wrote, "have a quick Sense of the Profit of their Labour, and will bestow their Cost & Pains in proportion to the Worth of the Subject Matter and the Benefit they gather from their Industry."[53]

Trade, like justice, had become no respecter of persons. All comers were theoretically welcome. Moreover, recognizing the voluntary aspect of buying and selling in an expanding market, the defenders of an enlarged, freer commercial life were forced to take account of the mutuality of trade, even that between foreigners. Despite the fact that his balance of trade theory implicitly justified efforts to beat out foreign competition in prized markets, Thomas Mun recognized that reciprocity was the rule of trade. Cautioning against carrying frugality too far, he noted that if Englishmen did not use foreign goods they could not expect to vend their own commodities. When he attacked the idea of overvaluing foreign coin in order to attract it to England, he pointed out that such action would break "the laws of entercourse, and would soon move other Princes to perform the same acts or worse against us." Proposing a kind of commercial golden rule, Mun concluded that, when in doubt about the results of an action, Englishmen could predict what foreigners would do in their countreis by observing their own proceedings.[54]

Mun's contemporary, Misselden, had an even more positive view of the irenic possibilities of trade. Instancing the winds' different directions as proof of divine justice in supplying means for everyone to get necessities, Misselden

52 *Is not the hand of Joab in all this?*, 1676, pp. 7, 12, Ks 1473.
53 [Briscoe], *A discourse of money*, 1696, p. 22, 80, K 1936.
54 *England's treasure by forraign trade*, 1664, p. 80, K 1139.

claimed that trade was pleasing to God because it bound people together.[55] John Battie announced that there was no greater enemy to trade than war.[56] William Potter in *The key of wealth* claimed that men's enjoyment of outward goods would be greatly enhanced with greater freedom and speed in commercial exchanges.[57] In *England's safety*, Henry Robinson urged that merchants sell as cheaply as they could and find ways to make other nations cooperate. It is to our benefit, Robinson said, "that monies bee plentiful also in such Countries where we carrie our commodities to sell." Counseling moderation to his fellow Englishmen, he conjured up the fear that they become like Alexander the Great "who having neare conquered the whole world, wept because there was no more left for him to conquer."[58] Even Ireland's prosperity should be desired, John Houghton wrote, for "'tis better for England to have Ireland Rich and Populous, than Poor and thin."[59] Flailing out at the Spanish and Portuguese for restricting entrance to their New World possessions, Rice Vaughn prophesied that "future times will find no part of the Story of this Age so strange, as that all the other States of Europe . . . have not combined together to enforce a liberty of Trade in the West Indies; the restraint whereof is against all Justice."[60] Trade had the same benign qualities for Roger Coke:

> But though all Nations be not of the same Religion, yet all Nations subsist in Society and Commerce; and as every man stands in need of being supplied by another, so does every Country. To restrain therefore the Society and Commerce of Nations to those of the same Religion, is to violate an Institution of God in the con-

[55] [Misselden], *Free trade*, 1622, p. 25, K 392.
[56] [Battie], *The merchants remonstrance*, 1645, p. 2, Ks 822.
[57] [Potter], *The key of wealth*, 1650, p. 3, K 815.
[58] *England's safety*, pp. 51, 57-58.
[59] *A collection of letters*, 1681-83, p. 43, K 1539.
[60] *A discourse of coin and coinage*, 1675, p. 134, K 1394.

versations of Humane Society, and to deny the benefits which places mutually receive from one another.[61]

From this conception of trade Coke was able to criticize the Navigation Acts. "Without question," he wrote, "our Plantations and Ireland too would have been much increased and inriched by a Free Trade, more than by this restraint, and by like Reason the Trade of England too would have been much more and the Nation much more enriched."[62] Advocates of the Navigation Acts did not draw upon the balance of trade for their support, but rather from traditional rivalries. As the author of *England's exchequer* explained of English, Dutch, and Spanish relations, "though there were no open hostilitie, yet is there a politique secret warre, by striving to undermyne and beate each other, out of their trades."[63] And Benjamin Worsley, who has been credited with an instrumental role in the creation of the navigation system, similarly conjured up for his readers a powerful Dutch nation animated by the desire to engross the trade of the whole world.[64]

The association of trade with amicable foreign relations followed logically from Thomas Mun's grand design of an international trade in goods moving from seller to buyer through Coke's "Society and Commerce of Nations" no longer knit together by the same religion. This pacific vision, however, did not dominate economic thinking in the Restoration. By the last years of the 1660s and throughout the 1670s a different prescription for economic growth and national prosperity appeared. The new ideas represented the manufacturers' rather than the merchants' point of view. The theme of a fundamental mutuality of trade, which suggested to some the oneness of the world of trade, was built upon the assumption that the national "super-

61 *England's improvements*, 1675, preface, K 1380.

62 *A discourse of trade*, p. 33.

63 *England's exchequer*, 1625, p. 7, Ks 567.

64 [Worsley], *The advocate*, 1651, pp. 1-4. For a discussion of Worsley's career, see Farnell, "The Navigation Act of 1651," p. 445.

fluities" (whose exchange commerce facilitated) were unique to each country. The diversity of the world's production was presumed to underly the amicability of trading relations, but in fact England's closest neighbors—Holland and France—were also the country's principal competitors in the woolen trade. The struggle for markets, especially with the French, suggested to the clothiers that rivalry more than reciprocity dominated foreign traffic. In their pamphlets the pleasant idea of exchanging unwanted commodities was replaced with more aggressive proposals for protecting English interests. Trade that had earlier been "the life of a State," with manufacturers as "the sinewes of Trade," became instead the handmaiden of the English industry which employed the poor and raised the value of land.[65] The economic freedom and international circulation of goods depicted in the writings of the entrepreneurial merchant came under critical attack. The wealth and prosperity of this kingdom rests chiefly on our manufacturers, Samuel Fortrey announced, because, as he explained, they employ people, keep them industrious, and produce what can be sold abroad for obtaining "what ever for use or delight is wanting."[66]

As early as 1641 Lewes Roberts had detailed the advantages of manufacturing, but his emphasis had fallen upon the increase of value involved in bringing "the original substance" to its finished state. Noting that some princes were "not satisfied with those materials, that grow amongst themselves," he explained how they imported raw materials for their people to work up "much enriching themselves, and honouring their Countrey." Roberts instanced Florence, the Dutch and Manchester manufacturers "who buy the Yarne of the Irish, in great quantity, and weaving it returne the same againe in Linnen, into Ireland to sell; neither doth the industry rest here, for they buy Cotten Wooll, in London, that comes first from Cyprus, and

[65] [Battie], *The merchants remonstrance*, p. 1.
[66] *Englands interest*, p. 21.

Smyrna."[67] After 1660, however, the awareness of competition for markets dominated writing about manufacturing. The increase in England's productive capacities and the careers and fortunes tied up with this increase made the fate of England's industrial exports a question of general concern. New theories of economic development published in the Restoration were sharpened on the whetstone of rivalry with France.

Fortrey's pamphlet in 1663 provided the English reading public with the first statistics pinpointing the imbalance in England's trade with France. To demonstrate how injurious an unrestricted trade with the French was, Thomas Culpeper, Jr., struck out on a new analytical path by calling attention to how dependent an activity trade actually was: "as trade, without improvement of Land, with us would be abortive, so without Manufacture, it must starve at Nurse." In his writings the French became dangerous neighbors because they forced a pattern of disadvantageous trade on the English.[68] Thomas Sheridan underscored his anxiety by announcing that he feared peace more than war, for with France peace was but a preparation for war.[69] The assumed overbalance in the French trade struck these writers as evidence of what might be spent on domestic goods rather than as an indication of how the English might sell to the French as much as the French evidently sold to them. Bringing together two different indices of economic capacity, Sir William Petty took Fortrey's £1.5 million annual trade debt to France and the rebuilding of London after the fire as proof that English craftsmen could produce £4 million of goods in four years without lessening

[67] *The treasure of traffike*, pp. 31-32. Roberts has been credited with first mentioning the cotton manufacturing in Manchester, but John May, *A declaration of the estate of clothing*, 1613, K 323, deserves that distinction.

[68] *A discourse*, 1668, p. 10, K 1215.

[69] [Sheridan], *A discourse*, 1677, p. 139, K 1453.

other production and thereby supply to English consumers what they bought from the French.[70]

Although Fortrey's summary of the imbalance of the French account was exaggerated, the repetition of his figures in other pamphlets indicates their impact.[71] Contemporaries either believed that English consuming habits represented a threat or they seized on the pervasive hostility to the French in the Restoration as a means to check the drive for economic individualism and free trade. What is significant in the development of social thought was the predisposition of those in industry to take a defensive stand toward economic growth and to argue instead for retrenchment in consumption. Rejecting the definition of trade as a benign exchange of superfluities, the manufacturers' tracts concentrated upon the husbanding of national resources rather than the cultivation of trading opportunities. The specter of England's deindustrialization was raised amid recommendations for mobilizing English economic forces and crippling the woolen industry of European competitors.

The flood of clothiers' pamphlets in the 1670s conjured up a far different picture of the trade world than the one the merchants lived in. International amities gave way to muscular patriotism. Spokesmen for the weavers and clothiers talked crisis rather than expansion, enrichment, and the satisfaction of desires and wants. Their posture was aggressive; their vocabulary militant. Their analysis of England's economic situation started with the assumption that prosperity began not with England's commercial prowess but rather with the protection of English industry. They did not have confidence that the kingdom would prosper if natural economic laws were allowed to operate. Rather, they stressed that the merchants were profiting while the

[70] *Political arithmetick*, 1690, pp. 107-08, K 1741.
[71] See Margaret Priestley, "Anglo-French Trade and the 'Unfavourable Balance' Controversy, 1660-1685," *Economic History Review* 2nd ser. 4 (1951).

patrimony of the nation was wasted. Against the drift of merchants' thought, the manufacturers built a case for the clothing industry as the principal employer of the poor as well as the foundation for land values. Wealth did not appear in their tract as the result of individual efforts. Instead, only the shrewd management of economic activities would enable the English to preserve their economic position among formidable rivals who did not exchange goods for goods but cozened the English with luxury items sold for cash. Left on English shores were the cloths with which the king's subjects hoped to earn their daily bread.

Coupled with the descriptions of the new commercial threat posed by France was a rearguard action against the campaign to legalize a limited export of wool, a measure that English landlords evidently hoped would raise the price of raw wool. William Carter, the author of a half-dozen pamphlets sounding the alarm for the cloth industry, described how the English farmer would lose far more from the export of raw wool than he could possibly gain. In *The great loss and damage to England, by the transportation of wooll to foreign parts,* Carter included almost all economic groups—the king, merchants, clothiers, farmers, graziers, gentry, and all who depended upon trade—as potential sufferers from such a disastrous policy, "there being such a Connexion of Trades one to another, and the whole Trade being enlarged by the abounding of Laborious People." Carter also described the possibility that England might be reduced to becoming the supplier of raw materials to an industrialized France.[72] Joseph Trevers boasted that all the American mines of the Spanish king could not equal the riches from the "yearly revenue, that doth or may come into England" from commodities made from English wool. Like Carter, he traced the money in its circulation to farmers,

---

[72] 1677, n.p.; and *idem, England's interest by trade asserted,* 1671, pp. 8-15, K 1283. Carter left an account of his efforts to prevent the exportation of wool in *An abstract of the proceedings,* 1688, Ks 1625.

landlords, and shopkeepers.[73] Both Thomas Culpeper, Jr.,
and his opponent on the usury issue, Thomas Manley,
agreed on the pernicious nature of French rivalry. They,
too, shared the fear of English deindustrialization. Manley
argued that a repeal of the ban on wool exports—a measure
always sure to evoke anguish from the clothiers—would be
tantamount to an admission that England was not able to
manage her manufacturing. The result of abandoning the
woolen industry, he said, would be that the people would
live "on us or dye at our doors."[74]

Emerging clearly at the end of the 1670s was a rationale
for protective legislation that was to have long-range implications. Dealing comprehensively with England's economic
situation, William Petyt urged that the government encourage and superintend new manufacturing. Of particular
significance was his assessment of the East India trade.
Acknowledging that the Dutch exported bullion and prospered nonetheless, the author argued that the Dutch had
fewer people—and by implication less unemployment—and
that until that point was reached in England, coin—which
in this context meant capital—should be used to create
employment. Despite much that was conventional in *Brittania languens,* Petyt's sharp distinction between economic
growth and economic development captured lucidly what
the hard-hit clothiers had been saying in more florid prose.[75]
Thomas Firmin, recognizing the fact that rejecting a
neighbor's industry prevented the neighbor from buying
English cloth, agreed that: "the Exchange of Commodities
one Nation with another, is a very profitable way of Commerce, provided the Ballance of Trade be any thing equal;
which it is well known hath not been with France for some

[73] *An essay to the restoring of our decayed trade,* 1677, pp. 13-14,
K 1456.

[74] *A discourse,* 1677, p. 2, K 1442. For Culpeper's fears, see *A discourse,* pp. 10-11.

[75] [Petyt], *Brittania languens,* 1680, pp. 100-03, K 1521.

years of late: So that there is very great reason we should fall upon making such Cloth as we receive from thence."[76]

Another active supporter of the interests of English industry, Richard Haines, went even further with protection policies. In his view, the indispensability of English wool and fuller's earth raised the hope that England might destroy the woolen industry of her neighbors. Reasoning that all the wool currently grown in the world "is neither Burnt, rotted, nor any wise wilfully destroyed in any Nation wherever it grows" Haines concluded that the English could either work up the cloth or one of their competitors would. Such an heroic effort to corner the wool of the world would redeem itself in but a few years, Haines said, holding out an inviting prospect to his readers: "the more we convert in England, the less in other Nations; and the more they Decrease in their Manufactory, the more shall we Increase in the Wealth, Trade, Seamen and Navies of Ships, for the Strength and Safety of our Nation." Tipping his hat to arguments that both iron and linen could be bought more cheaply abroad, Haines acknowledged that "tis best husbandry to buy all commodities where they may be had most cheap," but added that if the English industriously set about it, they might in a short time change the situation.[77] Also dwelling on the need of foreigners for English and Irish wool, Thomas Sheridan drew the logical conclusion to the protectionist position: though they should burn English cloth, the buying up of the wool and manufacturing it "would not only maintain the Poor and habituat them to Labor, but be as great an advantage in the sale of that Manufacture, both at home and abroad, for the future, as the burning part of their Spices, is to the Dutch."[78]

Although writers in the 1670s continued to dwell on trade decay and favorable balances, there was a decisive shift of

---

[76] [Firmin], *Some proposals for the imployment of the poor*, 1681, p. 22, K 1534.

[77] *A breviat of some proposals*, 1679, p. 4, K 1491.

[78] *A discourse*, pp. 203-04.

emphasis in the tracts that came from the clothiers. It was not the decay of trade they lamented, but the decay of England's woolen industry. An unfavorable balance of trade became a euphemistic expression for the fears aroused by Dutch and French competition. The undifferentiated enthusiasm for wealth-producing activities, which marked the writings at mid-century, became suspect. Spokesmen for English manufacturing interests articulated a new model of economic development stressing the need to mobilize the national resources of labor and raw materials. The ideal of a national economic goal, which was slipping from sight with the merchants' endorsement of economic individualism, reappeared. Advocates of protection for the English cloth industry began emphasizing the importance of channeling economic efforts into those areas where the total economy would be helped. Most importantly, the underemployment of England's poor surfaced as a major problem. The development of the labor force affected public safety and determined the amount of taxation needed to support the poor. The problem was national in scope. The manufacturers held out the hope of absorbing the unemployed poor if supportive policies were adopted.

Growth and development in the Restoration brought with it more clearly defined conflicts of interest within England's capitalist economy. The theorizing about market relations coalesced into competing views of what constituted wealth. Where the merchants had rallied around the idea of promoting prosperity through unrestricted competition, the manufacturers doubted that England's economic future could safely be entrusted to private initiative. Merchants had suggested that the activity of many traders would stimulate both production and marketing. By selling at cheaper prices England could beat out her rivals. If large fortunes were hurt in such a course of trade, middling ones would, nonetheless, increase. Manufacturers, grappling with the problems of reducing costs to meet foreign competition, drew back from this encouragement of free trade. The trend toward economic individualism wavered under the assault of the anxious clothiers. The widely shared assumption that economic activities conformed to a determinable, natural order, however, required that interest groups provide a theoretical explanation for what they wanted. The scientific mode of observation and analysis, once adopted, created its own demands, and economic reasoning became integral to the modern transformation of England.

Six

The Poor as a Productive Resource

WORDS PLAY TRICKS ON US WHEN WE DESCRIBE
the past. We employ the same word as we move from century to century and thereby obscure a changing reality
behind an unchanging term. "People" is such a word. Used
in a discussion of England in 1500, the people would mean
common husbandmen and their families living in villages
where custom, ritual, and habit patterned lives, and common tasks for survival created fetters as well as bonds. A
hundred years later the people would include these same
husbandmen and their families occupying the traditional
agrarian roles of their forebears as well as thousands of
additional people, the surplus sons and daughters at the
end of three-quarters of a century of population growth.
Their sisters and brothers having filled the stations custom
had prepared for them, these supernumeraries were without
a place, without a prescribed life role. The most basic social
institutions of family and village had nothing to offer them.
They took to the roads as beggars and masterless men and
women or searched out upland meadows and forests where
they could establish a dwelling as squatters. Thus, at the
end of the sixteenth century the word people covered not
only the normal transmitters of a rural tradition but also
a new group of men and women who had been displaced by
the irreversible processes of social change.[1]

Population in England stabilized after the middle of the
seventeenth century, but economic forces continued to redistribute people and occupations across the countryside.
The commercialization of agriculture increased the number
of men and women who worked for wages, producing what

[1] For a general discussion of population growth in this period, see
J. D. Chambers, *Population, Economy, and Society in Pre-Industrial
England*, London, 1972.

Alan Everitt has described as a profound restructuring of agricultural labor. In those areas devoted to grain growing, farmers continued to lose their holdings and their common rights, but as agricultural laborers they remained in the traditional world of manor, church, and village. The introduction of new techniques involved the acquisition of skills, which they passed on to their children.[2] The laboring poor of the fielden areas clung to a way of life that was sustained right through the nineteenth century. Although long-term agricultural developments of the seventeenth century meant fewer permanent places for men and women for those who remained, adaptation to new ways of farming did not necessitate a break with the older social order. Even as the market intruded, the established relations between manor, church, and village persisted.

Those descendants of the sixteenth-century peasantry who became the squatters of the forests and wastelands or who moved out of the countryside and into the growing urban centers of London, Norwich, Newcastle, Bristol, Hull, Exeter, Manchester, Birmingham, Leeds, Sheffield, and Halifax, found their lives drastically reshaped.[3] Once uprooted from the traditional agrarian order, they had, unwittingly perhaps, joined the modernizing part of English society. Outside the stable rural parishes, lower-class English men and women entered a world where patrons were few and employment uncertain. They got agricultural jobs as part of a migratory, seasonal work force and by-employment according to the vicissitudes of the cloth and colonial trades. Many of them moved to London, some no doubt catching hold of opportunities created by a maturing commerce and a developing industry.[4] Others traveled in a

[2] Alan Everitt, "Farm Labourers," in Joan Thirsk, ed., *The Agrarian History of England and Wales, 1500-1640*, vol. 4, Cambridge, 1967, pp. 435ff.

[3] Peter Clark and Paul Slack, eds., *Crisis and Order in English Towns, 1500-1700*, London, 1972, p. 30.

[4] E. A. Wrigley, "A Simple Model of London's Importance in Chang-

constant search for work following with their feet the course of English economic expansion. Henceforth, the people of England—that undistinguished portion of the population whom contemporaries described as poor, landless, necessitous, able, or idle—could be divided between those whom the changes of the century dislodged and those who stayed put.

The famous Elizabethan Poor Law of 1601 introduced a measure of stability into the lives of the most destitute. The last years of the sixteenth century had witnessed dearths of famine proportions. Grain shortages were precipitated by bad harvests, but the widespread suffering also reflected a breakdown in the distribution of food. The Poor Law established the principle of taxing the well-off for the relief of the needy, naming parishes as the effective administrative units.[5] A writer in the 1680s summarized its provisions succinctly as "work for those that will Labour, Punishment for those that will not, and Bread for those that cannot."[6] Outdoor relief was henceforth made available to ward off starvation, but the able-bodied poor could be set to work on terms beyond their control. In seeking help from the parish they lost part of their civil liberties.

In 1662 when the Poor Laws were reconfirmed in the Restoration, a new provision enabled the overseers of the poor to deny relief to those in the parish who had been born elsewhere, but reforms in 1691 permitted those in need to claim settlement outside their place of birth if they had established themselves in a parish through employment or

---

ing English Society and Economy, 1650-1750," *Past and Present* 37 (1967).

[5] Charles Wilson, *England's Apprenticeship, 1603-1763*, New York, 1965, pp. 348-50. See also H. L. Beales, "The Historical Context of the *Essay on Population*," in David Victor Glass, ed., *Introduction to Malthus*, London, 1953.

[6] Richard Dunning, *A plain and easie method shewing how the office of overseer of the poor may be managed*, 1686, Preface.

tax paying.[7] Enjoined to work or be punished, the poor who fed the pool of occasional labor in the city and migratory labor in the country were acutely aware of their dependence upon formal outdoor relief. Unlike their peasant ancestors they were freer from tradition and faced a range of choices, some of which occasionally led to upward mobility. On the other side of the coin, they were more exposed to the vagaries of the harvest, the fluctuations of foreign markets, and the investment preferences of the propertied men who alone could offer employment. As day laborers they were vulnerable to economic trends, which meant in fact being vulnerable to a social void—an absence of lord, master, or employer at critical times throughout the year.[8] The introduction of national legal charity at the beginning of the seventeenth century established a permanent connection between the needs of the unemployed and the economic planning of their betters, a vital link, as it turned out, between the initiators of economic change and the victims of its social dislocations.

The amorphous laboring class, set loose from the traditional moorings of the peasantry, presented a new phenomenon to contemporaries. The men who wrote about these poor evaluated them in terms appropriate to their own participation in a developing economy. Themselves detached from the social precepts of old, agrarian England, these writers struggled to find a place in their vision of the future for the sturdy beggars and able-bodied poor whose idleness seemed both a puzzle and a promise. As we have seen, other economic analyzers of the period had created a model of the national economy that gave a sense of place to enterprising investors and improving landlords. Without criticizing the distribution of property or power in the kingdom, economic pamphleteers repeatedly hailed the value of disciplined, economic effort in appraising the

---

[7] James Stephen Taylor, "The Impact of Pauper Settlement 1691-1834," *Past and Present* 73 (1976), 50-52.

[8] Karl Polanyi, *The Great Transformation*, New York, 1944, p. 88.

various elements in their society. In doing so, they articulated a model for the society that provided—at least theoretically—a place for the persons displaced by the seventeenth-century's changes.

When it is said that "People are the Wealth of a Nation," Sir Dalby Thomas wrote, "It is only meant, Laborious and Industrious People, and not such as are wholly unemploy'd, as Gentry, Clergy, Lawyers, Servingmen, and Beggars, etc." In this categorizing Thomas was echoing Bacon's injunction not to overburden the nation with clergy or nobility.[9] The idea that only laboring people could increase wealth became a truism and found its way into discussions on immigration and taxing policies. Flailing out at the vulgar opinion that "popular feastings and good fellowship" are in the interest of the nation, Slingsby Bethel charged such hospitality with dulling wits, spending time and making men "unfit for action and business which is the chief advancer of any Government."[10] In a similar vein, the author of *The art of good husbandry* dismissed all explanations for the decay of trade such as the export of wool or import of foreign manufacturing as circumstantial compared to the failure to appreciate the value of time. "It is," he explained, "the industrious hand that enricheth the land, and not the contriving pate. The wasps and hornets, by their rapine, bring to their nests more honey at once than the industrious bees can at many times; and yet, for all this, they usually die for want in the winter; whilst the industrious bees, by continual labour and improvement of time, gather sufficient to serve themselves in the winter, and can afford their masters a liberal share out of their plentiful stock."[11] In his

[9] [Thomas], *An historical account of the rise and growth of the West-India collonies*, 1690, p. 2, K 1749. For Bacon's statement, see J. M. McNeill, ed., *Bacon's Essays*, London, 1959 (originally published in 1625), p. 41.

[10] [Bethel], *The present interest of England stated*, 1671, p. 12, K 1281.

[11] Joan Thirsk and J. P. Cooper, eds., *Seventeenth-Century Economic Documents*, Oxford, 1972, pp. 97-98.

Treatise on taxes, William Petty made explicit his view that landlords were parasitical and tenants productive. Taxes, Petty said, could transfer wealth "from the Landed and Lazy, to the Crafty and Industrious."[12] William Sheppard recommended the excise because it taxed according to whether or not one was extravagant.[13] The "trade of taxes," as Defoe styled it in *Taxes no charge*, could actually pluck money from pleasure spenders and give it to the wretched, whose spending would "terminate in the hands of Industry and Trade."[14]

A few publications came forth with the traditional defense of the spending of the nobility and gentry by rationalizing the need for pomp and circumstance in a monarchy. The Court should be exempt from strictures against luxurious dress, said the author of *Englands vanity*, "for it seemeth to me, that our Saviour hath granted some kind of dispensation to Princes, and their Retinue, (for the Honour of Kingdoms, and Governments) to appear as Gloriously as themselves please, or can."[15] Far more aggressively, Edward Chamberlayne said that in all Christian monarchies men of "Courage, Wisdom, Wealth, etc. have been judged fit and worthy to enjoy certain Priviledges, Titles, Dignities, . . . above the Common people." Indeed, the shame of the nation to Chamberlayne was not that the nobility were idle and indulgent, but that sons of baronets, knights, and gentlemen found their way into trade.[16] Sir Dudley North, the father of the author of *Discourses upon trade*, defended the prudence of English nobles to spend largely, adding that traders depended upon it, but Sir Francis Brewster presented the most commonsensical view of the nobility as an economic force.[17] Agreeing with prevailing economic wis-

12 [Petty], *A treatise of taxes and contributions*, 1662, p. 18, K 1098.
13 *Englands balme*, 1657, p. 178.
14 [Defoe], *Taxes no charge*, 1690, p. 13, K 1729.
15 *Englands vanity*, 1683, p. 1, K 1577.
16 *Angliae notitia*, 1669, pp. 381, 435, K 1235.
17 [North], *Observations and advices oeconomical*, 1669, p. 126, K

dom that it would be far better for them to invest their incomes, he reasoned that since they would continue to spend their money in consumption, this extravagance should be recognized as preferable to hoarding. Despite these occasional digs at the habits of the traditional ruling class, the economic writings of the century furnish little evidence of a deep division between the capitalists associated with trade and manufacturing and those with landed wealth. Rather than challenge the sensibilities of their age, the economic writers tended to insinuate their commercial virtues into the older social outlook.[18] They saved their reforming interests for the poor whose labor they were compelled to organize and whose subsistence they underwrote through the poor rates.

The problems of the poor—their number, their habits, their opportunities for work and proper management—absorbed the attention of dozens of writers in the 1660s, 1670s and 1680s. The most significant change of opinion about the poor was the replacement of the concern about overpopulation at the beginning of the century with fears about a possible loss of people at the end. Where sending people to the plantations had been advanced at one time as a solution to the surplus mouths to feed, the colonial emigration was criticized more often than not after 1660. Roger Coke flayed the policy of allowing people to go to the colonies and refused to believe that the gains from sugar and tobacco production would compensate for the loss they represented.[19] William Petyt, the author of the influential *Britannia languens*, also blamed American growth for the de-

---

1245; and Brewster, *Essays on trade and navigation*, 1695, p. 52, K 1877.

[18] For instance, John Scarlett in the preface to his *The stile of exchanges*, 1682, told the story of a learned man in Italy who was advanced to high office on the basis of his learning, but was dismissed by merchants because he lacked letters of credit.

[19] *A discourse of trade*, 1670, p. 43, K 1260.

population of England.[20] Samuel Fortrey advised extreme caution in undertaking further plantations since England still had a "countrey sufficient to double our people, were they rightly employed."[21] Carew Reynell, concurring in Fortrey's estimate, said that twice the number of people could be contained "meerly by Inclosures" and with a million more, "we should quickly see how Trade and the vend of things would alter for the better."[22]

Since the same writers who deplored the depopulation caused by emigration spoke in the same pages of increases in unemployment—not one in ten has steady work in the city, one writer maintained—the concern with depopulation must represent an expectation of future growth rather than an observation of the present need for labor. Indeed, the Restoration writing on the poor offers compelling evidence of the existence of a vision of economic growth and development that took precedence over immediate concerns with the distress of the poor or the exactions of the poor rate. Such a vision helps explain how writers who acknowledged that half the people resorted to outdoor relief in any year could also recommend free immigration and civil concessions to alien residents. Idle, able-bodied English men and women presented themselves to entrepreneurs as two separable qualities: persons capable of work and idle persons, and more often than not they chose to affirm the value of increasing the national labor force and focus reforming attention upon the idleness.

The zeal for reforming the idle poor rather than losing them to other parts of the empire can perhaps partially be explained by the prevailing assumption that population density promoted prosperity. "Where the people are many, and the arts good, there the traffique must be great, and the Countrey rich," Thomas Mun set forth as an indisputable proposition in *England's treasure by forraign trade.* Mun's endorsement of cities stemmed in part from the con-

20 [Petyt], *Britannia languens*, 1680, pp. 153-54, K 1521.
21 *Englands interest*, 1663, p. 4, K 1337.
22 *The true English interest*, 1674, pp. 59-60, K 1369.

clusion that craftsmen earned more than husbandmen and in part from the observation that the most conspicuously prosperous country of the century was Holland where two to three million people were crowded into a very small area.[23] Similarly, in *An apology for the builder*, Nicholas Barbon defended new construction in London on the grounds that cities created employment and wealth, and that new buildings were: "instrumental to the preserving and increasing of the number of the Subjects; and numbers of Subjects is the strength of a Prince: for Houses are Hives for the people to breed and swarm in, without which they cannot increase."[24] Arguing for free entrance to foreigners, Samuel Fortrey agreed that "People and plenty are commonly the begetters the one of the other, if rightly ordered."[25] In a more systematic way, Sir William Temple offered the proposition that the riches of a country are a function of the ratio of people to land. "Trade begets Trade, as fire does fire, and People go much, where much People are already gone," a point he emphasized by relating Irish poverty to Irish depopulation.[26] Thomas Sheridan claimed that England was underpopulated and proposed taxes to encourage early marriages.[27] Making explicit his contemporaries' propensity to separate the population problem from the employment problem, Sir Humphrey Mackworth asserted that England did not have too many people unless they were unemployed: "I propose Employment, and there is no doubt, that the Consumption of the People is not so much, as the Product of their Labours, which is the real Riches and Strength of the Nation; And the more the merrier, like Bees in a Hive, and better cheer too."[28]

The hopes for turning around the problem of the poor

[23] *England's treasure by forraign trade*, 1664, p. 31, K 1139.

[24] [Barbon], *An apology for the builder*, 1685, p. 26, K 1608.

[25] *Englands interest*, p. 4.

[26] [Temple], *Miscellanea*, 1680, p. 100, K 1522.

[27] [Sheridan], *A discourse of the rise and power of Parliaments*, 1677, p. 180, K 1453.

[28] [Mackworth], *England's glory*, 1694, pp. 20-21, K 1850.

and converting a distasteful liability into a precious asset deserve analysis. Why were the pamphleteers of the Restoration so entranced by the possibilities of employing the growing number of unpropertied laborers in England? This optimism is all the more puzzling in that the dimensions of the problem of unemployment were well known. Writers frequently quoted the social statistics garnered by Gregory King, John Graunt, and Sir William Petty. Scholarly investigations of King's estimates, which found permanent form in his famous *Natural and political observations* have confirmed his grim picture of almost half the population being laboring people, out-servants, cottagers, and paupers whose annual expenditures exceeded their income.[29] Moreover, contemporaries had a pretty good idea how much the poor rates cost the nation each year, and estimates were widely published. Max Beloff has said that the poor rate yield rose from £665,000 to £900,000 between 1685 and 1701. In *Britannia languens*, published in 1680, the figure was put at £400,000. Mackworth published the figure of £700,000 per annum in 1694, and six years later James Puckle calculated that the poor rates plus charity amounted to £1 million per annum. In 1710 James Hodges raised it to £2 million.[30] Despite these well-circulated figures, not a single economic tract considered the problem of the poor to be insoluble or proposed any population checks or encouragements for migration to Ireland or the colonies. Indeed, for most of those writing on the poor, the discussion of poor rates was but a preamble to an appeal for a more rational use of poor funds rather than an indictment of the burden itself.

[29] King's figures are assessed in D. V. Glass, "Gregory King's Estimates of the Population of England and Wales, 1695," *Population Studies* 2 (1950); and more critically by G. S. Holmes, "Gregory King and the Social Structure of Pre-Industrial England," Royal Historical Society *Transactions* 5th ser., 26 (1976).

[30] *Public Order and Popular Disturbances 1660-1714*, New York, 1938, p. 208; [Petyt], *Britannia languens*, pp. 131-32; [Mackworth], *England's glory*, p. 24; [Puckle], *England's path to wealth and honour*, 1700, p. 2, K 2253; James Hodges, *Essays on several subjects*, 1710, pp. 5-6.

THE POOR AS A PRODUCTIVE RESOURCE

The 1640s witnessed the first spate of tracts on the poor. The political convulsions of the Civil War let loose a good deal of private theorizing about public issues, and the decade was ushered out with five consecutive harvest failures and a general trade depression that extended the misery to the urban as well as rural poor. William Goffe, Adam Moore, Leonard Lee, Samuel Hartlib, John Cook, Peter Chamberlen, Henry Halhead, Humphrey Barrow, John Moore, John Lilburne, Gerald Winstanley, and dozens of anonymous pamphleteers kept the plight of the poor before the reading public. Winstanley and Cook indicted the principles of private property by evoking a commitment from those "that have" to those "that have not," but the preponderance of the tracts narrowed their concern to the dilemma of those beggars who were enjoined to work but could find no employment. Charging the public with a lamentable indifference, the author of *Stanleyes remedy* attacked the provision whereby vagrants were to be sent back to their place of birth. "There are thousands of these people, that their place of birth is utterly unknowne, and they had never any abiding place in their lives, or ever retained in service, but were and are vagrants by descent." *Stanleyes remedy*, which was to become everyone's remedy, was to put the poor to work through a government-managed program. If only two persons got free goods in 9,725 parishes at 3d a day it would be, he calculated, a daily loss of over £243 which could be recouped through workhouses.[31] Hartlib, speaking more charitably of the need "that the godly and laborious poore may be countenanced and cherished," recommended the raising of a stock of hemp and flax for the poor to work on, a notion that suggested to him the likely savings of the £1 million that was spent each year importing linen.[32] Chamberlen argued that the land acquired by Parliament from the church should be retained to support a public works program for employing the poor

---

[31] *Stanleyes remedy*, 1646, pp. 2-5, K 702.
[32] [Hartlib], *The parliaments reformation*, 1646, pp. 1-3, K 692.

"and making such industrious as are not," while William Goffe detailed an ambitious plan for establishing, through funds from the poor rate, settlements near each fishing port. There trees could be planted for ships' timbers, and fishing factories erected where the poor could learn to make rope and sailcloth for cordage, nets, and sails. Like the others, Goffe urged that the poor be "encouraged, and mercifully dealt with, and kindly used." What is unusual is his awareness of the economic aspects of the problem. "What will be done with all those Goods so many Thousand Hands shall make more every year?" he asked, answering with a proposal to raise duties on foreign linen and sailcloth.[33]

Here in embryo are most of the schemes propounded for employing the poor during the rest of the century. The wasteful drain of money from a poor rate used to keep the idle poor from starving was pitted against the far-sightedness of raising a national stock to underwrite such things as a fishery, the draining of fens, clearing of wastelands, working up of flax or the spinning of wool by thousands of poor whose misery could thus be exchanged for a supportive competence while "turning the Great Burthen of this Land, into an equall Benefit."[34] Those like Thomas Firmin who concentrated on the benefits of putting the poor people to work on flax pointed out the advantages of developing an industry presently underdeveloped in England, while others who proposed setting the poor to spinning and weaving wool reasoned that working up all English wool would prevent its export to foreign competitors. The example of the Dutch, where people had "to work or starve," was frequently invoked in anticipation of scoffers. An equally insistent theme through this literature was that of the blamelessness of the poor who could find no work. Repeatedly exposing the problem of underemployment, the pam-

---

[33] [Chamberlen], *The poore mans advocate* [1649], p. 26, K 759; [Goffe], *How to advance the trade of the nation and employ the poor*, 1641, in *Harleian Miscellany*, vol. 4, London, 1745, p. 366.
[34] Sir Roger L'Estrange, *A discourse of the fishery*, 1674, p. 8, K 1362.

phleteers pointed to the need for by-employment for great numbers of poor Families "who only work if in the Countrey, at harvest."[35] Weavers' apprentices, too, were said to be thrown on the parish when their spell of employment was finished. The writers frequently treated their audience to calculations of the daily consumption, daily lost labor, daily savings when idleness was turned to industry. There is a recognition that the woolen trade suffered from frequent gluts and that linen worked up by the unskilled would have to be sold at a loss in order to outsell foreign competitors, but neither loss was counted as great as the dead loss of simple outdoor relief.

Writers frequently urged that jobs be found for the poor because the ability to work was a learned habit which must be husbanded as much as the laborer's time. In a 1600 pamphlet, Thomas Wilson described the success in Norwich when poor children were put at the stocking frame at the age of six, a story that was approvingly repeated in writings throughout the century.[36] What is significant is that the emphasis upon child labor fell upon the educational value of work. Thomas Firmin, who wrote two pamphlets describing his efforts to organize the poor in the parish of Aldergate, stressed the urgency of putting children to work at as early an age as possible. In his 1678 tract he reported children working at seven and eight. Three years later, he dropped the age to five. It matters not, he insisted "what you employ these poor Children in, as that you do employ them in some thing, to prevent an idle, lazy kind of Life, which if once they get the habit of, they will hardly leave." As usual the Dutch Republic was the exemplar nation, and Firmin maintained that few in Holland reached seven or eight years and remained a charge to parent or parish.[37] Similarly, Sir Francis Brewster decried the lack of

35 [Haines], *The prevention of poverty*, 1674, p. 5, K 1361.

36 *The state of England anno dom. 1600*, in F. J. Fisher, ed., *Camden Miscellany*, 1936, p. 754.

37 [Firmin], *Some proposals for the imployment of the poor*, 1681, p. 2, K 1534.

concern for the upbringing of children. What, he asked, was all the fuss about overaged beggars when at the same time London was "breeding up a greater number of Poor Children." Brewster recommended working schools for poor children in order to "Manure and Improve the first Sprouts as they come into the World."[38] James Puckle repeatedly conjured up for his readers the beggar children plagued by idle habits that rendered them "undisposed for labour." Touting a national fishery, Puckle warned that, without a due care for relief of the poor, the nation was continually being stocked with thieves and beggars.[39] Lamenting the fact that children grew up without moral or practical education, Richard Haines saw public workhouses as the means of employing children and reforming beggars and vagrants. To give them the means "to get an honest livelihood" mattered because "Idleness in Youth is the Weed plot of the Hangmans Harvest." Vehemently rejecting the charge that workhouses might become an expedient for enslaving the poor, Haines disavowed his complicity in "any such base and cruel Purpose," affirming instead his goal that the poor might be allowed to "mind their Business, Eat, Drink and take their Rest without anything to disturb their Peace."[40] Another reformer, Adam Moore, credited the poor with the readiness to "be reclaimed and refined to loyall and laudable courses" if they could but be given a stake in life, in this case a four-acre parcel to be carved from the estimated two million acres of commons and waste land in England and Wales.[41]

The educational value of work was kept clearly in focus by most of the writers on the poor. Thomas Manley's depiction of "the abused crutch of statute-maintenance" represented a rare repudiation of public responsibility for the poor. Rather it was the mismanagement of the Poor Laws

[38] *Essays on trade and navigation*, p. 60.

[39] [Puckle], *England's path to wealth and honour, passim.*

[40] [Haines], *Provision for the poor*, pp. 6-8, K 1465; Haines, *A breviat of some proposals*, 1679, p. 6, K 1491.

[41] *Bread for the poor*, p. 30, K 885.

and the failure to tackle the problem of training the poor that is criticized. Rather than raise a stock—by which writers meant capital—to put the poor to work, parishes were charged with paying as little as possible and setting the poor to begging.[42] Answering Manley, Sir Thomas Culpeper, Jr., retorted that "if you will take from the poor this crutch, you must withal cure their Lameness, and set them upright upon their own legs lest they lye too heavy at your doors."[43] Sir Matthew Hale, the jurist, indicted the English as a people for their short-sighted provision for the poor. By failing to promote cooperation among parishes, the Poor Laws left the impotent in distress and others exposed to the ups and downs of trade. Hale proposed a four-year stock to provide public work when private employment flagged. The principal benefit of such a program, he claimed, would be the educating and disciplining of the poor who could be taught to read and become industrious. Counteracting the idea that the people of some nations are more able than others, Hale claimed "if we had the same industrious Education, we should have the same industrious Disposition." Instead, as things stand, poor families "bring up their Children either in a Trade of Begging or Stealing, or such other Idle course, which again they propagate to their Children, and so there is a successive multiplication of hurtful or at least unprofitable people, neither capable of Discipline nor beneficial Imployment."[44] Thomas Culpeper also tackled the proposition of some people being by nature more industrious. All men, Culpeper explained, that were near in climate and meridian have "neer the same Principles of ingenuity." Differences after birth were caused rather by law, education, customs, and other accidents of life.[45] The Quaker reformer, John Bellers, enumerated the difficulties of the poor as bad parental education, incon-

[42] *Usury at six per cent. examined*, 1669, p. 24, K 1241.
[43] *The necessity of abating usury re-asserted*, 1670, p. 30, K 1261.
[44] *A discourse touching provision for the poor*, 1693, p. 12, preface, K 1579.
[45] *The necessity of abating usury re-asserted*, p. 27.

stant employment, no vent for what they did raise or make, and insufficient food to feed them for their labor. Bellers, perceiving that many of the poor were "supernumery in the Trade they were bred in" proposed colleges of industry to provide the poor with needed skills.[46]

Sir William Petty emphasized the urgency of finding employment for the poor by proposing such economically irrational expenditures as using tax money to set them to work building useless pyramids on the Salisbury Plain. Because the poor were hungry they must be fed, but the payment must be mediated through work, however useless, "to keep their minds to discipline and obedience, and their bodies to a patience of more profitable labours when need shall require it." It would be better "to bring the Stones at Stonehenge to Tower Hill" rather than allow workers to lose their faculty of laboring. Even as indiscrimate a tax as the poll tax was commended by Petty because it would encourage men with many children to set them "to some profitable employment upon their very first capacity, out of the proceed whereof, to pay each child his own Poll-money."[47] From the 1640s—when the poor first presented themselves as a social problem—to the end of the century, the need for employment and the role of employment in preparing the poor for socially useful tasks was reiterated in economic tracts. "It is certain that employment and competencies do civilize all men, and makes them tractable & obedient to Superiors commands," Peter Chamberlen wrote in 1649.[48] Four decades later, the idea was a cliché. "There is no adjourning labour," Daniel Defoe insisted, for the "Mechanical Arts in a few month will either lose the Men, or they their Trade by some other course of life."[49]

Historians have accused seventeenth-century economic writers of favoring a large population because of its influ-

---

[46] *Essays about the poor*, 1699, p. 4, K 2107.

[47] *A treatise of taxes*, pp. 13, 42.

[48] *The poore mans advocate*, p. 9.

[49] *Taxes no charge*, p. 16.

ence upon wage levels.[50] In fact the tracts display a welter of opinions about what influenced wages and what impact wages had on the habits of the poor and the rest of the economy. The restructuring of English economic life—both agricultural and industrial—brought an increasing number of workers into the ranks of day-labor. In the country the employment of casual laborers gradually replaced that of servants, and most late seventeenth-century industries grew up outside the guilds. Apprentices were more often than not simply wage-laborers, and cottagers could best be described as wage-laborers working at piece rates. The seasonal and cyclical interruptions in employer–employee relations enforced a certain social distance between the two groups. The old ideal of rich and poor linked by mutual needs was replaced by an ad hoc contractural relationship mediated by wage payments, but economic writers were not agreed on the value of low wages, and the most serious commentators recognized that wages and subsistence costs were inextricably bound together.

What clearly emerges as a commonly held view was that the poor—whether due to their own moral defectiveness or because of an idle life thrust upon them—did not possess those habits necessary to becoming participants in the future productiveness of England. "The enterprising business man of the day," as T. E. Gregory calmly noted, "was in conflict with the tendency of his employees to remain content with a fixed standard of comfort."[51] Understandably lacking the detachment of the twentieth-century scholar, contemporaries vented their rage at such "content." "The Poor, if Two Dayes work will maintain them, will not work Three," said Francis Gardiner, who claimed that manufactures were "never so well Wrought" as when wages were

[50] Richard C. Wiles, "The Theory of Wages in Later English Mercantilism," *Economic History Review* 2nd ser. 21 (1968), reviews this literature.

[51] "The Economics of Employment in England, 1660-1713," *Economica* 1 (1921), 50.

low, while in times of plenty workers "will spend the more in Drinking."[52] John Houghton reported to his readers that when "the framework knitters or makers of silk stockings had a great price for their work, they have been observed seldom to work on Mondays and Tuesdays but to spend most of their time at the ale-house or nine-pins."[53] Thomas Manley pungently portrayed the English workers' independence: "too proud to beg, too lazy to work, when 'tis either too hot or too cold, and will choose their own time and wages, or you may do your work yourself."[54] William Carter shared this view and said that the poor were so surly that they would often mar what they did. Those living within fifty miles of London were the worst, according to Carter, being idle, surly, and only willing to work "if two days pay will keep them a week."[55]

The harshest statements about the working habits of the poor came from the clothiers, who tended to view outdoor relief as a public underwriting of laziness. The author of *The grand concern of England explained* drew the most explicit relationship between wages and relief when he wrote that "handcraftsmen" get paid "what they please for their wages" because there are so few industrious workers, a deficiency that could be corrected by putting the poor to work manufacturing the staple commodities of the kingdom.[56] Both Thomas Manley and William Carter blamed high wages for England's declining competitiveness in the cloth trade. Manley set as a necessity "reducing the wages of servants, labourers and workmen of all sorts."[57] In *The linnen and woollen manufactory discoursed*, the author criticized a national linen manufacturing venture because

[52] [Gardiner], *Some reflections on a pamphlet*, 1697, pp. 16-17, K 1968. See chapter 7, n. 31, for a discussion of Gardiner's identity.

[53] As cited in E. P. Thompson, "Time, Work-Discipline, and Industrial Capitalism," *Past and Present*, 38 (1967), 72.

[54] *Usury at six per cent. examined*, p. 25.

[55] [Carter], *The ancient trades decayed*, 1678, p. 8, Ks 1464.

[56] *The grand concern of England explained*, 1673, pp. 61-62, K 1338.

[57] *Usury at six per cent. examined*, pp. 24-25.

it would injure the woolen industry "by diverting some that are now in it, and so raise the price of Spinning," adding, "nothing can retrieve our lost Trade abroad, but underselling our Competitors: so then we must labour to make ours as cheap as we can, and not set up another Manufactory, to bid who gives most for Spinners; a ready way to ruin the Clothing Trade of England" giving to spinners a pretence for standing "on their terms with their Masters."[58]

While no writers stepped forward with counterclaims of the poor's diligence and good manners, writers as influential as Sir Matthew Hale, Sir William Petty, Sir Josiah Child, Sir Thomas Culpeper Jr. and Sir Frances Brewster defended the poor from the blame of their own poverty, urging that instead of self-serving, short-range remedies a national policy for creating work be adopted. In *A plea for the bringing in of Irish cattel*, John Collins attacked the argument that it took high food costs to drive the poor to work. Pointing to London and other places, he explained that if you set provisions high to force people to work, wages must also be high, "and to make Provisions dear as a means to make the poor work, is the ready way to drive them into Foreign Plantations" where they might "have greater wages for their pains."[59] William Petyt held the same ground, arguing that high costs drove out potential workers. The people of England, he announced, are "naturally as ingenious, industrious, and willing to labour as any part of Mankind, so long as they can have a reasonable fruit of their Labours, which hath been evidenced by many former undeniable Experiences."[60] Similarly Sir Francis Brewster favored cheaper subsistence, which would make people willing to work because their wages would then be able to cover the expenses of life.[61] Obviously a jurist rather than

[58] *The linnen and woollen manufactory discoursed*, 1691, p. 8, Ks 1734.
[59] *A plea for the bringing in of Irish cattel*, 1680, pp. 3, 10-11, K 1515.
[60] *Britannia languens*, p. 46.
[61] *Essays on trade and navigation*, p. 54.

an employer, Sir Matthew Hale calculated among the benefits of his plans for a national stock to employ the poor that
his workhouses would offer a standard of good wages and an
alternative for workmen who otherwise were forced to accept wages below subsistence because masters took advantage of their need.[62] Both Petty and the anonymous author
of *Reasons for a limited exportation of wooll* drew attention to the unreasonableness of critics of outdoor relief not
to favor higher wages. As Petty put it, "it is unjust to let
any starve, when we think it just to limit the wages of the
poor, so as they can lay up nothing against the time of their
impotency and want of work."[63] A frequent critic of the
harshness of laws against the poor, Sir Thomas Culpeper Jr.
wrote that "to compel men to work is not the way unless
wages be propounded, For Industry cannot be forced by
Laws, it should be tempted with profit, or, at least, baited
with a subsistence."[64] "If the Poor were always certain of
Work, and Pay for it," Charles Davenent concluded, "they
would be glad to quit that Nastiness which attends a begging and lazy life."[65]

In such wide-ranging discussions of the poor, the absence
of any very strong disapproval of the Poor Laws is remarkable. Thomas Manley, who ascribed to such hardbitten
sentiments as "the fear of a loathsome disease rather than
virtue deters men from vicious practices," vigorously de-
nounced "the abused crutch of statute-maintenance," but
spoke equivocally of rescinding or better regulating it, and
his fellow clothier William Carter explicitly denied the ad-
visability of repealing the Poor Laws even though he
blamed the idleness of London workers for pricing England

[62] *A discourse touching provision for the poor*, pp. 18-19.

[63] *A treatise of taxes*, p. 3. In *Reasons for a limited exportation of
wooll*, 1677, pp. 3-4, K 1451, the author says that masters pay such low
wages that the poor "are only preserved from starving whilst they can
work."

[64] *A discourse*, 1668, pp. 15-16, K 1215.

[65] [Davenant], *An essay upon ways and means*, 1695, p. 143, K 1884.

out of the cloth market.[66] The overwhelming majority of pamphleteers confined their criticisms to the implementation of laws rather than the principle of legal charity. Despite the increasing burden on the ratepayers, writers showed far more concern with the long-range consequences of the present management of poor relief than with the costs of the commitment. Frequent complaints were lodged against the magistrates for their failure to provide work and enforce the laws against begging. Sir Josiah Child urged the repeal of the Act of Settlement because of the lifelong wandering habits of a large segment of the English poor. He also defended as understandable the tendency of the unemployed to congregate in London parishes where the variety of industries held out hope for jobs.[67] Others were less content to watch the poor streaming to London, and perhaps the landowners' interest in driving potential workers back into the country accounts for the failure to repeal this part of the Poor Law. According to James Puckle, "discontent, curiosity, hopes of greater wages, or of living lazier lives" drove people to London. There servant girls gave birth to bastards while in the countryside landlords were forced to pay higher wages to those who remained.[68] Sir Edward Dering blamed the Justices of the Peace for not apprenticing the poor to husbandry "whereby the whole race of farmers is almost utterly lost," and Sir William Coventry suggested that the laws "obliging poor people to give security to save the parish from charge" prevented many marriages, which in turn kept population down. However, like other critics, his recommendation called not for the repeal of the Poor Laws but for the erection of workhouses "where such as will not work for themselves may be compelled to work for others."[69]

---

[66] [Carter], *The ancient trades decayed*, pp. 9-10.
[67] [Child], *A discourse about trade*, 1690, p. 62, K 1725.
[68] *England's way to wealth and honour*, 1699, p. 29, K 2129.
[69] "Sir Edward Dering on the Decay of Rents in Kent, c. 1670," and

The idea of using revenues from parish taxes as a wage fund for setting the poor to work was enormously popular. These schemes variously called for a two- to four-year advance on the rates in order to maintain the poor and buy the stock for working-up wool, hemp, and flax, or for outfitting a national fishery. Tax support figured prominently in a variety of proposals, from financing river dredging to the rewarding of servants who continued in the same service for seven years. Proponents of such projects promised thus to convert a regular drain of income into eventual tax relief, but they saved their raptures for describing the transformation that would be wrought in the lives of the poor. As Jacob Viner has said of the eighteenth century, given the level of administrative skill of the English bureaucracy, such plans could appropriately be labeled as visionary.[70] However, the power of the vision should not be discounted. England alone among European nations had adopted a system of legal charity. The Poor Laws had institutionalized public support for both able-bodied and impotent poor. Whatever precedents the legislation reflected, recognition of the permanence of the need and the national scope of the obligation influenced economic thinking while the laws themselves made the plight of England's displaced persons a legitimate public issue. In this protracted discourse self-appointed critics and reformers sketched out the dream of a fully productive society. Population growth, the attraction of foreign capital and skills, the education of pauper children, and the adoption of a uniform code of economic virtues were summoned to the task. The pervasive conviction that England could produce more if resources were better managed provided an economic incentive to reorganize public charity. Almost without exception the writers of the

---

"Sir William Conventry on the Decay of Rents, 1670," in Thirsk and Cooper, eds., *Seventeenth-Century Economic Documents*, pp. 86, 80.

[70] "Man's Economic Status," in James L. Clifford, ed., *Man Versus Society in Eighteenth Century Britain*, Cambridge, 1968, p. 45.

tracts drew attention to the lack of employment opportunities and found in the idea of work—even make-work—the essential basis for social stability and economic growth.

The emancipation of property owners from most forms of political control over the use of their land and money had shifted the source of economic planning from regulations shaped by the past to private decisions oriented toward the future. Where earlier the disposal of a harvest or the pursuit of a trade had been conditional upon the likely social impact, the acceptance of near-absolute property rights had driven a wedge between society and the economy. With the curtailment of political oversight over economic life, the formal link between the material resources of the country and the people to be sustained by them had been cut. The commonwealth had become an aggregation of private wealth. Even husbandmen and craftsmen had acquired the competitive values of the market. John Cook claimed that the poor farmer was more resentful of the restraint of profit during the time of dearth than members of the gentry. "Let me sell as deare as the Market goes" is the sentiment he ascribed to the husbandmen.[71] Another writer charged ordinary weavers with a similar contempt of control. Seldom would they take apprentices as the law enjoined, he wrote, hiring servants for a year or less, heedless of the excess of laborers they produced by "this expeditious way."[72] But the mutual dependence of rich and poor, workers and employers, had not come to an end; it had only changed its form. Propertied Englishmen enjoyed the liberty to change tenants, withdraw their stock, and discharge workers, but they were not free from concerns with the poor as a source of labor, for labor was an integral part of their organization of resources. This realization, so obvious in the writings on the poor, represents the infusion of the outlook of those who had embraced the productive ideal into public thinking on charity.

[71] *Unum necessarium*, 1648, p. 8, K 731.
[72] [W. Smith], *An essay for recovery of trade*, 1661, p. 5.

The unwelcome hordes of masterless men at the beginning of the century appeared to the most concerned of their betters seventy years later as a pool of badly managed labor. Economic changes had disentangled agriculture and industry from the web of social obligations of village, manor, and guild but, like so much in England's new market economy, the free laborer was but a potential resource. In the countryside, as Alan Everitt has pointed out, many of the laborers in fielden villages adjusted to commercial farming without geographic displacement. Even the specialized skills of an improved agricultural technology were passed from generation to generation in a reworking of family customs. The other part of the propertyless—perhaps two-fifths of the whole population—became those visible poor who could be described as both laboring and idle because the same person could expect at any time to be either. For them modernization brought an ambiguous social position and a radical break with the customary preparation for social tasks. No longer viewed as peasants and not yet part of an industrial proletariat, the floating population of poor uprooted men and women represented a problem of staggering proportions. From this perspective the English Poor Laws created a kind of holding pattern. The provisions neither implied that the poor possessed claims upon society's material resources nor interfered with long-run hopes for making the idle self-supporting. In every sense the chronically underemployed of England's propertyless people were supernumeraries and recognized as such. The hands once needed— or at least occupied—in feeding the English population were now a burden because provisions were plentiful and could be had through the labor of fewer men and women. In one of his many hypothetical calculations Sir William Petty conjured up a nicely rounded population of one thousand, one hundred of whom raised the necessary food and clothing for the whole, another eight hundred of whom worked in manufacturing, trading, and the professions, with one hundred left unemployed. While this tenth is considerably smaller than the indigent two-fifths in Petty's day, the moral to which his calculations pointed is significant: although society did not need their labor, it could not afford to let them be idle. As there was food enough, they must be fed, but only if they worked so that the connection of support and labor be firmly fixed in their minds, bodies, and habits.[73] In this hypothetical situation Petty had reduced to its starkest form the problem of supplying artificially the socialization process that a later age would characterize as natural: the schooling of labor under the schoolmaster of need. Jobs offered social roles in a market society, but economic development lagged. The increased capacity to produce food was not matched by an expansion of work in commerce and industry. Even with a stable population between 1630 and 1730, the growth of the sixteenth century could not be absorbed by the economy, yet the economy with its new orientation toward productivity represented the single most powerful integrating institution in the society. What made the poor a national issue in Restoration England was their tenuous position. They had been expelled from a traditional order and as yet were only conditionally and occasionally needed in the new economic structure growing up outside the old.

In a seminal article on labor in seventeenth-century England, D. C. Coleman has argued that circumstances, more than policy considerations, accounted for contemporaries' obsession with the problems of unemployment.[74] Coleman's description of the relevant circumstances focused upon the limited output per worker, the high dependency ratio in a population squewed toward youth, and the vulnerability of the production processes to natural disasters. In such a situation, he maintained, it would be natural to connect

[73] *A treatise of taxes*, p. 12. See also N. G. Pauling, "The Employment Problem in Pre-Classical English Economic Thought," *The Economic Record* 27 (1951).

[74] "Labour in the English Economy of the Seventeenth Century," *Economic History Review* 2nd ser. 8 (1955-56).

prosperity with the more efficient mobilization of the working population. While Coleman's assessment of the production possibilities of the English economy at that time was a welcome corrective to the notion that prevailing ideas existed in a vacuum, it does not explain why the grim realities of underemployment and limited output did not evoke despair or discouragement, prescriptions for retrenchment, or counsels to rely on providence. Where in this situation is the source of the imperturbable faith in the potential productive capacity of England's idle hands that is consistently expressed? Contemporaries not only wanted employment for the unemployed; they wanted still more people. In the nineteenth century when the full industrial possibilities of a revolution in mechanical power were apparent, Thomas Malthus and his circle drew only the most pessimistic conclusions from the fact of a growing population, but over a century earlier when fully half of the population was underemployed, the reformers, mathematicians, jurists, clothiers, merchants, and publicists who wrote on economic topics seemed able to perceive only the potential plenty that could come from surplus men and women. This expectation shaped the relations between the poor and those members of the propertied class who committed their hopes for England to a future of increased material wealth and worldwide commercial dominance. What they saw in the idleness of the poor was a waste, but this perception of waste depended upon a vision of economic efficiency. In fact, England had too many people. These people had too few demands upon their time and skills. The internal and international markets through which English products were distributed were frequently clogged with too many goods and too few consumers, but the optimism about efficient management of the poor continued. In vain did a writer like Edward Littleton inveigh against the neglect of demand. Referring to the plethora of schemes for employing men and women in fishing and linen trades "and other projects of the like nature," Littleton shrewdly commented that these projecters "would do well to contrive a way, how the People imployed in them may make wages. For unless they do that, they do nothing. There is nothing," he concluded, "more easy than to find out unprofitable Employments."[75]

The persistence of schemes for the employing of the poor through a national stock suggests that, despite the awareness of trade gluts, the idea of an incremental expansion of human production was too compelling to be restrained by the mundane consideration of the limits of the existing market. In the realm of imagination the obvious want of material goods among most people, coupled with the possibility of organizing the labor of those no longer producing their own subsistence, was enough to sustain dreams of a larger laboring population. This vision hovers in the background of countless pamphlets. "The Time of labouring and industrious People well-employed, is the best Commodity of any country," James Puckle wrote, going on to indulge himself in the fancy of a fishery absorbing each vacant moment of "all our disbanded soldiers, poor prisoners, widows and orphans, all poor tradesmen artificers, and labourers, their wives, children and servants."[76] Manufacturing, which earlier in the century had appeared as a kind of adjunct to commerce, became instead the principal engine of wealth and the employer of those who, as John Cary described it, must otherwise "lie heavy on our land."[77] Laying the misery of the poor at the door of the inefficient overseers, another pamphleteer waxed eloquent on the wonders that could be wrought by a reorganization of the management and taxing system of poor relief, when "Those that whil'st unhiv'd were a Swarm of Droans and Pest to the Society, become (oh a Miracle) Industrious Bees, each contributing something to the support of the General."[78]

[75] [Littleton], *The groans of the plantations*, 1689, p. 34, K 1700.

[76] [Puckle], *England's path to wealth and honour*, pp. 31-32.

[77] *An essay on the coyn and credit of England*, Bristol, 1695, dedication, K 1947.

[78] *Proposals for the better management of the affairs of the poor* [1681], p. 4, K 1545.

Even more seductive was the dawning realization that art could produce more than nature. Much that was written on unemployment was a celebration "of the miraculous Power of Industry, and of those prodigious Acquirements which Human Nature is capable of attaining to, by laborious and an indefatigable Pursuit."[79] Considering that England at the time had the structural characteristics of an underdeveloped nation and that since time out of mind its economy had operated with severe limitations in output, the expectation of greater productivity is significant, as is the absence of doubt that a revolution in work habits could be effected. The writings on the poor advertised the fact that irregularly employed parents could not be relied upon to prepare their children for lives of productive toil. In a society in which more and more social tasks were being delegated to persons acting in their own interests, the collective concern of private commentators indicates an emerging upper-class consciousness. The idle hands that once struck observers as ready for the devil's work increasingly engaged attention for their potential conversion to useful occupations. As the students of factory discipline have detailed, factory owners with constant employment to offer completed the education of the "surly" English poor, but sustained debate on the need and the likely social consequences of adequate training led to the recognition that between the dislocations of the past and the expectation for the future must be thrown a bridge for the dependent poor.[80] The analysis of the employment problem gives evidence that a group—perhaps a class—of men was prepared to assume the leadership in England's modernization. At least inferentially, they recognized that the increase in private ownership

[79] *A discourse of the necessity of encouraging mechanick industry*, 1690, p. 15, K 1730.

[80] See N. McKendrick, "Josiah Wedgwood's Factory Discipline," *Historical Journal*, 4 (1961); Keith Thomas, "Work and Leisure in Pre-Industrial Society," *Past and Present*, 24 (1964); and E. P. Thompson, "Time, Work-Discipline, and Industrial Capitalism."

of property that gave them a wider ambit of freedom also tied their future aspirations to the behavior of those without property. If they did not make explicit their personal involvement in the transformation of the old peasantry into a new working class, they nonetheless indicated that the prosperity they hoped to profit from would be compromised as long as the potential working capacity of the people was neglected. What emerges from their writings is the constructive role that hopes of productivity played in linking rich to poor in a nation whose only comprehensive purpose was the development of its material resources.

Seven

A New Argument for Economic Freedom

IN ITS MOST ELEMENTAL FORM THE THEORY
of the balance of trade is little more than a truism. Be the
spender a nation or a private person, if more goods are
bought than sold, the difference must be made up in payment. As Charles Wilson has pointed out, the main features
of the balance-of-trade theory were set forth with admirable
clarity in the mid-sixteenth century tract *A discourse of the
commonweal of this realm of England*, and they could be
read without significant alteration two centuries later in
Matthew Decker's *Essay on the causes of the decline of the
foreign trade*.[1] It would be a mistake, however, to conclude
from this observation that between these terminal dates the
theory received the same emphasis or served the same purposes, for at the end of the seventeenth century most of the
theoretical assumptions of this explanation of how countries
grow wealthy had been effectively challenged and the idea
of favorable balances declared outmoded. The fact that economic writers like Decker, Josiah Tucker, and Malachy
Postlethwayt still drew upon balance-of-trade notions in
the eighteenth century owes more to social and political
considerations than to the sterility of economic reasoning
through two centuries of dramatic change in the English
economy.

When in the depression crisis of the 1620s Mun called
upon the balance-of-trade imagery he did so to make one

[1] "Trade, Society and the State," in E. E. Rich and C. H. Wilson,
eds., *The Cambridge Economic History of Europe*, vol. 4, Cambridge,
1967, pp. 499ff; and Jacob Viner, *Studies in the Theory of International
Trade*, New York, 1937, pp. 60-61. Bruno Suviranta, *Theory of the
Balance of Trade in England*, Helsingfors, 1923, pp. 21-22, notes that
an officer of the mint in 1381 drew attention to the need to have a
favorable trade balance before specie could be kept in the country.

principal point: that money passively followed the exchange of goods through the circuitous channels laid out by the settling of trade accounts in international commerce. His aim was not to explain the benefits of a favorable balance of trade but rather to scotch the patrimonial notion that the depression in the cloth trade could be cured by official regulation of the rates for exchanging coins. Here, as we have seen, Mun argued in the strongest possible terms that neither royal control of the exchange nor statutory restraints on merchants would make any difference. Considering the havoc the contemporary round of debasements and devaluations was playing in England's markets abroad, his assertions must be viewed in part as facts called forth by wishes.[2] Mun served the merchants' interest well, however, by offering an elegant theory about long-run trends that could be used to criticize the cavalier actions of princes. The balance-of-trade theory quickly became an explanation of a dynamic rhythm in international commerce, which held out hope of both growth and development. Merchants with money could search out home commodities to be sold abroad and their drive for profit could promote the advantageous disposal of agricultural surpluses, foster industrial efforts, and fetch from foreign parts goods that could be resold in a spiraling pattern of profit and investment.

From the 1620s onward the association of wealth with a favorable balance of trade was connected with this prospectus for developing England's productive resources.[3] In a published speech to Parliament, Sir Robert Cotton noted England's windfall profits from the Thirty Years War but stressed that trade must be increased through new ventures like the growing of hemp and flax on newly drained fenland and the working-up of linen cloth to make England the "outfitter to all Europe." Extolling the new draperies, Cot-

[2] J. D. Gould, "The Trade Depression of the Early 1620s," *Economic History Review*, 2nd ser. 7 (1954-55), 89ff.

[3] This point is developed in R.W.K. Hinton, "The Mercantile System in the time of Thomas Mun," *ibid.*, 287-88.

ton pointed to their superior trading potential over the traditional English woolen cloth, which "serves but one cold corner of the World."[4] Without traffic, as Lewes Roberts put it, natural riches go to waste and are not sent out to bring back other necessities, and John Keymer, in advice attributed to Sir Walter Raleigh, lamented the fact that English traders pursued an "unprofitable course of merchandising" while failing to achieve the full manufacturing of home-bred commodities.[5]

Thus, the simple proposition about what happened when a country exported more than it imported became in the early seventeenth century a theory of economic growth that emphasized the initiating role of the merchant, the superior force of commercial factors over political ones in determining the flow of money, and the capacity for a growing foreign trade to increase the importation of specie. The tensions and contradictions in the balance-of-trade notion were those implicit in a theory of economic growth that detailed only the producing–selling side of the economic equation. Mun, however, did not totally neglect the reciprocal nature of international trade. In *England's treasure by forraign trade* he warned that legislation aimed at foreign merchants would only provoke retaliation and that too much frugality in the English consumption of foreign goods would inhibit the capacity of foreign countries to purchase English goods. These possibilities, however, were left in a kind of conceptual limbo, and the enunciation of Mun's fully articulated description of a worldwide commerce served principally as a memorial to the merchants' prowess and a warning to princes and law givers about the new age in which "necessity or gain will ever find some

[4] *Sir Thomas Roe his speech in Parliament,* 1641, p. 11, K 598. See chapter 2, note 38.

[5] *The treasure of traffike,* 1641, p. 11, K 595; [John Keymer], *Sir Walter Raleigh's observations touching trade and commerce with the hollander, and other nations,* 1653, p. 36, K 892.

means to violate" legislation inimicable to profitable enterprises.[6]

The rambling discussions of agricultural improvements and industrial expansion that characterized writings during the Interregnum were replaced by much more sharply focused economic arguments during the last three decades of the seventeenth century. Despite the substantial increase in both the wealth and the productive capacity of England after the Restoration, economic writers became more critical of one another. The rivalry of the Dutch and the French in European cloth markets put the English clothiers in a permanently defensive posture that made the world of trade look more like a struggle for survival than a shared cornucopia. In their hands the competitive implications of the idea of favorable balances became the most salient. As one writer put it, the "Increase and Wealth of all States, is evermore made upon the Forreigner for whatsoever is gained by one Native from another in one part of this Kingdom, must necessarily be lost in another part, and so the publick Stock nothing thereby Augmented."[7] According to Samuel Fortrey, "the onely way to be rich, is to have plenty of that commoditie to vent, that is of greatest value abroad; for what the price of anything is amongst our selves, whether dear or cheap it matters not; for as we pay so we receive . . . but the art is when we deal with strangers, to sell dear and to buy cheap and this will increase our wealth."[8] The worst of the situation was that England's rivals seemed to have learned these lessons better than England—at least in the eyes of the clothiers. The French used high tariffs to exclude English goods in their home markets and beat out

[6] [Mun], *The petition and remonstrance of the governor and company of merchants of London, trading to the East Indies*, 1628, p. 9, K 454.

[7] *Certain considerations relating to the Royal African company of England*, 1680, p. 1, K 1513.

[8] *Englands interest*, 1663, p. 29, K 1337.

the English elsewhere by cheap manufacturing. The Dutch throve by dint of industry and enlightened policies. Like most troubles, the blows to the English woolen trade had come in clusters. The anonymous author of *The Linnen and Woollen Manufactory Discoursed* specified five: German success in selling their coarse woolens to the Venetians for the Turkey trade; the prohibition of English woolens in the French market; the increase of woolen manufacturing by England's neighbors; the domestic popularity of silks and calicoes, which displaced the demand formerly supplied by Tammies and Sayes; and the decline of the Irish market.[9]

Under the pressure of these adversities the clothiers called for a rigorously enforced national trade policy and summoned the principles of the balance-of-trade theory to their support. Where Thomas Mun had made much of the self-sustaining interaction of international commerce, they used his theory to justify restrictions, a program that necessarily required suppressing the idea of a mutuality of interests among trading nations. In their hands the notion of an unfavorable balance was cast as a national evil to be warded off by legislation. English economic writers had repeatedly praised the Dutch for promoting prosperity through formal policies. Dutch policies, however, promoted the expansion of trade, with the Dutch getting a proportionately larger share in the increase of international productivity. The clothiers had a narrower vision. Trading activities in England were to be subordinated to those commercial endeavors that either set the poor to work or utilized the products of English land. Even imports of sailcloth and cordage, important to English shippers, were to be excluded and the English poor set to work on flax and hemp to supply the loss. In the writings of the clothiers, England was conceived of as a giant corporate undertaking, each part contributing

[9] 1691, pp. 7-8, Ks 1734. See also *An abstract of the grievances of trade which oppress our poor*, 1694, p. 2, K 1830.

to the well-being of the cloth industry, which alone could lure to England the gold and silver that constituted true wealth. Agricultural improvements should be aimed at producing cheap victuals that would permit low wages which would make English cloths competitive in international markets. Funding of poor rates would create a national stock for the employment of the poor. The wealth of England was indeed to be squeezed from foreigners as earlier dreams of expanding trade contracted to the goal of economic self-sufficiency and competitive muscle in world cloth markets. The rationale for securing cooperation from the rest of the nation rested upon the definition of wealth as a store of treasure procured through a favorable balance of trade most easily accessible through the careful management of England's woolen industry.

In popularizing these ideas, William Carter, Carew Reynel, Thomas Manley, Samuel Fortrey, Richard Haines, and John Pollexfen focused attention upon production in such a way as to obscure the dynamics of consumption. The conspicuously wasteful spending of the rich and the costly maintenance of the poor encouraged the notion that foreign markets alone could return wealth to England. Exchanges in the domestic market were described as mere transfers of money and consumption a necessary evil at best.[10] Referring nostalgically to the days when English goods went far and fetched back silver and gold, Richard Haines lamented present times when "all that our Goods

---

[10] For contemporary assertions that selling to one another is "mere consumption" without enrichment, see Thomas Culpeper, Jr., *A discourse showing the many advantages which will accrue to this kingdom by the abatement of usury*, London, 1668, pp. 2-3, K 1217; John Cary, *An essay on the state of England in relation to its trade*, Bristol, 1695, pp. 1-4, K 1870; [John Pollexfen], *England and East-India inconsistent in their manufactures*, 1697, p. 20, K 2042; *The profit and loss of the East-India-trade*, 1700, pp. 8-9, K 2262; *Certain considerations relating to the Royal African company*, p. 1; and Sir Francis Brewster, *Essays on trade and navigation*, 1695, p. 50, K 1867.

and Money bring in is soon consumed, and comes as it were to the Dunghill, whilst our Wealth becomes a prey to other Nations."[11] Inhibited by this general perspective from studying demand as elastic, the unexamined assumption prevailed that spending at home should be curbed and opportunities for profit exploited abroad. The logic of this position—even if it left unexplored the role of demand— was flawless. Domestic consumption detracted from the store of English capital through luxury buying and the support of the poor. If these were kept to a minimum, England would be able to increase exports. Foreigners would be the consumers, to England's profit.

Such an explanation of wealth-producing activities fitted well with the endemic political rivalries of seventeenth-century Europe and invested the balance-of-trade theory with the patriotic appeal of joining Englishmen in a cooperative effort against outsiders. From this perspective, members of society did not compete with one another, but rather participated in the collective enterprise of selling surplus goods abroad. Where the balance-of-trade theory failed was in its inability to explain the prosperity and development that had become conspicuous by the 1670s. In the closing decades of the seventeenth century, real income, domestic spending, and foreign exports rose together. From John Graunt in 1662 to William Petty in 1682 to Charles Davenant in 1696 the growing wealth of England drew comment.[12] Every index of economic growth showed an advance: agricultural output, capital investment, imports from the Indies and the New World, the range and

11 *The prevention of poverty*, 1674, p. 12, K 1361.

12 K. G. Davies, "Joint-Stock Investment in the Later Seventeenth Century," *Economic History Review*, 2nd ser. 4 (1952), 284-85; for contemporary comment see [Charles Davenant], *An essay on the East-India-trade*, 1696, p. 17, K 1954; Sir William Petty, *Political arithmetick*, 1690, pp. 96-100, K 1741; and [William Carter], *The great loss and damage to England by the transportation of wool to forreign parts*, 1677, p. 12.

quantity of home manufacturing.[13] Most striking was the abounding evidence of a rise in the level of domestic consumption. What had happened to the store of wealth consumed by the London fire? Contemporaries saw it splendidly replaced before their very eyes. The rebuilding of London was but the most spectacular testimony to the fact that Englishmen generally were enjoying a higher standard of living. Gregory King, building on Petty's estimates of twenty-three years earlier, calculated the quarter-century gain in national wealth at 23 percent.[14] Foreign trade increased by 50 percent and estimated gains in income were 8 percent.[15] Daniel Defoe hailed the period since 1680 as a projecting age when men set their wits to designing "Engines, and Mechanical Motion," a propensity greatly encouraged, he noted, by stockjobbing. Subsequent research has confirmed Defoe's accuracy: between 1660 and 1700, 236 patents for inventions were issued in England, 64 of them between 1691 and 1693, a registration of ingenuity not matched until after 1760.[16] London's opulence attracted comments from admirers as well as rural critics who blamed the city for draining away everything from prospective tenants, hard cash, and unwed mothers to prodigal members of the gentry and nobility.[17] Defending the Church of England from the

[13] Charles Wilson, *England's Apprenticeship, 1603-1763*, New York, 1965, p. 185; R. M. Hartwell, "Economic Growth in England before the Industrial Revolution," *Journal of Economic History* 29 (1969), 25; E. A. Wrigley, "A Simple Model of London's Importance in Changing English Society and Economy 1650-1750," *Past and Present* 37 (1967), 51, 54, 61; and J. D. Gould, *Economic Growth in History*, London, 1972, pp. 156-77.

[14] Davies, "Joint-Stock Investment," p. 284.

[15] William Robert Scott, *The Constitution and Finance of English, Scottish and Irish Joint-Stock Companies to 1720*, vol. 1, Cambridge, 1912, p. 496.

[16] *An essay upon projects*, 1697, pp. 24-25, K 2024; Davies, "Joint-Stock Investment," p. 285.

[17] Stephen Primatt, *The city and country purchaser and builder* [1667], p. 4; [Charles Davenant], *An essay upon ways and means of*

charge that the spending of prelates before the Civil War had ruined trade, the author of *Ananias and Saphira discover'd* pointed to the happy configuration of luxury spending, enhanced trade, and prosperity visible in London in 1678.[18] Edward Chamberlayne regaled his readers with the prosperity of the city where the ships "by their masts resemble a forest." Notwithstanding fire, pestilence, and war, he continued, the citizens of London recovered in a few months.[19]

From the English manufacturers' point of view the most distressing aspect of this conspicuous prosperity was the display of East India fabrics. English men and women had acquired a taste for the light, airy muslins and printed calicoes, which touched off a craze. The East India Company, one of the last of the great monopoly joint stock trading enterprises, cultivated the English market with great entrepreneurial skill. Free trade in bullion after 1663 permitted the company to expand its operations and by 1680 it was exporting £500,000 annually.[20] In the early years of the 1670s the company dispatched English artisans to the Far East to show the Indians how to design patterns to English tastes. What had begun as the inconspicuous use of cotton for suit lining grew rapidly into a pervasive display of printed draperies, bedspreads, tapestries, shirts, and dresses.[21] According to John Pollexfen the popularity of

---

supplying the war, 1695, pp. 116-17, K 1884; [Carter], *The ancient trade decayed*, 1678, p. 8, Ks 1464 (republished in 1681 as *The trade of England revived*, Ks 1533); [Nicholas Barbon], *An apology for the builder*, 1685, p. 2, K 1608; "An essay concerning the decay of rents and their remedies" [1670], in Joan Thirsk and J. P. Cooper, eds., *Seventeenth-Century Economic Documents*, Oxford, 1972, pp. 80-82.

[18] *Ananias and Saphira discover'd*, 1679, pp. 5-6, K 1475.

[19] *Angliae notitia*, 1669, pt. 2, p. 207, K 1235.

[20] Suviranta, *The Theory of the Balance of Trade*, p. 7; *A true relation of the rise and progress of the East-India company* [1697], in Walter Scott, ed., *A Collection of Scarce and Valuable Tracts*, vol. 10, London, 1815, p. 648.

[21] *Ibid.*; *The great necessity and advantage of preserving our own*

Indian wares reached all ranks in society, "from the greatest
Gallants to the meanest Cook-Maids, nothing was thought
fit, to adorn their persons, as the Fabricks of India."[22] The
taste, another warned, would spread to the colonies where
people "will imitate the Gentry of England."[23] The clothiers
blamed the East India Company for causing widespread
distress as Bengal silks displaced English silks and Spitalfield silk throwers were thrown out of work. The preference
for cheap Indian cottons over German linens meant, critics
said, that Germans could no longer afford to pay for English woolens.[24] The popularity, versatility, and competitive
advantage of imported Indian fabrics prompted woolen
industry spokesmen to mount a vigorous campaign to ban
Indian imports. Because they appealed to the balance-of-
trade argument in this effort, its theoretical weaknesses
were well advertised. Some company defenders tried to turn
the theory to their own account—Charles Davenant, for
instance, argued that cheap imported textiles "freed" more
woolens for exports—but other writers moved outside the
balance-of-trade logic altogether.[25] In this they were aided
by certain older strains of economic reasoning, which had
emphasized the importance of demand as a stimulant to
industry and through industry to greater productivity.

In *Considerations upon the East-India trade*, Henry
Martyn made a frontal attack on the whole notion of
artificial stimulation of the employment of English laborers. Conceding that Indian imports "abate the price of

manufacturing, 1697, pp. 6-8, K 2019; *The clothiers complaint*, 1692,
p. 36, K 1784; and [Pollexfen], *A discourse of trade and coyn*, 1697,
p. 106, K 2040.

[22] [Pollexfen], *A discourse of trade, coyne, and paper credit*, 1697,
p. 99, K 2041.

[23] *Reasons humbly offered for the passing of a bill for hindering
the home consumption of East-India silks, bengals &c.*, 1697, p. 7.

[24] *A true relation*, p. 648; *The profit and loss of the East-India trade*,
p. 23; and *The clothiers complaint*, p. 36.

[25] As quoted in P. J. Thomas, *Mercantilism and the East India
Trade*, London, 1963, p. 81.

English manufacturers," he maintained that this actually promoted growth in other segments of the economy.[26] Laborers who bought Indian cottons would have more money available from their wages to spend on those items produced more efficiently by the English. Even if English laborers were thrown out of work, he continued, the greater competition for jobs would drive down wages and hence lower the cost of other English products. Pursuing his cost-advantage theory, Martyn stressed that any law that forced the English to consume only English goods forced them to pay more for their needs than was necessary. He likened this to rejecting the benefits of new inventions or the obvious savings from the division of labor, or even to spurning gifts of wheat if God sent them.[27]

Martyn explored the relation between earning and purchasing power with unprecedented analytical skill. He carried one step further a line of inquiry that had already attracted John Houghton, Dalby Thomas, Francis Gardiner, Nicholas Barbon, Dudley North, Roger Coke, and several anonymous pamphleteers. In the 1680s and 1690s these writers had explored the role of demand, the importance of consumption and the economic stimulus of individual initiative. They saw England not as a giant workhouse but rather as a giant market whose individual members had differing needs. Always inferentially, sometimes explicitly, they extolled competition and the freedom that promoted it, seeing in both new avenues to productivity.

With the focus of attention passing to internal market relationships, the conflicts between manufacturers and merchants, which the predominating concern with foreign trade had so long obscured, finally stood out. As John Pollexfen noted critically, East India Company spokesmen had given up justifying their trade with claims that their profits were made through the reexporting of goods to Eng-

26 [Martyn], 1701, pp. 62, 73-76, K 2310.
27 Ibid., pp. 50-52.

land's rivals and acknowledged that half their volume was consumed at home.[28] This admission required a defense of domestic consumption which of necessity undermined the whole structure of ideas associated with the balance of trade, because it challenged the idea that wealth was specie that could only be secured from the settling of favorable accounts. A new definition of wealth was in order. When the maverick spirit of fashion revealed itself in the craze over printed calicoes the potential market power of previously unfelt wants came clearly into view. Here was a revolutionary force. Under the sway of new tastes, people had spent more, and in spending more the elasticity of demand had become apparent. In this elasticity, the defenders of domestic spending discovered the propulsive power of envy, emulation, love of luxury, vanity, and vaulting ambition. As long as demand was viewed as more inelastic than elastic, the static conception of wealth held good. England then could grow richer only by selling a larger share of her surplus abroad, that is, by controlling a larger share of the international market. Once consumption was analyzed as a constructive activity, the connections could be made between incentives to work, greater purchasing power, larger production units, greater efficiency, and higher levels of spending—a self-sustained momentum for economic growth, which did not rely on favorable balances.

Writing in 1690, Nicholas Barbon bubbled over with the possibilities of unlimited demand: "The Wants of the Mind are infinite, Man naturally Aspires, and as his Mind is elevated, his Senses grow more refined, and more capable of Delight; his Desires are inlarged, and his Wants increase with his Wishes, which is for everything that is rare, can gratifie his Senses, adorn his Body, and promote the Ease, Pleasure, and Pomp of Life."[29] From Dudley North came a similar expression: "The main spur to Trade, or rather

[28] [Pollexfen], *England and East India inconsistent in their manufactures*, pp. 3-4.
[29] [Barbon], *A discourse of trade*, 1690, p. 15, K 1720.

to Industry and Ingenuity, is the exorbitant Appetites of Men, which they will take pains to gratifie, and so be disposed to work, when nothing else will incline them to it; for did Men content themselves with bare Necessaries, we should have a poor World."[30] Less euphorically, Francis Gardiner allowed that frugality was no doubt a commendable thing, but, having made this concession, noted that "where People grow Rich, they will spend more largely, and it is better they should do so than to slacken their Industry and Diligence in Trade."[31] These sentiments even crept into the writings of conventional balance-of-trade writers like John Cary, who affirmed that the growth of pride and luxury was the principal quickener of trade and extended its influence to "our poor in England," who would spend more on clothes and furnishings when they were paid more and hence increase the consumption of the very goods they manufactured.[32] An early convert to the power of consumption, John Houghton asserted that "Our High-Living is so far from Prejudicing the Nation, that it enriches it." Describing the deadly sins as economic virtues, Houghton said

30 [North], *Discourse upon trade*, 1691, p. 14, K 1767.

31 *Some reflections on a pamphlet, intituled, England and East-India inconsistent in their manufactures*, 1697, p. 2, K 1968. The authorship of this anonymously published pamphlet is usually attributed to Gardner. However, the sentiments are very close to those of Alderman Gardiner of Norwich whom J. Keith Horsefield, *British Monetary Experiments 1650-1710*, Cambridge, Mass., 1960, p. 52, says was consulted by the Privy Council on the question of recoinage. Horsefield also lists two tracts by Alderman Gardiner in his bibliography: *Some remarks on a report containing an essay for the amendment of the silver coins*, 1695, and a manuscript, "Alderman Gardner of Norwich his Proposal about Amendment of the Coyn" [1695], in the Goldsmith's Library, University of London, vol. 62, "Recoinage of 1696." A contemporary pamphlet [Samuel Grascomb], *An account of the proceedings in the House of Commons*, [1696], K 2008, lists Fran. Gardiner of Norfolk among those voting on the recoinage issue and, according to Horsefield, Locke attributed *Some remarks on a report to* "———. Gardiner."

32 *An essay on the state of England*, Bristol, 1695, pp. 143ff, K 1870.

that "those who are guilty of Prodigality, Pride, Vanity, and Luxury, do cause more Wealth to the Kingdom, than Loss to their own Estates."[33] "Desire and Wants increase with Riches," Barbon observed, "a Poor Man wants a Pound; a Rich Man an Hundred."[34]

Not content merely to catalog the psychological stimulants to demand, these writers drew attention to the specific economic function of each emotion. Foreign imports were justifiable because they dazzled people with their novelty and promoted industry by way of the acquisitive instinct. Analyzing the rationale for banning foreign imports, Barbon explained that it was based on the fallacious idea that if Englishmen could not buy foreign luxuries, they would consume domestic goods. This is not true, he said, because it "is not Necessity that causeth the Consumption, Nature may be Satisfied with little; but it is the wants of the Mind, Fashion, and desire of Novelties, and Things scarce, that causeth Trade."[35] Dalby Thomas made the same point when he objected to those who wanted England to live on its own without imported luxuries. They are not the source of sin, he said, but "true Spurs to Virtue, Valour and the Elevation of the mind, as well as the just rewards of Industry."[36] Competition prompts men to invent things to reduce labor costs, Martyn asserted: "If my Neighbour by doing much with little labour, can sell cheap, I must contrive to sell as cheap as he."[37] John Houghton disputed Samuel Fortrey's strictures against French imports by point-

[33] *A collection of letters for the improvement of husbandry & trade,* 1681-83, pp. 59, 52, K 1538.

[34] *A discourse concerning coining the new money lighter,* 1696, p. 3, K 1931. In praising Barbon for his astuteness in gauging the importance of fashion, William Letwin, *The Origins of Scientific Economics,* London, 1963, p. 63, emphasizes too much the singularity of Barbon's assessment of fashion's economic power.

[35] *A discourse of trade,* pp. 72-73.

[36] *An historical account of the West-India collonies,* 1690, p. 6, K 1749.

[37] *Considerations upon the East-India trade,* p. 67.

ing out that even foreign luxury items satisfied genuine consumer demands and made people work harder.[38] Daniel Defoe, while equivocal about free trade, did attribute the increase in useful inventions to the fact that merchants and marine insurers, hurt by losses during the French war, had had to "wrack their Wits for New Contrivances, New Inventions, New Trades, Stocks, Projects, and any thing to retrieve the desperate Credit of their Fortunes."[39] North described envy as a goad to industry and ingenuity, even among the lowest orders. When the "meaner sort" see people who have become rich they "are spurr'd up to imitate their Industry." Even the man who beggars himself emulating his neighbor is a national benefactor, for the nation gains "from the extraordinary Application he made, to support his Vanity." Rejecting sumptuary laws, North commended consumption for its stimulus to trade. The nation "never thrives better, then when Riches are tost from hand to hand."[40] Fashion, Barbon explained, promotes trade because it "occasions the Expence of Cloaths, before the Old ones are worn out."[41]

Behind these endorsements of early obsolescence and conspicuous consumption lay a new confidence in society's productive powers. Where Adam Smith would use the self-sustaining power of consumption without extolling it, these

[38] [Houghton], *England's great happiness*, 1677, pp. 5-6, K 1431.

[39] *Essay upon projects*, p. 6.   [40] *Discourses upon trade*, p. 15.

[41] *A discourse of trade*, p. 65. See also Houghton, *Letters*, p. 36. N. G. Pauling, "The Employment Problem in Pre-Classical English Economic Thought," *The Economic Record* 27 (1951), 57, reasons that Coke, Barbon, North, Petty, and others assigned to the rich a moral obligation to spend freely in order to provide employment for the poor. While employment is often cited as a consequence of greater domestic consumption, Coke, North, and Barbon—like Martyn, Gardiner, and Houghton—present their case in the context of a comprehensive theory of economic growth. For the position that economic writers in this period were totally incapable of conceiving that "the wealth of the world as a whole could increase," see Eli Heckscher, "Revision in Economic History: Mercantilism," *Economic History Review* 1st ser. 7 (1936), 48.

writers of the 1690s actually praised prodigality. "A Conspiracy of the Rich Men to be Covetous, and not spend, would be as dangerous to a Trading State, as a Forreign War," Barbon proclaimed.[42] When Pollexfen, an unreconstructed balance-of-trade thinker on the Board of Trade, used the old moralistic arguments against luxury consumption, Gardiner rebutted him with the statement that "There is no other use of Riches but to purchase what serves our Necessity and Delight."[43] The dour disapproval of self-indulgence was countered with the happy intimation of a new society of buyers and sellers. North, Martyn, Thomas, Houghton and Barbon were endorsing the upward striving of the poor and turning the enjoyment of a higher standard of living into both the motive and the end of productivity. Dalby Thomas, in fact, explicitly distinguished between the spending of laborers and of the idle rich, the first contributing to the nation's wealth, the latter not.[44] It took just such a liberal reworking of theories of economic development to provoke Humphrey Mackworth's salute to population growth: "the more the merrier."[45]

Appreciation of the desirability of English consumers' having access to cheap East Indian imports involved looking at society as an aggregation of self-interested producer-consumers. The boldest proponents of free trade adopted this new conception and advanced a theory of economic growth based upon it. However, although they saw individual competition as advantageous to the economy because it promoted greater industry and a restless search for profitable investments of time and money, they still believed in a basic reciprocity of interests among the participants in both internal and international markets. The author of the Preface to North's *Discourses upon trade* put the case well

[42] *A discourse of trade*, p. 32; see also Houghton, *Letters*, pp. 52-53; and Thomas, *An historical account*, p. 6.

[43] *Some reflections on a pamphlet*, p. 7.

[44] *An historical account*, pp. 10, 3.

[45] [Mackworth], *England's glory*, 1694, pp. 20-23, K 1850.

when he wrote that: "the whole World as to Trade, is but as one Nation or People, and the loss of a Trade with one Nation, is not that only, separately considered, but so much of the Trade of the World rescinded and lost, for all is combined together."[46] This view of the mutually beneficial aspects of trade rested upon the conviction that the world's resources for creating wealth were presently undeveloped. Recognizing how the balance-of-trade theory led to a different conclusion, Barbon criticized the analogy between private estates and national economies. Conceding that a person could not spend more than he earned, Barbon explained that this was because an estate was finite, "but the Stock of a Nation [is] Infinite, and can never be consumed; For what is Infinite, can neither receive Addition by Parsimony, nor suffer Diminution, by Prodigality." Developing the idea further in *Discourse concerning coining the new money lighter*, Barbon described the "infinity" of national wealth as coming from the regularity of harvests, the perpetual increase of cattle and of mineral wealth: "if we consider a Nation as consisting of a Body of People, the Inhabitants may be made richer or poorer; but it is not by consuming the Stock of the Nation, but for want of improving the Stock. It is not by Trading, but for want of Trade. That Nation is accounted rich, when the greatest number of Inhabitants are rich. And they are only made rich by Industry, Arts, and Traffick."[47] "Why should not we by incouraging Arts and Sciences, get Mony from others," John Houghton asked, "as well as they from us? Are we the only Apes and Fools of the World? Doth not most parts of it, where Civiliz'd, love Fynery?"[48] In condoning the trade in luxuries there was an accompanying recognition of the elasticity of demand, which could be stretched through new

[46] p. viii. William Letwin, in "The Authorship of Sir Dudley North's 'Discourses on Trade,'" *Economica* 18 (1951), suggests that Roger North wrote the Preface to his brother's essay.

[47] *A discourse of trade*, p. 6; *A discourse concerning coining*, p. 48. See also [Gardiner], *Some reflections*, pp. 18-19.

[48] *Letters*, p. 61.

applications of industry and ingenuity. This conclusion persuaded writers to reject the "beggar thy neighbor" policy implicit in the balance of trade. It also focused attention upon consumption and the satisfaction of wants rather than possession of treasure as the aim of economic activity. Since riches serve individual purposes, Francis Gardiner concluded that "some Goods are more acceptable in some Countries, at some times, than Money."[49] Similarly, Roger Coke argued that "the Wealth of every Nation Consists in Goods more than Money, so much therefore as any Nation abounds more in Goods than another, so much richer is that Nation than the other."[50]

The economic reasoning that came to a head with the rash of publications in the 1690s was totally incompatible with the balance-of-trade theory of economic growth. While all but a few writers believed that foreign trade contributed to national prosperity, they did not stress the capacity of foreign trade to attract specie but fixed instead upon the more liberal benefits of a larger market and a greater variety of commodities. Where the balance-of-trade theory had begun with a definition of specie as wealth and led step by step to the vaunted favorable balance of trade as the only means to attract that one elixir of economic life, writers in the late seventeenth century recognized that gold and silver were commodities like corn, cloth, and cattle and could as easily be sold for the one as vice versa. This stress upon the commodity nature of specie led to the conclusion that it was not anything specific that constituted wealth but rather the capacity to purchase what one wanted. Not only had the idea of wealth as a tangible substance been metamorphosed into a psychological satisfaction—Nicholas Barbon even noted that the only truly wealthy man was the one who wanted nothing[51]—but the variety of products coursing

[49] *Some reflections on a pamphlet*, p. 7.

[50] *A detection of the court and state of England*, vol. 1, 1694, p. 522. See also [North], *Discourses*, p. 17.

[51] *A discourse concerning coining*, p. 3.

through European entrepots suggested endless variations on a theme of economic exploitation.

The switch from a static goal to a dynamic capability reinforced the tendency to analyze commerce as a process rather than a program. Since the satisfaction of wants could take place within an internal market as well as through international trade, some men began to deny that domestic exchanges were sterile, thus removing that distinction between the international and internal markets that formed so crucial a part of the balance-of-trade theory. Once the capacity for satisfying wants through domestic trade was recognized, the members of society became important on both sides of the economic equation. They were viewed as both consumers as well as producers, and the linkage of psychological drives to productive activities suggested a rhythm of expansion not possible as long as demand was presumed to be inelastic or only profitable when indulged in by foreigners.

This development in economic reasoning gave contemporaries a much surer grasp of the way in which the market mechanism actually worked. Without recourse to equations, the most imaginative of the economic writers in the Restoration were able to express through descriptions the way in which bargains were reached, prices determined, and regularities imputed to the richly textured social activity of buying and selling. Barbon laid bare the "invisible hand of the market" when he explained that it is the trader who takes care to provide a sufficient quantity of the goods for man's needs. And how does he find out how much to provide? From the market, "that is, by the quick selling of commodities, that are made ready to be sold."[52] Houghton, with similar simplicity, explained how the market was widened. "Our height," he said:

> puts us all upon an industry, makes every one strive to excell his fellow, and by their ignorance of one an-

[52] *An apology for the builder,* pp. 32-33.

others quantities, make more than our markets will presently take off; which puts them to a new industry to find a foreign Vent, and then they must make more for that market; but still having some overplus they stretch their wits farther, and are never satisfied till they ingross the trade of the Universe.[53]

More ingeniously, another pamphleteer explained why investments in land and trade tended toward equilibrium: "the interest of Trade and Land are the same, for the mutation frequently happens; the Moneyed Man to day is a Landed Man to morrow; and the Landed Man to day becomes a Moneyed Man to morrow: Every man according to his Sentiments of things turns and winds his Estate as he pleaseth, and as he fancies will be most Advantagious to him . . . some would Sell till money grew scarce to Purchase, and Land plenty to Sell, and then the Scales would turn, and it would fall again."[54] At an even more sophisticated level, Henry Martyn suggested that even if cheap East Indian imports threw men out of work, the price of wages would be abated by the increase of laborers and thus drive down the cost of production, but consequently by reducing the amount of labor through inventions might "without abating any Man's Wages abate the price of Manufacturers."[55] Barbon used this same appreciation of the echoing influence of events in the market to explain the fall in rents. Low rents, he said, probably came "from the great improvements that are made upon the Land in the Country . . . by which means the Markets are overstock'd and furnished at a cheaper rate than those Lands can afford, who have had no advantage from improvements."[56]

[53] *England's great happiness*, pp. 10-13.

[54] *Some thoughts concerning the better security of our trade and navigation*, 1695, p. 4, Ks 1905. Sir Dalby Thomas may be the author of this pamphlet, because the British Museum copy is bound with his letters from Cape-Coast Castle, sent in 1704.

[55] *Considerations upon the East-India trade*, pp. 62ff.

[56] *An apology for the builder*, p. 25.

The interrelatedness of wage rates, prices, and the supplying of markets received increasing attention in the last quarter of the century. The naive optimism that agricultural improvements and putting people to work in any way possible would contribute to the general welfare gave way to an appreciation of the losses as well as gains involved in any particular course of action. The prolonged experience with depressed grain prices prompted writers to search out the influences upon sales. Important new insights about the impact of a world trade in food were lodged in Sir William Petty's simple statement that husbandmen's wages must not be allowed to rise or else rents would fall since prices could not go up without food being imported.[57] The same sense of how the market distributed economic returns appeared in a speech by Sir Richard Cocks on the problem of anticipating returns when the landlord sets the rents of his tenants:

> if they [prices] sink and continue so to do lower than we expected when we made the bargain, then he is broke. If they rise and continue to do so, then I am at a loss; for though men have their rent paid in silver and gold, it is in effect but wool, beef, mutton, butter, and cheese; and when commodities are very low my tenant pays me more wool, etc., than he could raise of my land, which must ruin him. When corn, wool, beef, etc., rise without any visible cause, as scarcity or the unseasonableness of the year, then my tenant does pay me . . . as we agreed to, but this advance of price is a cheat that is come between us . . .[58]

From the market and the market behavior of participants some writers went on to explore that most elusive of all

[57] *Political arithmetick*, p. 33. This work was published posthumously and was circulated in manuscript after its composition in 1677.

[58] "Manuscript of speeches and views on public affairs by Sir Richard Cocks," [1698], in Thirsk and Cooper, eds., *Seventeenth-Century Economic Documents*, pp. 102-03.

economic concepts, demand. As early as the 1620s Rice
Vaughn had made precise the role of demand in creating
value. "Use and Delight, or the opinion of them," he wrote,
"are the true causes why all things have a Value and Price
set upon them, but the Proportion of that value and price
is wholly governed by Rarity and Abundance."[59] Little
effort was made to go beyond Vaughn's expression until the
flowering of economic analysis in the closing decade of the
century. Then Barbon, Houghton, Gregory King, and John
Law carried the subject as far as it was to go until the
nineteenth century. In his two pamphlets, *A discourse of
trade* and *A discourse concerning coining the new money
lighter*, Barbon probed most thoroughly the nature of market value. Starting from the axiom that the value of all
wares arises from their use and hence things of no use have
no value, he proceeded to bring together all the factors
influencing the establishment of price. Use gives values, the
wants of the body and the wants of the mind create use and
"the Price of Wares is the present Value; and ariseth by
Computing the occasions or use for them, with the Quantity
to serve that Occasion . . . [hence] there is no fixt Price or
Value of any thing." However, he cautioned that "the Value
of things depending on the use of them, the Over-pluss of
Those Wares, which are more than can be used, become
worth nothing." Recognizing that the cost of production
must form a part of value, Barbon offered "two ways by
which the value of things are a little guessed at," which are
the price the merchant sets upon his wares reckoned in
prime cost, charges, and interest and the price that the
artificer sets, which is reckoned by the cost of the materials
and his time, which in turn are conditioned by the skill of
the artificer and the demand for his time. "But," Barbon
summarized, "things are just worth so much, as they can
be sold for."[60]

[59] *A discourse of coin and coinage*, 1675, p. 19, K 1394. See p. 49, n. 39.
[60] *A discourse of trade*, pp. 13-20; *A discourse concerning coining*,
pp. 2-8.

From Barbon's construction it was but a short step to John Law's very sophisticated analysis in *Money and trade consider'd*. Where Barbon had left the concept of demand as the occasion for use expressed through the market, Law was even more precise. The value of goods cannot be determined according to their quantity in proportion to their vent, he explained, for demand will influence price even if the supply remains the same. Using the example of French wines, he said that a 100 tons of wine will sell at a higher price if there is a demand for 500 instead of a demand for just the 100. Here Law revealed the inadequacy of reckoning prices by the mere quantities of silver and goods, which William Petty had attempted to do. As Law put it: "The Vent of goods cannot be greater than the Quantity, but the Demand may be greater." He concluded his analysis of price by saying that demand is more of a determinant of price than supply because the supply of most things increases with demand. Since money was essential as a wage pool for increasing the supply of goods to meet demand, Law argued that nations should increase the money supply to just the amount necessary to stimulate the economy to full pitch.[61] In the work of a gifted statistician, Gregory King, the force of demand revealed itself also through the fluctuation of grain prices in times of dearth. Where the quantity theory of price implied that prices would rise proportionally to diminished supplies from harvest failures, King's calculations showed more of a geometric progression in prices under the pressure of shortages. Demand, in other words, had a disproportionate influence upon price.[62]

[61] [Law], Edinburgh, 1705, pp. 4-6, 20-21, K 2463.

[62] King's statistics were published in [Charles Davenant], *An essay upon the probable methods of making a people gainers in the ballance of trade*, 1699, K 2114. For a discussion of the importance of King's work see Raymond de Roover, "Scholastic Economics: Survival and Lasting Influence from the 16th Century to Adam Smith," *Quarterly Journal of Economics* 69 (1955), 161-90. Pierre Goubert, *Beauvais et Le Beauvaisis de 1660 à 1730*, pt. 2, Paris, 1960, p. 73, tested King's theory.

While trade had always been described as an exchange of surplus goods, the balance-of-trade theory prejudiced the role of demand. By claiming that increased exports alone brought back gold and silver, which constituted the only true wealth, writers who emphasized the necessity of securing a favorable balance neglected consumption and consequently the reciprocity of commerce. However, in the hands of others the word itself underwent change from the "mere consumption" of the 1660s. It became the "true end" of producing and trading efforts in Dalby Thomas's writings and the economic activity most likely to produce growth in those of Houghton, Barbon, North, Martyn, and Gardiner.[63] Man as a consuming animal with boundless appetites capable of driving the nation to new levels of prosperity arrived with this literature of the 1690s. By going behind the new tastes and exploring economic behavior, these writers discovered a human dynamic in the market mechanism. Unlike the number of working days in a person's life, ingenuity and industry mobilized to serve desire appeared almost limitless. Since men and women could only satisfy their new wants by increasing their purchasing power, the desire for material comforts had produced an incentive to be more competitive in the market. From such a spring the economy could function without outside direction. Where earlier writers had recognized the impact of taste and delight upon the market price of items, they never saw the effect of these influences upon total demand nor did they move to an appreciation of the role of domestic consumption as a stimulant to production and to total national

[63] For its derogatory usage see Thomas Culpeper, Jr., *A discourse, shewing the many disadvantages which will accrue to this kingdom by the abatement of usury*, 1668, p. 2, K 1215, and [Slingsby Bethel], *The present interest of England stated*, 1671, p. 12, K 1281. Frequent and nonpejorative use of the word begins with Houghton in 1681, e.g., *Letters*, p. 36, where he writes that if "an English-man be brought to Earn and Consume 10 l [£10] a year more than he was wont . . . it is as good as the Coming in of a Foreigner so qualified." See note 10 above for other references.

growth.[64] This required a new definition of wealth and a new model of economics as a self-sustaining complex of internal relationships in which foreign trade represented accessibility to desired goods instead of the principal driving force.

Several fresh observations about economic activity in general had long been gestating in the imagination of Restoration writers. First of all there was a sense of new levels of spending and conspicuous rises in the standard of living. Both the number and the volume of items commonly exchanged triggered the notion that the wants of mankind were limitless, and with limitless wants came the corollary that new levels of human exertion might be called forth by the hope of gratifying desires. "There are more hands employed to provide . . . Things that promote the ease, pleasure and pomp of life," Barbon wrote, than there are to supply those "first natural necessities from hunger, cold and a house."[65] Clearly, too, the new levels of demand were communicated through the market, which everyone relied on for information. Contemporaries also observed that the increase in demand made possible efficiencies in production. Defoe described the "wracking of wits" for new inventions, contrivances, and trades, and Henry Martyn anticipated Adam Smith with a description of the division of labor in the making of watches when he made his point that an increase in demand led to an increase in the number employed to meet that demand.[66] But far from fearing that all

[64] See [Sir William Petty], *A treatise of taxes & contributions*, 1662, pp. 66-68, K 1098, for an example of the failure to explore the influence of demand. For a discussion of this question see Marian Bowley, "Some Seventeenth-Century Contributions to the Theory of Value," *Economica* 30 (1963), pp. 122-39.

[65] *An apology for the builder*, pp. 5-6. Louis Dumont's contention in *From Mandeville to Marx*, Chicago, 1977, p. 63, that Adam Smith drew his favorable evaluation of self-love from Bernard Mandeville's *A fable of the bees* (1714), should be considered in the light of these earlier writings.

[66] *Essay upon projects*, p. 7; *Considerations upon the East-India trade*,

this individual, innovative activity would produce the anarchy long imputed to undirected human effort, the economists of the Restoration obviously applauded what they saw. The positive construction they put upon the independent decision making of market participants represented nothing less than a major reevaluation of the role of self-interest in social relations.

Running through the observations on trade in the last half of the century was a steady commentary on the motive of gain. From being a lamentable human tendency, which rendered men and women unfit for unsupervised living, it became the major cure for idleness, the most accurate guide to market decisions, and the unseen regulator of the body of commerce. After detailing how butchers, brewers, drapers, mercers, bricklayers, carpenters, and plasterers serve each other's needs—"for Trade is nothing else but an exchange of one mans labour for another"—Barbon claimed that they had a natural tendency to "out-live and out-vye one another in arts . . . [which] forceth them to be industrious and by industry they grow rich."[67] "There can be no Trade unprofitable to the Publick," the preface to North's *Discourse upon trade* announced, "for if any prove so, men leave it off," adding that wherever traders thrive the nation thrives.[68] An anonymous pamphleteer explained how manufacturing and commerce had given an economic incentive even to those "who have no Propriety in the Soil" because, as he

---

pp. 68-72. See Sir William Petty, *An essay concerning the multiplication of mankind*, 1686, p. 40, K 1640, for a similar peroration on the division of labor.

[67] *An apology for the builder*, pp. 32-33. *Martyn*, in *Considerations upon the East-India trade*, pp. 70-72, maintained that the more variety of artists involved in any manufacturing effort, the less would be left to the skill of a single person. Gardiner, in *Some Reflections*, p. 10, said increases of industrial labor would make production cheaper because workmanship would be "carried on to such a degree as it is capable to be improved."

[68] p. viii.

said, trade had given them "a distinct and peculiar Interest in the General Wealth of the Nation, by the several Benefits accruing to themselves." His conclusion speaks to the role of self-interest: "and every Man's private Interest is the strongest persuasive to the promotion of his own Concerns."[69] The necessity that Thomas Mun had ascribed to the flow of goods and payments, writers in the 1690s located in the inexorable motive of gain. "The Hopes of Gain may be said to be the Mother of Trade," John Pollexfen declared, from which he deduced that "Arguments from Interest ought to be taken for as good Proof as Demonstration."[70] John Locke's demonstration of the futility of statutory limits on interest rates was calculated according to a similar persuasion. "Since it's impossible, to make a Law that shall hinder a Man from giving away his Money or Estate to whom he pleases, it will be impossible," he concluded, "by an Contrivance of Law, to hinder Men, skill'd in the Power they have over their own Goods" from purchasing money at whatever rate they deem necessary.[71]

In the inexorability of human beings acting out of self-interest, the economic analysts who had boldly pursued the role of demand had found a sheet anchor for the rough sailing involved in speculations about human passions. Having probed into the psychology of envy, competition, desire, and imaginary wants, they had carried their investigations of market relations well beyond the safe limits of trade as "the exchange of superfluities." The undeniable subjectivity of desire had been turned into an objective and measurable force by assuming a constancy in human beings' market behavior. This intellectual stance of the writers in the late seventeenth century is responsible for economics becoming the first of the social sciences. Under the pressure

[69] *A discourse of the nature, use and advantages of trade*, 1694, pp. 8-9, 12, K 1842.

[70] [Pollexfen], *A discourse of trade, coyne, and paper credit*, p. 2.

[71] [Locke], *Some considerations of the consequences of the lowering of interest*, 1692, pp. 1-2, K 1792.

of searching for the relevant cause-and-effect relations in the market, these Restoration economists had built up a body of assumptions that enabled them to manipulate their data. Without using a special language of economics, they had nonetheless begun to assess market variables, to distinguish between independent and dependent factors, and to lay bare the regular, the constant, and the lawful in the particular round of buying and selling that unrolled each day before their eyes. The increasing sophistication of approach is evident in a wide variety of tracts. Sir William Temple, for instance, writing on the reasons for Dutch prosperity, breathed the spirit of the social scientist when he dismissed Dutch industry as an explanation, "For if we talk of Industry, we are still as much to seek what it is that makes people industrious in one Countrey, and idle in another."[72] In a similar vein another pamphleteer argued against the example of the Dutch by insisting that countries could not be compared in a vacuum. Their specific situation needed investigation and, this done, observers would be able to see that despite the success of the Dutch in acting one way, success would not attend the English because there were other causes at work to produce different effects.[73]

Concerns about taxation had a particularly important influence upon economic analysis. The amount of money raised from taxes grew in the last decades of the century, particularly during the war King William waged against Louis XIV. The burden of taxation was exacerbated by the fact that commerce itself was constantly readjusting income through shifts in the price of corn, cattle, wool, and tin. At the same time the growing complexity of trade and finance meant that the so-called invisible wealth of money, annuities, and stock made landed taxpayers restive under old-fashioned tax policies. Others spoke out against the retention of feudal dues for copyholders who had to pay their

[72] *Observations upon the United Provinces,* 1673, p. 187, K 1349.
[73] *A discourse of the duties on merchandize,* 1695, p. 24, K 1888.

share of the excise granted to the king in return for the abolition of feudal dues on the land held of the king. Also vocal were representatives of the West Indian interests who protested against the heavy duties loaded on sugars. Under these pressures an endless stream of tax schemes issued forth from the London presses. Income taxes, sales taxes, room taxes, taxes on bachelors, taxes from felons, and a variety of special taxes on consumption all found their champion. Working through this mass of fiscal inventiveness is the interesting assumption that tax equity required a respect for income, not person or property.[74] One of the most artistic and ambitious of the tax equalization efforts was a broadside devoted to a chart showing the amount each county paid in the land tax of 1693 and the subsidies of 1697 as a proportional fraction of their parliamentary representation.[75] Again, the role of the market surfaced in the discussions of customs levies and excise taxes, when supply and demand were described as determining which party to the bargain would bear the imposition.[76]

In the descriptive and analytical literature of the Restoration, economic processes were presented as mechanical and impersonal. The distribution of rewards that went on in the social and political realms may have represented responses to personality, whim, coercion, or deceit, but the market was presented as impervious to such influences. There, desire

[74] Reading the full titles for the publications in the 1690s in the *Catalogue of the Kress Library*, Boston, 1940, and the *Catalogue of the Kress Library: Supplement*, Boston, 1967, will convey a sense of the diversity of proposals. For specific mention of copyholders, see [Thomas Sheridan], *A discourse of the rise & power of Parliaments*, 1677, pp. 175-76, K 1453.

[75] John Smart, *A scheme of the proportions the several counties in England paid*, [1697], K 2049.

[76] [Edward Littleton], *The groans of the plantations*, 1689, p. 9, K 1700; [Sir Richard Temple], *An essay upon taxes*, 1693, p. 67. K 1826. See also William Sydenham, *To the knights, citizens, and burgesses* [1696], Ks 1979; *The true cess*, 1691, K 1778; W. Canning and J. Birquet, *A proposal . . . to raise four millions of money* [1696?], Ks 1921; and *A proposal for an equal land-tax*, 1691, Ks 1739.

found its master in the fixed terms of buying and selling in open competition. The market took the passions of ambition and envy and turned them into the steady drive for profit.

Two widely shared beliefs about commercial life enabled men to convert economic observations into a predictable science: the motive of gain and what could be called the theory of interchangeable participants. A theme with many variations, this theory was given its pithiest expression by Charles Davenant, who explained that the market price of a bushel of corn would prevail over any legislative interferences:

> because if B will not give it, the same may be had from C & D or if from neither of them, it will yield such a price in foreigne Countries; and from hence arises what wee commonly call Intrinsick value. Nor can any law hinder B, C & D from supplying their Wants [for in the] Naturall Course of Trade, Each Commodity will find its Price . . . The supream power can do many things, but it cannot alter the Laws of Nature, of which the most originall is, That every man should preserve himself.[77]

Davenant had laid bare what gave consistent force to a system of apparent free choice; if one person did not follow his self-interest to drive down a price or drive up a rate, someone else would. With this realization, economic writers had discovered the underlying regularity in free market activity. Where moralists had long urged that necessity knows no law, the economic analysts who pursued price back to demand had discovered a lawfullness in necessity, and in doing so they had come upon a possibility and a reality. The reality was that individuals making decisions about their own persons and property were the determiners

[77] "A memorial concerning the coyn of England," 1695 in Abbott Payson Usher, ed., *Two Manuscripts by Charles Davenant*, Baltimore, 1942, pp. 20-21.

of price in the market. The possibility was that the economic rationalism of market participants could supply the order to the economy formerly secured through authority.

John Locke, who in some people's minds was associated with the deplorable position that laws running athwart the profit motive were ineffectual, understood well the fragile underpinnings of an exchange economy. Commerce was more than anything else a system of promises: to buy, to sell, to lend, to work, to pay, to redeem. Commercial exchanges were made in trust, and yet the motive for exchange was acknowledged to be self-interest. If people could be expected to cheat or lie in pursuit of their profit, how could those great enterprises be undertaken that required confidence that others would perform their duty. Legislators, Locke wrote, would be well advised not to require oaths—such as in customs transactions, where they expect them to be broken—for "Faith and Truth . . . is the great Bond of Society" and if "the Custom of straining of Truth (which Mens Swearing in their own Cases is apt to lead them to) has once dipt Men in Perjury, and the Guilt with the Temptation has spread it self very wide, and made it almost fashionable in some Cases, it will be impossible for the Society (these Bonds being dissolved) to subsist."[78]

Locke was not alone in having a utilitarian conception of honor. Indeed, in the Restoration writings on commerce this secular spirit of capitalism had preempted all expressions of glorifying God through work. "Every Man in a Society or Common-wealth, even from the King to the Pesent," Thomas Sheridan claimed, "is a Merchant, and therefore under a necessity of taking care of his Reputation."[79] Sir William Coventry attributed the house building in London to the fact that "many are concerned in repu-

[78] *Some considerations*, p. 4. For a fascinating account of Robert Boyle's use of market concepts see J. R. Jacob, "Restoration, Reformation and the Origins of the Royal Society," *History of Science* 13 (1975).

[79] [Sheridan], *A discourse of the rise & power of Parliaments*, 1677, p. 225, K 1453.

tation to build their houses, lest they should be thought unable to build, which to trading men would be an utter undoing."[80] Another writer emphasized that "tradesmen live upon credit, buy much upon trust" and, he continued, "as they buy upon credit, so they must sell upon trust."[81] Another wondered that "the very awe of the power of Credits" had not inhibited a critic of the bankers from "falling foule upon so sacred a thing."[82] Sir William Temple tied public and private faith together when he declared that "as Trade cannot live without mutual trust among private men; so it cannot grow or thrive to any great degree, without a confidence both of publique and private safety."[83] This recognition of the chain linking credit to trust and trust to a pervasive commitment to the performance of obligations led to many schemes for rationalizing commercial practices.

These exhortations to act honorably in trade combined with recommendations not to rely on laws where gain was at stake, however, reveal the uneasy tension between the practical and the ethical. John Briscoe neatly encapsulated the problem when he described why sureties for good behavior provided stronger bonds than conscience, religion, and honor, "because in these," he said, "we are sure there may be Hypocrisie, but in Interest we know there is none."[84] The dilemma created by accepting the rightness of pursuing one's interest in situations where mutual dependence was essential could be resolved only by uniting self-interest to the faithful performance of promises. This required that those who engaged in market transactions identify with the whole commercial system. Concern for the immediate

[80] "Sir William Coventry on the Decay of Rents, 1670," in Thirsk and Cooper, eds., *Seventeenth-Century Economic Documents*, p. 83.

[81] *The grand concern of England explained*, 1673, p. 51, K 1338.

[82] *Is not the hand of Joab in all this?*, 1676, p. 15, Ks 1437.

[83] *Observations upon the United Provinces*, p. 190. The persistence of the problem is noted by A.J.P. Taylor, *The Origins of the Second World War*, London, 1961, p. 30, in the effort of the Allies to bind the Germans through the "sanctity of contract."

[84] [Briscoe], *A discourse of money*, 1696, p. 136, K 1936.

bargain had to give way to an appreciation of the future course of trade. Only then could the abstraction of a trading world and one's involvement in it take precedence over the benefits of any single transaction. From one perspective the whole body of economic literature served this purpose, explaining and describing the workings of the economy in such a way that its invisible communications network could be grasped as something real, much as the solar system seems real if understood.

What is remarkable about the exploration of self-interest in the tracts on trade and agricultural improvements is the openness of discussions of human behavior, which elsewhere in England were proscribed. The political philosophy of Thomas Hobbes was considered a scandal in the Restoration just because he asserted that it was only self-interest that forced human beings to form governments. The popularity of Hobbes' ideas and their congruence with observable social behavior made church and university authorities intent upon suppressing his works and discouraging his converts from proclaiming his philosophy.[85] Yet the economic pamphleteers not only suggested that self-interest ruled in human affairs, they laid the footings for the construction of a new social reality built upon the positive implications of that universal human tendency to seek one's own good. Even the name of Hobbes was drawn into their arguments. "All men by Nature are alike," Sir Josiah Child declared, adding for proof, "as I have before demonstrated, and Mr. Hobbs hath truly asserted, how Erroneous soever he may be in other things."[86] In Hobbes' *Leviathan* there was also that preoccupation with the problem of men's

[85] Quentin Skinner, "The Ideological Context of Hobbes's Political Thought," *Historical Journal* 9 (1966), 286-317; James L. Axtell, "The Mechanics of Opposition: Restoration Cambridge *v.* Daniel Scargill," *Bulletin of the Institute of Historical Research* 38 (1965), 102-11. According to Fredrick Siebert, *Freedom of the Press in England 1476-1776*, Urbana, Illinois, 1965, p. 1, government control of the press was particularly lax in the period 1685-1695.

[86] [Child], *A discourse about trade*, 1690, p. 125, K 1725.

keeping their promises when the only consistent motive Hobbes would acknowledge was the pursuit of their own desires.[87] However, whereas Hobbes had concluded that a common power was necessary to supply a short-range motive for the fulfillment of contracts, the endorsers of a liberal economic order at the end of the seventeenth century were willing to rely upon the punishments of the market itself. It was this vision of a new economic order that brought the free-ranging writings on the market economy into contact with the central political issues of the day.

Reflections on the consistency of economic behavior entered public discourse as observations tinged with cynicism. Malynes, Misselden, and Mun all conceded that the merchant doth "ever seek his profit." What gave this frequently reiterated statement its decisive role in economic thought was, first, the assertion that laws were unavailing when profit was at stake, and subsequently—and perhaps consequently—the attribution of this behavior to all human nature. "Trade is in its Nature free, finds its own Channel, and best directeth its own Course," Charles Davenant intoned, adding later in an injunction against elaborate trade regulations: "Wisdom is most commonly in the Wrong, when it pretends to direct Nature."[88] Rejecting the notion that inexperienced traders would injure England's commerce, Sir Josiah Child remarked that "shop keepers are, like all other Men (led by their profit), and if it be for their Advantage to send out Manufactures, they will do it without forcing," and he continued, "if it be for their Profit to send over Money or Bills of Exchange, they will do that, and so will Merchants as soon and as much as they can."[89]

Such convictions about the behavior of shopkeepers and merchants permeated attitudes toward all men and women as commercial relations came to dominate economic life.

[87] *The Leviathan*, 1651, chapters 13-17.

[88] [Davenant], *An essay on the East-India-trade*, 1696, pp. 25, 34, K 1954.

[89] *A new discourse of trade*, 1693, p. 86, K 1811.

Yet they began as observations, and contemporaries were aware that these writers were claiming for nature what had formerly been the province of politics. The author of *A discourse of the nature, use and advantage of trade*, for example, justified laws against usurers on the same ground as the existing statutes against ingrossers, regraters, and forestallers in corn. "The General Use of Trade," the author explained, "was never intended to be an occasion of inriching one man by the impoverishment of another, but to be a universal support to Mankind, by a medium of Traffick and Commerce," adding what was beyond dispute, that "the law has frequently interposed to oblige perverse and refractory Men to comply with such Rules and Measure in Trade, as have been thought most conducing to the General Good of a Nation."[90] In the same vein John Blanch attacked Child for suggesting that certain practices could not be controlled by law. An anonymous author attacked Locke's implication that he was "not under internal Obligation to any Laws, Human or Divine, if they cou'd be secretly and securely broken," claiming that there were still some in the world "who Worship God more than Money, and will not be Guilty of Extortion; as the taking more Usury than the Law allows, or any way making advantage of the Necessity or Folly of others."[91] Blanch was a clothier who wanted the government to prevent the export of wool, and Locke's critic favored a statutory limit on interest rates, so both had a stake in opposing the view that economic transactions could not be effectively controlled by formal authority. The inexorability of human self-seeking was a contention not a discovery, but this confounding of inadequate laws with an irresistible human tendency led to a new social reality. When Davenant made the natural law "that every man should preserve himself" an

[90] p. 25.

[91] [Blanch], *The interest of England considered in an essay upon wooll*, 1694, pp. 92-94, Ks 1813; and *Sir Thomas Colepeper's tracts concerning usury reprinted*, [1709], p. 18, K 2618.

underpinning for the automatic setting of prices in the market, he funneled a whole range of indeterminant actions into a formal definition that ignored idiosyncratic and socially diverse responses. The economic analysts of the seventeenth-century who dogmatically asserted the supremacy of the profit motive were not only laying the groundwork for a science of economics based on predictable laws of human behavior, they were legitimating that behavior at the same time.

In moving to a consideration of demand, certain economic writers had taken their investigations back to the demander, that sentient being whose individual decisions daily set in motion the flow of goods and payments. In probing for the persistence motives of market participants they had touched the dangling nerve of contemporary speculations: what role to assign self-interest. With an abandon not tolerated in academic and ecclesiastical circles, they had urged the release of human desires and the damned-up economic energies behind them. Far from fearing the anarchy usually associated with unrestrained liberty, they had asserted a lawfulness about self-interested economic behavior that converted the idle into the industrious and the envious into the productive. The difficulty, of course, lay in the short-term disadvantages that investors and laborers might experience as the inexorable flow of trade passed them by. Because what was good for the whole could still bring loss to particular persons, the promptings of self-interest influenced men's response to this idea that there existed a naturally effective regulator which would enhance the nation's economic well-being better than manmade laws.

The cumulative effect of the outpouring of writings on the market in the last decades of the century was to advertise the operative cause-and-effect relations in trade and thereby heighten contemporaries' awareness of the differing effects of economic measures. Where the earlier emphasis upon attracting money through the profits of foreign trade suggested to a capital-hungry trading community that their fortunes rose together, the economic issues of the 1680s and 1690s made clearer the divergence of interest between those in commerce and those in manufacturing. For the merchants, the English people were as important as consumers as they were as producers, and the prosperity of the Restoration had witnessed a striking rise in the standard of living of the moderately well-off. The clothiers did not share in this prosperity, nor did rents show the rise that was so marked in returns on merchant capital. Another unfavorable economic indicator for the manufacturers and landowners was the steady climb in the poor rates. Against this background, spokesmen for the manufacturers were able to ignore the theoretical sophistication of their opponents and summon patriotism, common sense, and xenophobia to their cause. To make their case they developed a variant of the old balance-of-trade argument, and it is this form of the theory that gave Adam Smith his famous "paper tiger."[92]

Where once men saw trade stimulating industrial activities, at the end of the century clothiers said that manufacturing alone was capable of furthering trade and then only if trade were properly managed. Rejecting the mutuality between self-interest and national interest that justified free trade, the clothiers argued for restriction and protection. They made the impact upon manufacturing— and through it, employment—the key consideration in the formation of commercial policy. Listing all the deleterious effects of the East Indian trade, one author appealed to the landowners to support their bill for the "hindering the home consumption of East India silks" by arguing that the employment of people was the only way to give value to land since poor working people spend all of what they get upon the produce of land. "It is evident all over the World, where the Price of Wages is low, the value of Land is little; and where many People live, Land is most valuable."[93]

[92] *An inquiry into the nature and causes of the wealth of nations,* New York, 1937 (originally published in 1776), pp. 398-419.
[93] *Reasons humbly offered for the passing of a bill,* p. 4.

Englishmen, the author of the *The profit and loss of the East-India trade* said, must recognize how the East India trade had undermined the export of those English woolens which played so important a part in employing the poor. The English consumer should wear only those garments which will "most advance his own Estate, and support his poor Neighbour, and cause Mony to Circulate through every part of his Country, and thereby make the Inhabitants Pleasant, Easy, Chearful, Useful, Industrious and Pious."[94] Answering what must have been a current argument, one author denied that complaints against the consumption of East Indian wares could be compared to Norwich weavers grumbling about the competition from London silk throwers. Both these groups, he cautioned, were members of the same body and what was laid out with one was still in the nation, but all the Treasure laid out with the Indians was entirely a loss to the Kingdom.[95] Again the role of demand was neglected as industrialists urged the artificial stimulation of home investment: "I would to God all the Merchants in England would Employ their Stocks in setting up new Species of Manufacturers in England in Towns and Places where the Poor have no Employment."[96]

The manufacturers' position involved contradictions, like the touting of the benefits of the internal trade while simultaneously maintaining that it was theoretically sterile, but the central affirmations were mutually supportive. To deny one of them was to see the others fall: gold and silver alone constituted treasure; England had only native products with which to procure treasure from others; manufacturing greatly enhanced the value of native produce; economic freedom could not be relied upon to produce the greatest wealth for the nation because individuals could profit while the common well-being suffered; proper man-

[94] p. 23.

[95] *The great necessity and advantage of preserving our own manufacturies*, 1697, pp. 10-11, K 2019.

[96] *Reasons humbly offered for the passing of a bill*, pp. 17-18.

agement assured the favorable balance of trade that alone could produce treasure. At no point did the writers who responded to the East Indian threat answer the theoretical position raised by Barbon, North, Houghton, Martyn, or Thomas. Rather they pleaded the distress of the poor, the impossibility of competing with either Indian or European producers, and the need for patriotism in economic matters as well as political ones. "I hope I need not use many Words to convince any Man that the Riches and Strength of England proceed from Manufactures," the anonymous author of *England's danger by Indian manufactures* began, going on to detail the havoc wrought by calicoes in Suffolk and Norfolk, where "the Masters break, Journeymen run away having no Trade . . . some Starve to Death at Home with their Wives and Children, Multitudes turned upon the Parishes, Houses empty, Prisons full, Landlords forced to pay their Taxes for their Houses themselves all-a-like, whether inhabited or empty."[97] Others stressed the unfairness of searching out a "place which can undersell our own commodities" and enrich "the great mogul of India by employing his poor."[98] Pamphleteers repeatedly stressed that England had no other way to gain riches "than by vending a greater Value of her Commodities in Foreign Markets, than what she expends in merchandizes imported from abroad."[99] The position was put forward succinctly in *The great necessity and advantage of preserving our own manufactures*: England has no mines, but her lack of gold and silver can be supplied through sheep's wool, which can be improved further through home manufacturing. If woolens are worn at home, the expense of foreign imports is eliminated; if sent abroad, all is clear gain to the nation. The definition of gold and silver as the only true wealth represented the linchpin of the argument. Production for

[97] [Thomas Smith], *England's danger by Indian manufactures*, [1698], pp. 1-3, K 1717.

[98] *Reasons humbly offered for the passing of a bill*, p. 9.

[99] [Simon, Clement], *The interest of England*, 1698, p. 2, K 2071.

home consumption was extolled for raising rents, quickening the circulation of goods in the internal market, and relieving the burden of maintaining the poor, but it only entered the treasure equation because it provided substitutes for foreign imports.

Equally frank—or perhaps disingenuous—was the clothiers' admission that they could not meet competition. Cottons were said to replace almost anything woolen, and the cheapness of Indian production could not be matched. Whichever country sells its exports cheapest will gain the trade, they argued. Even in woolen manufacturing, the Irish, the Dutch, and the French outstripped the English. The Irish lived cheaply, the Dutch were notoriously frugal, and the French used state power to secure advantages in world markets. The very salient conflict of interest between manufacturers and certain merchant groups led to an explicit disavowal of the harmony of interests that Barbon, North, and others had asserted. Merchants, Pollexfen wrote, may thrive from importing luxuries, but the nation as a whole does not.[100] Private hands can grow rich while the kingdom loses, Defoe concluded, and instanced those in the French trade who "were no better than Robbers of the Kingdom, in carrying away our Treasury."[101] "What is everybodies is no bodies business," became for Francis Brewster an answer to cries for economic freedom. The lack of proper ordering in trade was depicted as a scandal, and the need for government in trade was compared to the laws that secure private property itself.[102] John Cary distinguished between trades useful to the public and those "managed only for private Man's Advantage."[103] The homiletic analogy between the private person and the nation, which Barbon had tried to scotch, reappeared: "The case of a Nation is like that of a private man . . . if he's Extrava-

[100] *England and East-India inconsistent in their manufactures*, p. 48.
[101] [Defoe], *Taxes no charge*, 1690, p. 12, K 1720.
[102] *Essays on trade and navigation*, 1695, p. 47, K 1867.
[103] *An essay on the state of England*, Dedication.

gant, there must be some Restraint laid upon him, or else he'll soon ruin his Estate and beggar his Family."[104]

When the clothiers vehemently divorced private profit from society's gain, they were not echoing an old sentiment so much as they were launching a new counterattack against the liberal ideas that had been circulating as freely in England as East Indian calicoes. Their balance-of-trade arguments should also be distinguished from those used by Mun and Misselden to oppose mandated exchange rates in the 1620s. In the flow of trade Mun had found the imagery with which to oppose the patrimonialism of the Stuarts. In the hands of even more sophisticated economic analysts that flow had suggested that wealth consisted of a capacity rather than a possession. This idea led to the belief that the road to prosperity lay with expanding markets and encouraging consumption. The political corollary to this theory was that individuals were best left to their own in making economic decisions and that government could foster prosperity by protecting the environment favorable to enterprise. The traditional notion of Englishmen being secure in their persons and property had been subtly shifted to include wealth-making activities. As Sir William Temple observed, trade might thrive under "good Princes and legal Monarchies" but not under an arbitrary or tyrannical government for "this extinguishes Industry."[105] None of the champions of economic freedom had repudiated the advantages of favorable trade balances. Rather, they rejected the political restraint justified in the name of the balance-of-trade theory.

[104] *An answer to the most material objections that have been raised against restraining the East-India trade,* [1699], p. 1, K 2106.

[105] *Observations upon the United Provinces,* pp. 189-90.

Eight

A Crisis Over Money

A GOOD DEAL OF MEANING IS CONDENSED IN the simple word, money. Money is a store of wealth and therefore provides a way for satisfying future needs and deferring pleasure. Money is capital, the means of giving force to one's economic plans, the link between present potential and future actualization, as well as the access to enterprise. Money is also cash, an avenue to gratification and conspicuous display. Money is above all power over goods and services, and the extent of this commercial power grew as the market steadily intruded into areas of social life previously constrained by customary arrangements, social mores, or political authority. Money gave contemporary writers a great deal of trouble, for it presented both real and conceptual problems. The range of money's power had grown markedly. The increase in the number and kinds of market exchanges, with money as their measure, was perhaps the most striking social fact in the latter half of the century. Dependence upon commerce made communities vulnerable even as standards of wealth rose. Integral to this new vulnerability was the accessibility of money. Theoretically there is never an insufficient supply of currency. Actually England suffered chronically from coin shortages.[1] The major conceptual difficulty lay with finding a definition of money that would be adequate to the many new roles it played during the decisive decades of growth and development. "Everything can be bought with money,"

[1] B. E. Supple, *Commercial Crisis and Change in England, 1600-1642*, Cambridge, 1959, especially pp. 8-15, deals extensively with this new commercial vulnerability. See also Bruno Suviranta, *The Theory of the Balance of Trade in England*, Helsingfors, 1923, pp. 56-62; and J. D. Gould, "The Trade Depression of the Early 1620s," *Economic History Review* 2nd ser. 7 (1954-55), 83-88.

wrote Rice Vaughn.[2] Henry Peacham lamented that "whosoever wanteth money is ever subject to contempt, and scorn in the world, let him be furnished with never so good gifts, either of body or mind."[3] In an otherwise dreary little tract, Edward Leigh conjured up the American Indians to vivify the paradox of money. It "answereth for all things," yet the Indians spat out English coin after biting it because they "would not part with their Commodities for Money, unless they had such other Commodities as would serve their use."[4] Money became an extension of personal authority, an economic tool, a means of organizing other people's activities, an allocator of resources, a claim upon goods, and a good in itself. Money was wealth—something fixed—as well as a measure for determining values in exchange—something fluid.

Money represented values in the calculation of the equivalents upon which all exchange depended. But exactly who agreed upon the number of money units needed to stand for the commodity bought? This determination was disturbingly obscure. Prices were established through a consensus of value determinations. The widening of markets— that is the enlarging of the geographic area through which goods passed—meant that while any market participant could decline a sale or purchase, the existence of alternative sellers and buyers limited the importance of his or her decision. The impact of the individual decision was diluted. Each participant was an independent exchanger vulnerable to the decisions of others. The act of exchanging was a voluntary one but, as all aspects of economic life became commercialized, most people were forced to seek the gratification of their needs through the market. Increasingly, men and women directed their efforts toward the production of marketable commodities, and the investments of

[2] *A discourse of coin and coinage*, London, 1675, p. 57, K 1394.

[3] *The worth of a peny*, 1667 (originally published in 1647), p. 14, K 1200.

[4] *Three diatribes*, 1671, p. 36, K 1293.

their time, effort, and hopes of gain became hostages to commercial norms. The desire for money and the private power the market had created brought into being a new social reality as well as a different economic organization. As more personal effort was directed toward the production and consumption of goods, more hours were spent laboring and organizing the labor of others, spending and calculating how to get more to spend. Not only were economic decisions relative to ownership, occupation, utilization, and reward arrived at through market exchanges but these exchanges became the arbiters of purpose, power, and privilege in the society at large. As the goal of production for gain became preeminent in English society, money became the vital connection between human purposes and material means. It acted throughout the century as the solvent of traditional social arrangements. Money bought out customary tenants; money bought the labor of another; money invested in shares produced more money; money kept in a vault put other forms of payment in circulation. As the common denominator of such disparate things as a day's labor, a family holding, a shipment of exotic fabrics, or the cost of a loan, money seemed capable of measuring all value or, conversely, if something could not be so measured, it seemed to have no value.

Seventeenth-century economic writing began with the concerns over the drain of coin during the two depressions of the 1620s and ended with the crisis over recoinage in the 1690s. Between those dates English writers produced an increasingly sophisticated analysis of money. Definitions of money also provided the context for a struggle for economic power—first between public authority and private entrepreneurs and subsequently between conflicting economic groups. Much of the fighting was waged through competing descriptions of reality, where money was dealt with simultaneously as an analytical concept, a psychological force, and a practical problem. As a practical problem, however, it pressed most heavily, so the really fruitful discussion on money clustered around major issues: the shortage of coin, particularly during the depression of the 1620s; the pressure for more working capital, ending finally with the establishment of the Bank of England in 1694; and the crisis of clipped coins, which prompted the famous recoinage of 1696.

Despite the popular notion that the precursors of Adam Smith were bullionists, the polemics of the 1620s actually witnessed the defeat of the bullionist position and the triumph of the balance-of-trade explanation of money flows.[5] The true bullionist position is hard to grasp, but it involved several associated ideas: gold and silver alone constitute wealth; their value is wholly intrinsic; exchanges of specie can only be fraudulent, for they depend upon debasement, devaluation, or the surreptitious addition of interest to supply a motive for the exchange. The bullionists' critics broke through their rigid formulation, as we saw in chapter two, by asserting that the quickening of trade created wealth by enhancing commercial profits. Money in the analysis of balance-of-trade theorists was the medium of trade, valued as much for its utility as its story of wealth. Because of their emphasis upon international commerce, those writers in the middle years of the century who used the balance-of-trade

[5] Jacob Viner, *Studies in the Theory of International Trade*, New York, 1937, pp. 4, 11-19, 50-57, is consistently critical of mercantilist ideas. Charles Wilson, D. C. Coleman, J. D. Gould, R. C. Blitz, Herbert Heaton, Barry Supple, R.W.K. Hinton, and Richard Wiles, publishing their research within the last twenty-five years, have gone a long way toward rehabilitating the reputation of so-called mercantilist writers, but none more effectively than Suviranta in *Theory of the Balance of Trade in England*, pp. 118ff, where he instanced quotations from seventeenth-century writers that ridiculed bullionism in practically the same words as J. R. McCulloch had ridiculed them in *A Select Collection of Early English Tracts on Commerce*, London, 1856, p. vii. Suviranta is not correct, however, when he says (p. 154) that balance-of-trade proponents made all factors of production subservient to the single one of the balance, neglecting thereby the economic value of land. From Mun's *Discourse of trade* in 1621 onward, seventeenth-century writers discussed the fundamental importance of agricultural improvements.

model to explain the origins of wealth took into account also the difference between bullion and coin. While they recognized that silver constituted a universal standard and the principal source of value in coin, they also realized that because payments were made in the coin of a particular country that meant the demand for the products of a certain country would produce a demand for the coin of the same country. The silver content—the intrinsic value—might remain constant in a particular coin like Dutch guilders while an increase in the demand for Dutch goods or shipping services would cause an increase in the demand for guilders just because they were the legal tender in the Dutch Republic, that is, because of their extrinsic value. Money, or the rate of exchange, as Mun said, had a price determined like any other price by demand and supply. The distinction between the extrinsic and intrinsic value of money became critical again with the recoinage issue which absorbed the attention of economic writers and members of Parliament in the closing years of the century. Then the great architect of political liberalism, John Locke, reasserted the bullionist position. In the intervening years, it was the nature of money as capital that attracted most interest.

More than anyone else, Mun had made explicit the difference between wealth, capital, and currency when he explained that melting down plate or devaluing currency would create more coin, "yet should we be nothing the richer," something that could only be achieved through investments in trade that returned profit and enhanced the value of land by carrying off its produce.[6] In contradistinction to the bullionists' goal of acquiring wealth through building up deposits of specie, the balance-of-trade proponents clearly used the word money to mean working capital, which set in motion the trade that brought profits in coin back into the country. This explanation shifted attention from bullion to the commodities it could pur-

[6] *England's treasure by forraign trade*, 1664, pp. 52-55, K 1139.

chase. Money became the passive follower of goods and hence important for its instrumental value. "For what begot the Monies which we sent out, but our Wares?" Mun asked rhetorically.[7] Rice Vaughn put the point a little differently when he noted that since everything could be bought for money, that country that had money could get everything else.[8]

Vaughn's emphasis upon money's command over goods led logically to a consideration of what determined price, a question that penetrated the heart of the market economy. For the pure bullionist, goods and specie, locked in an equilibrium, determined price without any influence from the buyers and sellers. Displaying a quantifier's peculiar blindness to those aspects of reality that cannot be numbered, Sir William Petty captured the essence of this point of view when he attempted to figure out the relative value of silver and corn by imagining the same number of men working to produce each.[9] The elusive role of demand rendered such speculations inadequate to the task of explaining observable market phenomena, however, for the supply of specie and commodities could only determine prices in conjunction with what purchasers actually bought. "Whatsoever the value of Money be in other countreys, they will spend no more of your Commodities than they have use for," Vaughn noted.[10] Similarly, Mun argued against the notion that England could attract more coin by charging foreigners more for their wares, since English merchants had to compete with foreign goods in pursuading buyers to purchase them.[11] Recognition of the relevance of market

[7] [Mun], *The Petition and remonstrance of the governor and company of merchants of London, trading to the East Indies*, 1628, p. 21, K 454.

[8] *A discourse of coin and coinage*, p. 54. An unusually astute observer like Vaughn could perceive that prices would respond differently to demand for goods and to alterations of the currency (pp. 156-59). See also Supple, *Commercial Crisis*, pp. 211-15.

[9] [Petty], *A treatise of taxes & contributions*, 1662, pp. 23-24, K 1098.
[10] *A discourse of coin*, p. 158.   [11] *England's treasure*, pp. 18ff.

behavior was an important breakthrough in the effort to understand economic relations. It, more than anything else, distinguished the balance-of-trade advocates from the bullionists early in the seventeenth century and prepared the way for the adumbration of a liberal economic order in the Restoration. Since the bullionists held that it was the substance of gold and silver that was valuable, they concluded that money did not differ from gold and silver, both having an intrinsic value only. Money was just another form of gold and silver, and the sovereign's mint privileges served to insure the purity and content of the coin. This definition of money introduced a certainty that value was real and unchanging. In the marketplace where men and women were buying and selling Dutch herring, French wines, and English tin, however, the price of goods changed frequently. In international trade, moreover, it was possible to see that the price of money changed also for, if English goods were in demand abroad, that demand would first be expressed in a demand for English coin and a demand for English coin would register itself in a more favorable exchange rate for shillings. What might have remained obscure in a trade using the same currency could not long be hidden in international commerce: price was a reflection of value and value was a reflection of desire and desires changed with time and place, originating not with sovereigns but with buyers and sellers, ordinary people. Preferences, so hard to grasp in an age used to the overriding and inelastic need for food, revealed themselves through the differing prices of coins and bullion in foreign commerce. Throughout the century this perception acted as a goad to theoretical speculation. It also prompted a man like Mun to write that princes might oppress, lawyers extort, usurers bite, prodigals waste, and merchants carry out good, but treasure would still follow trade "by a Necessity beyond all resistance."[12]

This was a truth that the international trade had made

12 *Ibid.*, pp. 218-19.

particularly salient. The extent of the world market had removed it from the control of the single sovereign, and keeping watch over the bargaining of individual subjects was beyond the bureaucratic resources of any seventeenth-century ruler.[13] Despite the voluminous body of edicts and statutes, the influence of formal power declined with the spread of commerce. Explicit rules gave way to informal understandings, and the internal mechanism for distributing rewards—that is profits—acted as the motivating force at the point of participation. The operation of the market was too large and too small for traditional authoritarian direction. A single transaction could extend through the space of the globe and the lapse of a year, yet the connecting links were a letter dispatched, an instruction given, or two human beings engaged in a few minutes' negotiations. The secularization of economic life owed much to these circumstances for, without an enforcing authority, the actions of self-serving merchants and exchangers became the subject of legitimate investigation because they determined the flow of goods and money coursing through the markets of the world. This line of reasoning introduced an impersonality to economic relations that underplayed the specific influence of any particular person. What was critical to this new conception, however, was the belief that profit seeking was so uniform a drive that it could be taken as a regularity of nature.

The pamphleteering of the 1620s had begun with a lament over the coin shortage and ended with an interpretation of market relations that emphasized that the trade in goods—the exchange of surpluses—was the dynamic force in commerce, not the desire for coin. In the next half-century this emphasis upon commodity exchanges led in two diverging directions. One group of writers built on the

[13] There is an interesting discussion of the mutual exclusivity of political and commercial empires in Immanuel Wallerstein, *The Modern World-System*, New York, 1974, pp. 178-97. See also Suviranta, *Theory of the Balance of Trade*, pp. 103ff.

idea that wealth was the satisfaction of wants. With this definition, the mutuality of commerce became more important. As William Potter wrote, "the effect of all Trading, is but the parting with Commodities for such Money, Credit, or valuable Consideration, as procures other Commodities or Necessaries . . . whereby each mans Ware being transmitted from himself he in conclusion receives other Ware or Necessaries for it." "It follows," he then concluded, "that the more Commodity they after this manner transfer . . . the more they receive each from other."[14] Such a definition of trade necessarily undermined the idea that silver and gold had a special, imaginary quality, and for men like Potter this recognition of the interchangeability of goods through money opened up the whole prospect of finding money substitutes to increase the amount of capital. Moreover, if the end of trade was the exchange of goods instead of the accumulation of gold and silver, then internal trade was not necessarily sterile and development of the home market could be as important to a nation's prosperity as an expansion of world trade. The second and more familiar line of thinking retained Mun's emphasis upon foreign exchanges along with the conclusion that only the expansion of the volume of foreign trade could increase the nation's wealth—a rationale for legislation designed to stimulate England's productivity. Consideration of demand remained undeveloped in the work of Samuel Fortrey, William Petty, William Petyt, and John Pollexfen, and the distinction between extrinsic and intrinsic value of money lost its sharpness as the danger of official regulation of the exchange passed.

In Fortrey's widely read *Englands interest* the author acknowledged the interchangeability of goods and money, but retained the idea of the superiority of money, or specie. The greater the increase in commodities, he wrote, "the richer may we be, for money and all foreign commodities

---

[14] *The key of wealth*, 1650, p. 2, K 815.

that come thither are only bought by the exchange of our own Commodities."[15] Fortrey's often shrewd analysis of economic relations still gave primary place to money, putting Fortrey among the more conventional balance-of-trade thinkers of the Restoration, who favored restrictive legislation to enhance artificially England's ability to achieve a favorable balance of trade against her trading partners. Petty was also specific about the aim of economic life: "The great and ultimate effect of Trade is not Wealth at large, but particularly abundance of Silver, Gold and Jewels, which are not perishable but are Wealth at all times, and all places." From this he deduced that the wealth of every nation consisted chiefly in the share it had in the foreign trade with the whole commercial world rather than in the "Domestick Trade, of ordinary Meat, Drink, and Cloath etc. which [bring] in little Gold, Silver, Jewels and other Universal Wealth." However, he did recognize that "almost all uses may be answered several wayes . . . [so] that novelty, surprise, example of Superiours, and opinion of unexaminable effects do adde or take away from the price of things."[16] Emphasizing as they did the exchange of superfluities from one nation to another, these writers neglected the development of the internal market and ignored the factors differentiating currency movements within the country from those settling international accounts. Thus, John Cary warned against the danger of an overbalance of imports "fit only to be consumed at home." Instead, trade should be managed so that English products were exchanged for "bullion, or commodities fit to be Manufactured again . . . or some Staple Commodity allowed by all to have the same Intrinsick Value."[17] This emphasis upon the intrinsic value of both money and goods led to the

[15] 1663, p. 14, K 1337.

[16] *Political arithmetick*, 1690, pp. 19, 82, K 1741; *An essay concerning the multiplication of mankind*, 1686, p. 41, K 1640; and *A treatise of taxes*, pp. 70-71.

[17] *An essay on the state of England*, 1695, pp. 2-3, K 1870.

implication that value inhered in them as objects rather than in the attitudes of buyers toward them. Policy proposals dealt with means of stimulating manufacturing for exports, which would contribute to that all-important favorable balance. If money did not procure trade, in their thinking, the supply of goods did.

The idea that the end of effort and industry was the satisfaction of wants rather than the accumulation of wealth led to a totally instrumental conception of money which emphasized that extrinsic value of a coin conferred by a people's confidence that "it would pass." If money was something the government placed its stamp upon, then government authority could issue paper money, circulate its own debts, debase the amount of specie in given coins, or change the denomination of coins. The latter course of action enjoyed a certain patronage in the 1670s, when expectations of prosperity and improvement seemed to have outpaced the real growth being registered. Since all concurred that more money was a good thing, an ardent band of pump primers began writing in favor of quickening trade through increasing the money supply even at the cost of inflation. An indefatigable pamphleteer, Richard Haines, wrote a variety of tracts to push his favorite scheme, a 25 percent devaluation of English shillings. All that was involved was a message from the king to the mint officers to turn out a fifth more shillings from the same weight of silver. Far from finding the enhanced cost of settling foreign accounts an objection, Haines and his supporters praised devaluation because it would discourage the import of foreign wares and leave the field of the domestic market to English producers. Foreign merchants would no longer be able to compete, and home manufacturers would "unavoidably find quick and good markets." Not only that, the owners of plate would rush to the mint to have their silver coined, and the king would pocket the savings from circulating the lighter coins.[18] Clearly, here the domestic market

18 [Haines], *The prevention of poverty*, 1674, p. 16, K 1361. See also

took precedence over foreign trade. "A Domestick Trade is for the good of the whole Nation," the author of *The use and abuses of money* announced, adding "whereas the Forein Trade, as it is now managed, and in the hands of a few particular persons, and most of them foreiners, can never prove for the publick good of this Kingdom."[19]

Daniel Defoe offered a variation to the theme of quickening trade through increases in the currency with his idea of artificially speeding up the circulation of money. In *Taxes no charge*, Defoe developed the novel argument that there was more treasure at home than obtainable in overseas trade if the government would but adopt tax policies aimed at plucking money from the debauched and the miserly. Taxes, Defoe maintained, in what was probably the first endorsement of deficit financing, put money in fast circulation because they went to support the king's Court and soldiers' and sailors' pay, "by which means the Money of the Kingdom, like the Blood in the Veins, has its regular, circular motion, and every Member in the Body is warm'd and refreshed by it." Defoe's zeal for circulating money through the economy was so great that he labeled misers worse criminals than robbers, for they "lock up the Tools of the Industrious" while thieves are only guilty of "a wrong transferring of Riches"; the community is wronged by the miser and only particular persons by the robber, he concluded.[20] Although many proponents of inflationary schemes recog-

---

Provision for the poor, 1678, K 1465 and *A breviat of some proposals*, 1679, K 1491. It was in response to these proposals that John Locke added a section to his *Some considerations of the consequences of the lowering of interest*, 1691, pp. 134ff, K 1792 because, as he wrote, "I hear a Talk up and down of raising our Money."

[19] 1671, Preface, K 1303.

[20] 1690, pp. 15, 27, K 1729. The Tory writer, John Nalson, had suggested this idea in *The present interest of England*, 1683, p. 24, K 1586, when he explained that it was the want of "due Circulation of the Money that is in the Nation" which caused scarcity of money. Taxes, he observed, would be the best way to provide that circulation.

nized the effect of money on prices, their general belief was that the increase in the volume of trade and velocity of money exchanges would leave everyone better off. "No nation can have too much money," according to Hugh Chamberlen and Dalby Thomas, because, "as money encreaseth, so do the Uses of it, for plenty of Money raiseth the price of Land, in Rent and Purchase . . . Plenty of Money encreaseth the number of People, by encrease of Business, and that makes Consumption, of which, there can be no end, if there be the means, for Five Men can consume, if they have the means, more than Five Hundred that have it not."[21] Another inflationist, Robert Verney, maintained that the increase in currency would "probably make a greater and quicker Trade by Increase of Consumption, whereby the number and Estates of the Rich will be Augmented, and the Number and Necessities of the Poor diminished."[22] Humphrey Mackworth, exuding a similar confidence, said that when "Money is plentiful, a Man that gets a Hundred pounds a Year can better pay ten pounds, than a man with ten pounds can pay 10 shillings."[23] Money in this context seemed to be the conveyor of confidence, the wheedler of savings, the raiser of expectations. It quickened trade as hope quickens life, setting in motion a chain of positive forces in the economy: a willingness to buy, to lend, to invest, which led back to purchases and the employing of the idle poor, which in turn promoted the sales that made easier the paying of interest, rents, and taxes. The upward cycle of economic expansiveness evidently was so familiar that it could be invoked in a pamphlet by a phrase or two:

[21] *The proposal for a general fishery*, [1691], p. 2.

[22] [Verney], *Englands interest; or the great benefit to trade by banks or offices of credit*, 1682, p. 6, K 1556. The conspicuous and favorable connotation of the word "consumption" is significant in the light of the conventional balance-of-trade view that consumption ate up goods that might be exported for the return of profits. For other pamphlets that use consumption in a constructive way, see chapter 7, n. 55.

[23] [Mackworth], *England's glory*, 1694, pp. 18-19, K 1850.

"paying the landlords rent," "bringing cattle or corn to the market," "enabling the poor to earn their bread." More significant than the content of these proposals was their indication that the growth of the domestic market was generating its own interest groups and that the importance of foreign trade was beginning to recede a little.

The number of pamphlets written to describe schemes for increasing the money supply suggests also that opportunities for investments had outdistanced the accumulation of capital in Restoration England. Although twentieth-century economists have criticized these writers for their failure to see that an increase in money would lead only to a rise in prices, historians have suggested that the demand for working capital may have short-circuited the money–price relationship by diverting specie immediately into investments. More money, as R.W.K. Hinton has pointed out, could have produced more goods rather than higher prices if it became capital before currency, a consequence that contemporaries evidently anticipated when they argued that more money would produce lower prices because it would first produce an increase in the number of goods. Their search for an alternative to specie amounted to a search for an alternative to stored wealth.[24]

Samuel Hartlib's ideas, developed through several publications, provide an insight into prevailing notions of the relation of currency to capital. Without explicitly addressing the relation of money to prices, he explained that additional supplies of money in the from of bank credit would of necessity lead to an increase in agricultural improvements, manufacturing, and trade (i.e. investments), it being "an infallible Rule, that money being that, which every man (his petty occasions supply'd) seeks to employ in

[24] "The Mercantile System in the Time of Thomas Mun," *Economic History Review*, 2nd ser. 7 (1955), 282-87. K. N. Chaudhuri, *The English India Company*, London, 1965, p. 207, notes the real shortage of working capital that plagued the East India Company in the early years of its operation despite the high returns from its voyages.

Land, Trade, at Interest, or some such other way, as may make him a yeerly return of gain, the more there is of money in any Nation, the quicker also must all those wayes be, wherein money is ordinary imployed."[25] Extolling funded credit, Edward Ford claimed that it was the Dutch banks with credit that had advanced "their little Country (not so big, nor fruitful as one English County) from Poor Distressed States, to be Hogans-Mogans, all by a real cheat, for no considerate man can believe that they have so much Money in their Banks, as they give out bills for." Working from the same premises as Hartlib, Ford defined the end of money as the adjustment of contracts. Since "all Tokens of Accompt are valued according to their portableness," Ford concluded that land security or the funded public debt would serve better than anything else and would raise a circulating medium available at once to the landowner "whereby he may improve his Land, or lend his Money to such as can well pay him six per cent and gain enough."[26]

Elaborating on the theme of money's short-range token value, Francis Cradocke also proposed a land bank since its security would be sufficient "to supply the intervall of time between the selling of one Commodity and the buying of another." It would in time, "evacuate the use of Money."[27] Humphrey Mackworth echoed this expectation. "Now, Money," he wrote, "is but a medium of Commerce, a Security which we part with, to enjoy the like in Value . . . and such is a Bank-Bill, it will obtain what we want and satisfie where we are indebted, and may be turned into Money again when the Possessor pleaseth, and will be the Standard

[25] [Hartlib?], *A discoverie for division or setting out of lande*, 1653, p. 28, K 878. Although the publication of this pamphlet can be traced to Hartlib, it may have been written by Cressy Dymock. For a discussion of the writing of the works attributed to Hartlib, see Charles Webster, "The Authorship and Significance of 'Macaria," in *idem*, ed., *The Intellectual Revolution of the Seventeenth Century*, London, 1974.

[26] *Experimented proposals how the king may have money*, 1666, pp. 1-3, 4, K 1175.

[27] [Cradocke], *Wealth discovered*, 1661, pp. 15, 19, K 1067.

of Trade at last."[28] With security, bank credit could not only become the standard form of money but all agreed it it could provide capital in advance of the actual accumulation of specie. Projecting the hope of development upon everyone from the king to the "industrious Husband-man [who] under-manages his land" Mark Lewis claimed that his bank model would draw upon all forms of credit in the nation at large and render English more productive by relieving Englishmen from making uneconomic decisions when they were pressed by the want of money.[29] The anonymous author of *The use and abuses of money* detailed the theory behind increasing the money supply. Since everyone must extend six months' credit, everyone's "Money in the mean time lies dead," he explained, yet with ready money each could be improving his wealth, even farmers, who have but one season a year, "by breeding a Stock of Cattel, fatting them, or the like, every man in his own way."[30]

The dual roles of money as stored wealth that could be used as capital and money as a token of security during the interval when actual goods were being exchanged led some men to push hard for an official registry, which would make public all encumbrances on real property. Andrew Yarranton claimed that land registers would restore honor and honesty, which "is the basis of all trade."[31] While most land registry proponents included among its benefits the stopping of fraud, what really stirred their imagination was the idea of using the landed wealth of England for raising an equal sum in loans that would be so secure that the debts could become a form of currency. Assuming a pressing demand for capital, one writer bemoaned the loss to the nation of the capital of those people whom age, sex, or sloth elim-

[28] *England's glory*, p. 5.

[29] [Lewis], *Proposals to the king and Parliament*, 1678, pp. 23-25, K 1466.

[30] 1671, p. 20, K 1303.

[31] [Yarranton], *England's improvement by sea and land*, 1677, pp. ii, 29, K 1459.

inated from trade. He compared them "to one of the Wheels of a Clock that is Rusty, and thereby impedes the whole Motion."[32] Another claimed that a register would attract the money of foreign creditors.[33] All these pamphlets made explicit that it was security that gave currency to money. As Sir Josiah Child noted, the Dutch were able to borrow cheaply without laws limiting the rate of interest because they had laws enforcing the public registry of all transactions on land. For, Child explained, "Money is not so much wanting in England as Securities, which men accompt Infallible."[34] Writing a score of years later, Child claimed that a law making debts transferable would "effectually encrease the useful Stock of the Nation, at least one third part."[35] Andrew Yarranton claimed that it was essential "that there should be some security established, whereby men should be encouraged to lend that money to others which they know not how to make use of themselves."[36] Another writer sought the support of landed men themselves by appealing to their knowledge of how difficult it was to borrow money upon land "without City-Security."[37]

[32] *A discourse on the nature, use and advantages of trade*, 1694, pp. 14-15, K 1842. This had been the same point that Mun had made in *England's treasure*, p. 179, when he claimed that usury, far from hurting trade, enabled merchants to trade on credit using "the moneys of Widows, Orphans, Lawyers, Gentlemen and others . . . which themselves have no skill to perform."

[33] [Edward Chamberlayne], *Englands wants*, 1685, pp. 37-38, K 1617.

[34] [Child], *Brief observations concerning trade*, 1668, p. 19, K 1212. For an attack on the land registry proposals see *The brief observations of J. C. concerning trade and interest of money, briefly examined*, 1668, pp. 18-19.

[35] [Child], *A discourse about trade*, 1690, p. 110, K 1725.

[36] *England's improvement*, pp. ii, 21. Yarranton answers in this volume, p. 35, one of the principal critics of land registers, Fabian Philips, who wrote *The reforming registry*, 1662, Ks 1243.

[37] *The grand concern of England explained*, 1673, p. 10, K 1338. Without using the word "points" this pamphleteer refers to the fact that men must pay 3, 4, and 5 percent simply for procuring loans on land in addition to 10 percent for what is borrowed.

As in so many other economic debates of the century, the East India Company's peculiar trade of bullion for commodities stimulated self-serving defenses of the company, which had a generally liberating influence upon economic reasoning. It was in the interest of the East India Company to define money as a commodity, and this definition first appears in Lewes Roberts' *The treasure of traffike* where Roberts argued that when bullion was exported freely, it was never scarce, contrasting Spain with its mines and specie prohibitions to Florence with no mines, no restrictions, and plenty of specie.[38] Roger Coke, justifying the East Indian trade on grounds that the export of money returned a greater value of goods for trade, carried the theory a little further: "Money is that by which all Commodities are valued; and is of no other use: if therefore a man should give me 100 l. never to make use of it, I should scarce thank him for it. The most profitable use of money," he continued, "is so to buy, as to sell to profit."[39] Robert Ferguson, writing also to defend the East India Company, noted the inadequacy of measuring the nation's trade strictly in terms of gold and silver, "whereas in truth," he wrote, "the Stock and Riches of the Kingdom, cannot properly be confined to Money, nor ought Gold and Silver to be excluded from being Merchandise, to be Traded with, as well as any other sort of Goods."[40] And a quarter of a century later, Henry Martyn, another defender of the company, reversed Roberts' "predominancy" of specie over all other commodities and asserted that "Bullion is only secondary and dependent" upon the "true and principal Riches [which] are Meat, and Bread, and Cloaths, and Houses, the Conve-

[38] 1641, pp. 21-24, K 595. Suviranta, *Theory of Balance of Trade*, pp. 14-15, errs in saying that Samuel Fortrey was the first to refer to money as a commodity.

[39] *England's improvements*, 1675, pp. 57-58, K 1380.

[40] [Ferguson], *The East-India-trade a most profitable trade to the kingdom*, 1677, p. 4, K 1447. For a discussion of Ferguson's authorship of this pamphlet, see William Letwin, *The Origins of Scientific Economics*, London, 1963, pp. 33, 234.

niences as well as Necessaries of Life . . . These for their own sakes, Money, because 'twill purchase these," from which he concluded that bullion is "therefore by nature not so valuable."[41]

Since economic pamphlets, like the market that produced them, were the results of individual initiative, the writings on money might have continued to move in opposite directions had not the deplorable state of the English shilling precipitated a crisis in the 1690s. The need for recoining the badly clipped silver money presented Englishmen with a practical problem and an ideological issue. The practical problem was whether or not to change the silver content in the shilling. The ideological issue grew out of this, for slipped into this decision was a fundamental question about the relation of political authority to economic development. If money had only an intrinsic value arising from the universal desire for gold and silver, then the sovereign's control over the money supply was minimal, amounting to setting the terms for minting to a standard determined by universal consensus. If, however, the intrinsic value of money arose from its utility, then the extrinsic value of a coin's being legal tender became more important, and the public authority along with it.

English currency was complicated by a number of factors: there had not been a general recoinage since 1601 and the hammered silver shillings had been clipped for at least half a century; bullion prices of silver were higher than the mint price for silver so there was a constant incentive to convert coin to bullion; and gold was overvalued at the English mint where silver was undervalued, offering an incentive to work the mint for the advantage in selling gold and buying silver. Since 1663 silver brought to the mint for coining had been milled. This gave the new pieces an unclippable edge and a silver content nearly twice as much as the hammered shillings passing freely at face value. The incentive to real-

[41] [Martyn], *Considerations upon the East-India trade*, 1701, pp. 16-17, K 2310.

ize a profit by melting down the milled coins meant that few of them remained in circulation. The need for a circulating medium apparently had been so great in Restoration England that, despite the fact that average shillings had little more than half their designated silver content, they passed. The economy absorbed counterfeit coins as well without any significant variations in commodity prices or foreign exchange rates. All this changed suddenly under the multiple pressures brought on by King William's war.[42]

After a century of official neglect, the battered silver shilling became the object of intense concern during the crisis year of 1694. The successful establishment of the Bank of England had saved the king from imminent financial disaster, but the increase in bank notes precipitated a dramatic inflation, which many blamed on the low silver content of England's principal coin. Evidence that the government finally intended to undertake a general recoinage introduced panic to a situation already badly deranged by the speculation attending the lotteries and tontines that had helped pay the costs of waging war against Louis. The value of the shilling, which had passed freely for years, plunged suddenly. Prices soared, and gold guineas, which had commanded only 22 silver shillings in March of 1694, were selling at 30 shillings in June.[43] The need to

[42] Sir Albert Feavearyear, *The Pound Sterling*, Oxford, 1963 (originally published in 1931), p. 120. Feavearyear recounts Samuel Pepys' story of a counterfeiter working at the mint who, when discovered, was let off because his forgeries were so ingenious and with so little hurt because the money was as good as what commonly passed (*Diary*, 19 May 1663). See also D. W. Jones, "London merchants and the Crisis of the 1690s," in Peter Clark and Paul Slack, eds., *Crisis and Order in English Towns, 1500-1700*, London, 1692, pp. 333-38, for an interesting theory on the connection between wartime interruption of commerce and the establishment of the Bank of England.

[43] *Pound Sterling*, p. 129. Feavearyear emphasizes the credit expansion from the Bank of England's notes as the reason for the inflation, while William A. Shaw, ed., *Select Tracts and Documents Illustrative of English Monetary History, 1626-1720*, London, 1896, p. 8, and C. R.

retire the old hammered silver shillings was widely recognized. The new milling process could produce an unclippable edge, so there was a possibility of bringing clipping to an end and making counterfeiting more difficult. The problem, however, was how to recoin without a drastic reduction in the number of coins in circulation. If, as contemporaries estimated, the face value of the silver coinage was £5 million, but the silver content was closer to £2½ million, calling in and melting down the clipped coins and reminting them at the old standard would halve England's silver currency. Popular acceptance of clipped shillings had created this dilemma. If the old mint denomination were to be preserved in the new coins, how was the loss of currency to be made good and who would bear the loss: the government or the holders of clipped coin?

Serious engagement with the issue of recoinage began in 1694 when the Privy Council referred Lewis Gervaize's elaborate scheme for a two-year recoinage proposal to William Lowndes, secretary of the treasury.[44] Lowndes responded with a recommendation that the shillings be recoined with 25 percent less in silver content, that is, a reduction from the old official denomination. Unwilling to confine themselves to Lowndes' expertise, the Privy Council sought the advice of a number of other men, among them

---

Fay, "Locke versus Lowndes," *Cambridge Historical Journal* 4 (1933), have stressed the run on guineas and the panic associated with recoinage. See also P.G.M. Dickson, *The Financial Revolution in England*, New York, 1967, p. 348, for a discussion of the problems of war finance. Four very interesting contemporary observations on the problems of war finance are: [Thomas Wagstaffe], *A letter to a gentleman elected a knight of the shire*, 1694, K 1861; *A word in season about guineas* [1695], Ks 1911; *Some seasonable memorandums to supply the present want of money* [1695], Ks 1903; and *Only way to have the rents of England well paid* [1696], Ks 1964.

[44] "Papers relating to the British coinage and the mint, 1652-1769," *Add. Ms.* 18759, British Museum, 108-108 verso. Gervaize's proposal was later published anonymously as *A proposal for amending the silver coins of England*, 1696, K 1985.

John Locke, who vigorously opposed Lowndes' plan.[45] The sense of urgency created by the rapid inflation and the universal concern about the terms for recoinage made it a major public issue. Both Lowndes and Locke published their views, and the prospect of recoinage called forth a flood of pamphlets which finally made explicit the political issue lurking beneath the economic definitions. At last a practical decision had forced a public debate on the nature of money. For two years, contending pamphleteers addressed themselves to the question of whether money derived its principal value extrinsically from its being legal tender or strictly from its intrinsic, specie content. The economic reasoning of the past seventy years was boiled down in tracts and broadsides, which circulated freely.[46]

Lowndes' proposition was simple, but it is rather hard to grasp in an age accustomed to paper money. With money made out of precious metals, the denomination or name "shilling" was given to a certain weight and purity of silver. The designation was actually an order at the mint to accept silver bullion and mint it at a particular standard, in this case 5 shillings to the ounce of silver. Lowndes proposed to remint all silver coin with only 80 percent as much silver as the old standard and thus to bring the silver content into rapport with the market price of silver. The reminted silver coins, with new fluted edges, would then have roughly the same amount of silver in them as the old clipped coins. The mint would merely confirm the market and the new standard would produce 6s 3d worth of coin from an ounce of silver.[47] As long as bullion was worth more by weight than

[45] Peter Laslett, "John Locke, the Great Recoinage, and the Origins of the Board of Trade: 1695-1698," *William and Mary Quarterly* 14 (1957), 378-85. See also J. Keith Horsefield, *British Monetary Experiments, 1650-1710*, Cambridge, 1960, pp. 56-60; D. Waddell, "Charles Davenant (1656-1714)—a Biographical Sketch," *Economic History Review*, 2nd ser. 11 (1958-59), 280-81.

[46] Horsefield, *British Monetary Experiments* has an exhaustive bibliography.

[47] *A report containing an essay for the amendment of the silver coins*, 1695, pp. 79-81, K 1908.

English coin, Lowndes explained, silver would pass out of England to fetch a better price abroad, illegalities notwithstanding. Detailing how mint ratios had been altered in the past, Lowndes came up with a practical solution that would have left English coins at their current value and allowed the impact of the inflation already registered to abate slowly under the influence of a mildly deflationary recoinage.

In the eyes of John Locke, a government devaluation would rob all the creditors and landlords of the kingdom who had lent money or established rents when shillings bore a different denomination. The ideological impact of Locke's position went far beyond this observation, however, for Locke entered the recoinage fray with the assertion that legal tender in England had always been the full weight value of shillings. Since clipped coins passed for shilling value in the payment of taxes as well as in the marketplace, Locke's assertion had only a formal validity: the official indenture at the mint still called for the same amount of silver in the shilling. He did not rest his case on this formality. Instead Locke insisted in the most unequivocal terms that money could not enjoy a higher price than bullion since it drew its total value from the esteem conferred upon gold and silver by universal consent. Upon this ground the father of empiricism built the gold standard edifice that was to stand for the next two centuries.[48]

Locke's argument followed that of his earlier treatise against statutory usury limits. Legislation is unavailing because men will seek their own gain which, in both loan rates and money exchanges, is set in the market. Both interest and specie, Locke said, had a natural value that legislators and kings were unable to change.[49] The crucial and unrecognized difference in his reasoning about these

[48] *Further considerations concerning raising the value of money*, 1695, pp. 10-11, 23, K 1905. Locke had made these points earlier in *Some considerations*, p. 142, and of course in his famous *Second treatise of government*, 1689, sections 46-47. See also my "Locke, Liberalism and the Natural Law of Money," *Past and Present*, 71 (1976).

[49] *Some considerations*, p. 32.

two natural prices, however, was that in the case of interest rates Locke included all the forces affecting the supply and demand of lendable money, whereas in the case of money he defined coin in such a way as to exclude key factors in the determination of its market value. Mankind, Locke explained, had consented to put an imaginary value upon gold and silver. This unique and imaginary value had created the utility of money and raised a standard for the exchanging of all other commodities. Market values were thus set in relation to the quantity of gold and silver for which goods were exchanged: "by the quantity of Silver, Men measure the value of all other things."[50] There was only one source of value in coin, Locke was saying, and that was its specie content. Hence any change of denomination would be fruitless, and its perpetration by government a fraud. For Locke, shillings were silver in another guise and that guise was totally irrelevant to the value of the coin. This being the case, logically there was no possible way to affect the behavior of men in relation to silver coin by changing the mint ratio as Lowndes had suggested.

The basic assumption Locke built into his case was faulty: that men exchanged goods for quantities of silver.[51] In fact men exchanged goods for quantities of coin. The fact that coin was legal tender added value to the silver content as the acceptance of clipped shillings had demonstrated. Coin being separable from silver, it had a different market value depending, as the English experience had shown, upon such specific factors as the demand for particular currency and the standard at which gold and silver were minted in rela-

[50] *Further considerations*, p. 3.

[51] Shaw, in *Select Tracts*, pp. viii, 105ff, wrote that Locke's writings on money showed so little advance upon Henry Robinson that they would merit neglect were it not for their influence upon recoinage. T. B. Macaulay, *History of England*, ed. C. H. Firth, vol. 5, London, 1913-15, p. 2572, on the other hand, treated Lowndes' proposal as a moral lapse and even attributed to him the mistake of not recognizing that foreign balances were settled by weight rather than by denomination.

tion to bullion prices. If the quantity of silver alone measured the exchange of goods, there would have been no reluctance to use milled coins in daily trade, no melting down of coin, no export of bullion, no variety in the silver content of the variously clipped coin in circulation, no fluctuating relation between gold and silver coin. Locke's position involved the rejection of three discrete facts of English commerce in the 1690s: the acceptance of clipped coins at face value, the different price per pound of silver in English coin and silver in bullion, and the movement of gold and silver bullion in response to its own international market.

Locke's errors were obvious to the dozen or more writers who rushed into print to challenge the great philosopher. For the most part merchants and entrepreneurs, Locke's opponents were willing to start with the evidence that coin had a source of value in addition to its silver or gold content. This extrinsic value caused the divergence between coin and bullion prices. Breaking free from Locke's dogmatic association of money and specie, his critics were prepared to explore the idea of money as an independent market item, separable from specie, much as flour is separable from wheat. They began by reversing his cause-and-effect explanation for the use of money. Where he had said that mankind's esteem for gold and silver had created the utility of money, they said that the utility of having a medium of exchange had prompted the use and hence the value of gold and silver. Their refutations of Locke emphasized the role money played as a medium for trade rather than as an end in itself. At the same time their recognition of the difference between coin and silver enabled them to see that money was not always the passive follower of foreign trade balances that Mun had described. In fact, money had its own market. When there was an official undervaluation of silver, as at the English mint, then silver coins (like the full-weight milled ones) would be melted down and exported to a better market. Equally important, they distinguished between factors affecting money within the national economy and money in international exchanges, a distinction Locke categorically rejected. In short, they responded to the evidence of daily commercial life, which indicated that the value of money could be influenced by governmental policies as well as the expansion of private credit.

In one of the pithiest responses to Locke, Sir Richard Temple noted that time, place, and circumstance, as well as minting costs, the bullion price, and the demand for a particular national currency will raise or lower what Locke called the intrinsic value of money. "The Money of every Country, and not the Ounce of Silver, or the intrinsick value, is the Instrument and Measure of Commerce there," Temple wrote. Indeed, Temple said, the proposition that an ounce of silver will buy an ounce of silver is absurd since there would be no occasion for an exchange. It is the transformation of silver into coin that gives rise to the exchange of an ounce of silver for an ounce of coin, and the relative value of the two will depend upon the need for a particular form of silver, which in the case of coin is its extrinsic value as legal currency.[52] According to James Hodges, Locke's system of coin was built upon the "common error" of considering the estimate of worth to be equal to intrinsic value. Hodges reduced Locke's argument to a meaningless syllogism: silver is the measure of commerce by its quantity. The quantity is the measure of its intrinsic value, therefore the same quantity of silver must always be equal in value to the same quantity of silver. Asserting the contrary—that extrinsic value arose from a coin's capacity to circulate as a legal medium of exchange—Hodges declared that "Silver, considered as money, hath, speaking properly, no real intrinsick Value at all" for "the whole Value that is put upon Money by Mankind, speaking generally, is extrinsick to the

[52] *Some short remarks upon Mr. Lock's book in answer to Mr. Lownds*, 1696, p. 4, K 2004. For an account of Temple see Godfrey Davies, "The Political Career of Sir Richard Temple (1634-1697) and Buckingham Politics," *Huntington Library Quarterly* 4 (1940).

Money, . . . and hath its real Seat in those good things, which it is capable . . . to purchase."[53] Robert Murray, an ardent bank promoter, carried Hodges' point one step further. Affirming that the sovereign could change the value of money, he claimed that coin should in fact be considered "a particular commodity of our own product, since it is so, from the Stamp and the Authority by which it is done" rather than "an Universal Commodity" of a "different Nature" as Locke had maintained.[54] Addressing himself to the constituents of Parliament, another pamphleteer attempted to hoist Locke on his own petard. Quoting Locke on the uselessness of laws against the exportation of coin, the author said that since laws are unavailing against the natural disposition to seek gain, we must "make our Coin of such Value" as there shall be no advantage to export it.[55]

Nicholas Barbon charged Locke with failing to see the difference between silver as a commodity without "any fixt or certain Estimate that common consent hath placed on it," rising and falling in value "as other commodities" on the one hand, and money which is "the Instrument of Commerce from the Authority of that Government where it is Coined" and valued by men for its stamp and currency rather than the quantity of fine silver in each piece. By insisting that the value of money arose from an imaginary value placed upon silver and hence was determined by the quantity of silver in each coin, Locke was ignoring the fluctuations in the value of particular currencies and the impact of the demand for goods upon the value of money. Money, Barbon maintained, was a commodity like anything else and its value arose from its use. Plenty or scarcity in respect to their occasion or use determines prices, Barbon said, and the plenty or scarcity of one commodity will not alter the

[53] [Hodges], *The present state of England, as to coin and publick charges*, 1697, pp. 146-47, K 2029.

[54] [Murray], *Proposals for a national bank*, 1697, pp. 11-12, K 2043.

[55] *A letter humbly offer'd to the consideration of all . . . that have right to elect members to serve in Parliament*, 1696, pp. 8-9, K 1978.

price of another if they do not serve the same uses.[56] James Hodges also attacked Locke's insistence that prices were determined by the quantity of silver. Silver, Hodges explained in contradiction to Locke, receives its value in relation to what it buys. It does not have the same value if wheat is scarce, even if the quantity of silver remains the same.[57] Similarly, John Cary explained that the true value of silver cannot be said to rise or fall or be worth more in one place or another, for it always responds in relation to another commodity "because the Buyer must pay for the Commodities he wants, suitable to his Necessity, and their Scarcity; thus one Day a thing is worth an Ounce of Silver, which at another time is not worth half so much."[58]

Two crucial theories were entwined in the discussion of the value of money: one was the source of the value of money and the other was the connection between money and wealth. Although separable concepts, there were logically paired affinities. The early mercantile position had been that the accumulation of treasure in specie was the aim of economic life; people produced and exchanged in order to acquire money. Such a view naturally predisposed its holder to assume that coin was valued for its specie content. The second view focused upon the exchange value of money—its command over goods or in investments: "Land at Farm, Money at Interest, or Goods in Trade," as Dudley North put it.[59] Long before the coin crisis of the 1690s most English economic writers had abandoned the view that Locke defended, that is, that the money a man possessed represented his proportion of the world's gold and silver. Things useful to man's needs or his delight had become the assigned objects of economy activity. Money had been re-

[56] *A discourse concerning coining the new money lighter*, 1696, "the contents" and p. 7, K 1931.

[57] *Present state*, p. 142.

[58] *An essay, on the coyn and credit of England*, Bristol, 1696, pp. 11-12, K 1947.

[59] [North], *Discourses upon trade*, 1691, p. 24, K 1767.

conceived as a convenience in the process of exchanging what was not wanted for what was wanted. Francis Gardiner of Norwich, who was among those consulted by the Privy Council, wrote that the treasure of the nation consists not just in money, "but in Moneys Worth. Silver and Gold serve as the measure of other Commodities, and is valuable only in proportion to them."[60] Dalby Thomas set forth the uses of money with admirable clarity: "To distinguish rightly in these points we must consider Money as the least part of the Wealth of any Nation, and think of it only as a Scale to weigh one thing against another, Or as Counters to reckon Riches by, or as a Pawn of Instrinsick Value to deposit in lieu of any necessary whatsoever." He went on to define true, solid, and real wealth as the land and what is useful upon it or under its surface, but "the value of every thing useful to the necessities, Luxuries, or Vanities of Life," he explained, "is measured by the Industry and Labour either of Body or Mind, which is necessary to their Acquirement."[61] When John Houghton claimed that money is anything "the Government of each Dominion sets a mark and value on" and that coin "is good for nothing, but potentially is good for everything," he was expressing a common view on the subject, which made entirely reasonable his recommendation that goods rather than money be imported to balance accounts since "money is unable to satisfy any real human needs."[62]

Presumably, in Locke's logic, trade never would have

[60] [Gardiner], *Some reflections on a pamphlet intituled, England and East-India inconsistent in their manufactures*, 1697, p. 6, K 1968.

[61] [Thomas], *An historical account of the rise and growth of the West-India collonies*, 1690, pp. 2-3, 7, K 1749. It is interesting to compare Thomas's definition of the labor theory of value with that of Adam Smith, in *An inquiry into the nature and causes of the wealth of nations*, New York, 1937 (originally published in 1776), p. 30: "The real price of every thing, what every thing really costs to the man who wants to acquire it, is the toil and trouble of acquiring it."

[62] *A collection of letters for the improvement of husbandry & trade*, 1681-83, pp. 24-27, K 1538.

developed beyond commodity bartering had gold and silver not inspired a unique and universal admiration among mankind. Locke's opponents, who were attempting to account for the monetary fluctuations of the past decade, came to an opposite conclusion, money was valued because it was useful. To go one step further, its usefulness could be traced to its specific property of being the legal tender in the trade of a particular country, an extrinsic value added by sovereign authority. The Free Coinage Act of 1666, which had permitted anyone to bring bullion to the mint to be converted into coin at no charge, had greatly facilitated the conversion of bullion into coin. The profit to be made by feloniously melting down undervalued English silver coin into bullion for export had promoted the reverse conversion of coin into bullion. This movement of specie and money had driven a conceptual wedge between the intrinsic and extrinsic value of coin.

The passing at face value of clipped silver coins for three decades had forcibly impressed itself upon the thinking of contemporaries. Whereas the French had recoined their clipped coin in 1640 immediately after the invention of the mill (which could produce a fluted, unclippable edge), English silver currency—like so much else during the century of political upheaval—had been neglected. The Dutch had not recoined; they had continued to value silver coin by its bullion content, that is, by weight; but the establishment of the Bank of Amsterdam in 1609 had provided the country with a flexible currency through bank money. Failure to pursue either course in England had given rise to a situation in which the demand for money had made the utility of coin as currency more salient than its value as a unit of silver.[63] Lamenting the retirement of the old money, Sir William Hodges had concluded that "though the old money was exceeding bad, yet it served to Trade with, and go to Market: And as many use to say, if it was Leather, if

[63] Feavearyear, *Pound Sterling*, p. 121.

it would pass, it would serve."[64] In daily commercial trans-actions people had demonstrated that "that which would pass, would serve." Not the intrinsic but the extrinsic value predominated. The value-conferring role of the sovereign, banished by Edward Misselden and Thomas Mun during the famous debate on the Royal Exchange in the 1620s, had reappeared in the 1690s.[65] James Hodges could ask ingen-iously why people should object to the sovereign changing the value of money when the loss of an East India merchant-man or a dearth led similarly to the lowering of the value of their money in relation to corn purchases.[66] John Locke, the political philosopher, could not so easily accept this power over property.

Locke had attempted to dissociate the value of money—that is gold and silver—from the value of other commodi-ties. Goods were sought for their usefulness; gold and silver were given an imaginary and unique value by mankind but, because this value was universal, specie could serve as a pledge in the exchange of goods. Locke's opponents rejected this view. Barbon called it "a popular but false notion," Hodges "a Fundamental mistake in the Notion of Money," Henry Layton a simple "mistake."[67] Having participated in a sustained effort to master the relationships of a market economy, they had come to accept the fact that all value lay in the imagination. "Things have no Value in themselves," Nicholas Barbon said, "it is opinion and fashion brings them into use and gives them a value."[68] "There is no other use of Riches but to purchase what serves our Necessity and Delight . . . and some Goods are more acceptable in some

[64] *The groans of the poor*, 1696, p. 14, K 1970.

[65] For a discussion of this earlier pamphlet debate see Barry Supple, "Currency and Commerce in the Early Seventeenth Century," *Economic History Review*, 2nd ser. 10 (1957).

[66] *Present state*, p. 178.

[67] *A discourse concerning coining*, p. 40; *Present state*, p. 135; *Observations concerning money and coin*, 1697, p. 12, K 2031.

[68] *A discourse concerning coining*, p. 43.

Countries, at sometimes, than Money," as Francis Gardiner put it.[69] Locke's theory of the value of money was central to his concept of wealth and, as we shall see, his larger theory of natural law. Money that he defined strictly as gold and silver had a unique, universal, and imaginary value. All three qualities were important in his overall scheme. If money value was imaginary, it could not arise from utility. If it was unique, it could not be replaced. If it was universal, it could not be influenced by the extrinsic trappings of particular minting processes. Given these qualities, all men were willing to accept gold and silver as a pledge "to receive equally valuable things to those they parted with."[70] Uniquely desired, its accumulation could be the unquestioned aim of commerce, and only through trade could this accumulation be achieved: "In a Country not furnished with Mines there are but two ways of growing Rich, either Conquest, or Commerce . . . Commerce therefore is the only way left to us, either for Riches or Subsistence . . . Trade then is necessary to the producing of Riches, and Money necessary to the carrying on of Trade."[71] The argument was circular and outdated. Locke's view prevailed because of the harmony between his ideas and the interests of the parliamentary magnates, who decided that the clipped silver coin would be called in and reminted at the old standard.

[69] *Some reflections on a pamphlet*, p. 7.

[70] *Some considerations*, p. 31. Wrestling with the "imaginary" quality in the value of money, Locke in *Further considerations*, p. 23, added jewels to gold and silver as true treasure, but said they were inappropriate as money because their value was not measured by their quantity. [John Law], *Money and trade considered*, Edinburgh, 1705, p. 16, K 2463, specifically refutes Locke, saying that money does not have an imaginary value, rather silver in the form of money is more or less valued in terms of the demand for silver in that form, a point also made in *A method proposed for the regulating the coin* [1696], p. 1, Ks 1960.

[71] *Some considerations*, pp. 16-17. Further on (p. 32) Locke excluded bills of exchange as money "Because a law cannot give to Bills that intrinsic Value, which the universal Consent of Mankind has annexed to Silver and Gold."

In the 1620s the growing awareness of the importance of foreign trade to the English economy had called attention to the ability of specie to transcend national boundaries and impose its value upon the international market. The sovereign right to mint coin shrank before the sovereign passage of gold and silver from country to country in response to commercial transactions. By the 1690s, however, domestic trade, particularly in England's vastly expanded internal market, was absorbing an increasing amount of productive resources. The need for currency—any currency, apparently—had overcome the earlier use of specie content as a measure of value. The lesson of the two experiences had not been lost. Locke's critics correctly pointed out that coin partook of two sources of value: specie content and the status of being legal tender in a particular country. Neither, they insisted in contradiction to Locke, was unique; both sources of value were similar to that of other commodities that serve "our Necessity and Delight." As commodities, both specie and coin responded to their own markets. Because this was so, the balancing of trade could in no way solve the problem of the coin drain. With Locke in mind, one writer attacked those who "puzzle the Country with the Balance of Trade" and tell us " 'tis the Balance of Trade must make us rich" when in fact gold and silver are part of the balance.[72] Another pointed out that English importers "will sell according to the Denomination of Mony in England and not according to the Intrinsick value in Holland," adding that an adverse balance of trade was merely carried as a debt in any case.[73] Lowndes, Barbon, Hodges, Temple, and Vickaris all insisted that as long as there was a profitable trade in exporting undervalued English silver, the settling of other accounts would never solve the problem. Predicting the immediate melting down of a recoinage at the old standard, Henry Layton wrote that "nothing that

[72] *A letter humbly offer'd to the consideration of all . . . that have right to elect members in Parliament*, 1696, p. 22, K 1978.
[73] *A method proposed*, p. 1.

England can do is able to alter the price of Silver in other places of Europe, from whence we must acquire and obtain it."[74]

This dispute over the nature of money impinged upon the balance-of-trade view on growth. The essential point of the theory was that only a favorable balance of foreign trade, as Locke repeated, could attract gold and silver to a country without mines. As the analogy to a mechanical balance suggested, the balance of trade worked through automatic and autonomous adjustments. Monarchs and parliaments could not alter this economic order, although they could adopt policies to enhance its workings. A more subtle implication of this balance-of-trade analogy was that all market participants in England benefited or suffered equally from its operation since the nation as a whole grew rich from its total net balance of international accounts. By recognizing the differences between a money mechanism within the internal economy and the one used for settling international accounts, the devaluationists were able to discriminate among the effects of changing the mint ratio. At the same time, this discussion brought out into the open the way government monetary policies affected diverse economic groups.

Throughout the seventeenth century, Englishmen had felt the full force of the economic variables in a market society. New World silver imports had created inflation; increased demand for corn had forced up prices; employment had followed trade cycles; gluts had produced depressions; clipped coins had passed for their face value; inflation had eroded returns from rents and loans. The close observation of these new phenomena had sharpened their perception of economic interests. Despite the mercantilists' rhetori-

[74] *Observations*, p. 39. "When your Money is richer in substance, and lower in price than . . . the Silver in the Low Countries, how can you expect that the Merchant, who only seeketh his profit, will ever bring hither any Silver," Rice Vaughn had explained in *A discourse of coin*, p. 144.

cal claim that a favorable balance of trade brought uniform prosperity, astute commentators had discerned and advertised the differing effects of trade flows, money exchanges, and policies affecting agriculture, manufacturing, and commerce. When the wild price fluctuations of 1695 prompted Parliament at last to act on the problem of coin clipping, not all observers responded as theorists. For many the question was not how the nation would correct the situation, but rather who in the nation would benefit from the remedy. Reminding his "superiors" that the price inflation from West Indian silver had redounded to the benefit of merchant shopkeepers and tradesmen rather than the crown, church, nobility, and landed gentry, an anonymous pamphleteer urged the defeat of Lowndes' recommended devaluation.[75] While those who supported reminting at the old denomination tried to rest their case with Locke's argument that devaluation would be ineffective, they inconsistently argued that devaluation would help landlords and creditors who otherwise would be defrauded of their due if the currency were inflated.[76]

Lowndes had argued that changing the mint ratio would be the least disruptive policy since the denomination he suggested reflected the average silver content of the coins passing current at the time. Landlords and creditors would receive less value, but no less than in the present currency.[77] In a similar vein, Vickaris carefully weighed the different effects of raising a tax to make good the loss in clippings or raising the denomination as Lowndes had suggested, and concluded that the latter was preferable. He explained away the loss to landlords and creditors by saying that the tax would have been a loss to them as well.[78] Lewis Gervaize,

[75] *The proposal for the raising of the silver coin of England, from 60 pence in the ounce to 75 pence*, 1696, p. 11, K 1991.

[76] *Decus & Tutamen*, 1696, p. 27, K 1955; *Some considerations about the raising of coin*, 1696, p. 20, K 1998.

[77] *Report*, pp. 206ff.

[78] [A. Vickaris], *An essay, for regulating of the coin*, 1696, p. 26, K 2005.

although more concerned about the landed and the lending, advised devaluation, but proposed a limit of two years for the proposed new inflated mint denomination.[79] Drawing more polemical conclusions, Layton charged that Locke "extends his Care to Creditors and Landlords, not regarding the Cases of Tenants or Debtors; Men for this four or five years last past, have borrow'd many Thousand Pounds in Clipt Money, but he notes no unreasonableness or injustice in compelling them to pay such Debts again in heavy Money, perhaps of twice the weight."[80]

Richard Haines had pointed out earlier that "money is principally intended for the Conveniency of Traffique between persons of the same Nation onely, and to them it is all one, since the same is made Currant by Authority."[81] Lowndes had made explicit this fact when he explained that the common propensity to speak of money in terms of foreign exchange ignored its more common use in domestic trade.[82] The anonymous authors of *Decus & Tutamen* and *Letter from an English merchant at Amsterdam* recognized the difference, but did not draw connections between it and the effect upon various segments of the economy.[83] Vickaris,

---

[79] [Gervaize], *A proposal for amending the silver coins of England.* Other pamphlets supporting Lowndes were [Samuel Prat], *The regulating silver coin made practicable and easie,* 1696, K 1990; *Select observations on the incomparable Sir Walter Raleigh relating to trade, commerce and coin,* 1696; *Proposals concerning the coin* [1696?], Ks 1966; *A method proposed; A letter to two members* [1696], Ks 1957; *A letter humbly offer'd,* 1696, K 1978; *The right way to make money more plentiful,* 1690, Ks 1711; *Proposals to the Parliament* [1696], Ks 1968; *A word in season about guineas,* 1696, Ks 1912, in addition to those pamphlets by Temple, Barbon, Layton, Vickaris, Hodges, and Gardiner already cited.

[80] *Observations,* p. 13.   [81] *Prevention of poverty,* p. 19.

[82] *Report,* p. 74.

[83] *Decus & Tutamen; A letter from an English merchant at Amsterdam,* 1695, K 1882. *A letter to two members,* p. 1, claimed that *A letter from an English merchant* was the only piece on restoration acknowledged as worthy of comment and goes on to call it a "Counter-sham & fraud more for the interests of Amsterdam than London."

on the other hand, said that inflating the currency officially would have no impact upon the domestic economy except to discourage foreign imports, while Layton associated specific resistance to inflation with the fact that certain merchants would have to spend more coins of lighter silver to pay for foreign goods.[84] Once the terms of recoinage were known, broadsides argued its merits, some obviously holding out hope for a repeal. "I hear of no Provision made in the Coin Act for those who are unable to lend to the king," announced one, while *A letter of advice* remarked that if holders of coin lost by the recoinage at the old weight value, it was their fault to have accepted the bad money in the first place.[85] The conflicts of interest, cloaked by the balance-of-trade theory, stood forth briefly during the raging debates over recoinage.

The superior reasoning of the devaluationists had not convinced Parliament. English silver currency, with an estimated face value of £4.7 million, was reduced to £2.5 million, reminted at the old standard. During a six-month grace period, taxpayers and those willing to lend to the king could turn in their clipped coin for full face value.[86] The folly and disaster predicted by Locke's critics was realized in full. Much of the newly minted silver was melted down and sent abroad to realize a profit as bullion. The actual minting could not keep pace with the demand for a circulating medium, and wage earners and shopkeepers found themselves desperate for some kind of money. The halving of the face value of silver coin caused a drastic deflation. Prices fell, and landlords and creditors reaped the benefit. The reminting arrangements were peculiarly structured to reward the payers of direct taxes and the king's creditors. Others, the bulk of the population, could only exchange their clipped coins during the six-month period

[84] *An essay*, p. 24. See also *A further essay for the amendment of the gold and silver coins*, 1695, pp. 6-8.

[85] *A word in season*, p. 1; *A letter of advice*, 1696, pp. 31-33, K 1972.

[86] Feavearyear, *Pound Sterling*, p. 139.

of grace by selling them at a loss to the privileged taxpayers. Those who had no opportunity to unload or who had to hold on to some ready cash suffered the loss when the deadline came. The shortage of money pressed particularly hard on the poor. Rioting broke out in Kendal, Halifax, and among Derbyshire miners.[87] Even the government had difficulty paying its soldiers. Trade contracted under the cold winds of deflation and money shortages. Debtors and tenants saw their obligations increase overnight while money profiteers had another go at melting down English coin.

No specific, intended goal of recoinage was achieved except for Locke's abstract and novel one of turning a mint standard into an immutable fact of nature.[88] Considering the venerability of the gold standard in the next two centuries, it was the ironic triumph of mind over matter by one of the major architects of empiricism. The reminted silver did not provide England with a good currency; silver left the country, and the overvalued gold and vastly increased use of banknotes supplied the deficiency. It did not ease trade or make the war financing more convenient. Its burden did not fall, like the gentle rain, on rich and poor alike.

The rejection of Lowndes' proposal with its supporting army of pamphlets from nearly every economic theorist of the day pushes to the fore the question of ideology. What in Locke's formulations about money was more satisfying than that of his opponents? His contemporaries suggested the political significance of his definition of money: Locke's denial of the extrinsic value of coin carried with it a limita-

[87] *Ibid.*, pp. 140-43; Joan Thirsk and J. P. Cooper, eds., *Seventeenth-Century Economic Documents*, Oxford, 1972, pp. 708-09; and Max Beloff, *Public Order and Popular Disturbances 1660-1714*, London, 1938, pp. 98-106.

[88] Justifications such as that of C. R. Fay, "Locke versus Lowndes," pp. 147-48, that the loss of silver facilitated English merchants' preference for gold are not only debatable but demonstrate the fallacy of explanations—to use Peter Laslett's words—"in terms of unconscious anticipations": Laslett, "John Locke, the Great Recoinage, and the Origins of the Board of Trade," p. 397.

tion of government in economic affairs. Henry Layton, an opponent, criticized him for pretending that "the Government had no more power in Politicks than they have in Naturals."[89] John Briscoe, who accepted the existence of extrinsic value in coin, nonetheless urged, like Locke, that an unadulterated, unalterable standard be maintained because "[as] it is a mark of slavery, so is it the means of poverty in a State, where the Magistrate assumes a Power to set what price he pleases on the Publick Coin: It is a sign of Slavery, because the Subject in such Case lives merely at the Mercy of the Prince, is Rich, or Poor, has a Competency, or is a Beggar, is a Free-Man, or in Fetters at his Pleasure."[90] The fact that everything could be bought for money, as Rice Vaughn had observed, had implications that went far beyond the buying and selling of goods. It meant that the command over the goods, labor, and land of the nation had passed into private hands at the same time that money transformed into entrepreneurial capital provided the direction and scope for social change. Money in the market set policy in the nation at large. The definition of what constituted money was integral to the struggle for power that had gone on in England since the beginning of the century.

The recoinage question offered an opportunity for Parliament to reassert its control of the economy and at the same time to confront the ideological implications of the economic reasoning of the last two decades. Samuel Grascome, a famous nonjuror, published an angry account of the debates on the Coin Act, complete with an appendix on the division. In Grascome's view, landlords, mindful of their rents and indifferent to the course of trade, rammed through the deflationary recoinage despite the advice of Treasury Secretary Lowndes and dozens of other experts.[91] Here, as in

[89] *Observations*, p. 15.

[90] *A discourse of money*, 1696, p. 18, K 1936.

[91] *An account*, pp. 18-24. The account was written as though by a member of Parliament, but Grascome was not, although he obviously was in close touch with someone who was. The division he pub-

the controversy over East Indian imports, the divergence of interest between the merchants on the one hand, and the manufacturers and landowners on the other, revealed itself. When John Houghton dismissed money as a thing unable to gratify any human want he was calling attention to consumption as the natural end of economic activity and opening the way to a liberalization of social norms contradictory to the rationale for national economic policies designed to increase England's exports. This conflict focused attention upon the fact that members of society were both potential consumers and potential factors in the cost of production. The increase of consumption—so regularly invoked by seventeenth-century writers as a "quickening of trade"— came from avarice, vanity, emulation, and a growing taste for luxuries. The dilemma for the English entrepreneur was clear. The stimulation of domestic trade involved an expansion of the purchasing power of ordinary people and an acceptance of the motives that impelled them to consume. If markets were sought abroad, the dilemma was resolved. Thus, while policies supportive of foreign trade did not equally benefit all groups in England, it did advance the social interests of the upper class in general.

Locke's view of money, however, went far beyond the recoinage issue. It breathed new life into the moribund balance-of-trade explanation for economic growth, and it firmly imbedded the value of money in the substance of gold and silver. At most the recoinage could have been defended as a measure to restore faith in government, but Locke did not build his argument on such common-sensical grounds. Rather, against the collective wisdom of dozens of knowl-

---

lished was 205 yeas and 75 nos. Those counties with more members voting against the measure than for it were Bedfordshire, Cheshire, Derbyshire, Durham, Gloucestershire, Huntingdonshire, Norfolk, Oxfordshire, Shropshire, Somerset, Staffordshire, Sussex, Warwickshire, and Wales. Overwhelming affirmation of the Act came from the Cinque Ports, Yorkshire, Nottinghamshire, Northamptonshire, Middlesex, and Kent.

edgeable opponents, he maintained that wealth consisted of having more gold and silver, that foreign trade alone could achieve this for England, that gold and silver derived their value from a unique, imaginary, universal esteem, and that by the quantity of gold and silver people measured the value of other things. Such a formulation was deceptively simple for, while it did not account for the developments of the past thirty years, it did postulate that the distribution of wealth was contained in the order of things and therefore was not amenable to governmental interference. Thus, Locke's definition of money made way for the nineteenth-century belief in natural economic laws beyond the reach of political authority.

As Sir Albert Feavearyear observed, the most remarkable consequence of recoinage was a new sanctity in the thinking about money:

> This sanctity which Locke attached to the Mint weights was something new. Before his time few people regarded the weights of the coins as in any way immutable. The King had made them; he had altered them many times; and doubtless if it suited him he would alter them again . . . Largely as a result of Locke's influence, 3£. 17s. 10½d. an ounce came to be regarded as a magic price for gold from which we ought never to stray and to which, if we did, we must always return.[92]

As if to underscore this new sanctity, the majority in Parliament responsible for the Coin Act proclaimed its seriousness by singling out from the hundreds of recoinage publications Grascome's *Account of the proceedings in the*

---

[92] *Pound Sterling*, pp. 148-49. William Letwin has argued in *The Origins of Scientific Economics*, pp. 147-48, that Locke helped provide the scientific underpinnings to economic theory because he was "willing to consider the economy as nothing more than an intricate mechanism, refraining for the while from asking whether the mechanism worked for good or evil."

House of commons as "false, scandalous and seditious, and destructive of the freedom and liberties of parliament." Published anonymously, the pamphlet was ordered to be burned by the common hangman and his majesty urged to issue a proclamation promising a reward of £500 "for the discovery of the Author of that Libel!"[93]

Although the balance-of-trade theory provided an explanation for controlling wages and protecting domestic manufacturing, it had been under attack since the early 1680s and clearly was rebutted by almost all of the tracts on recoinage. What it lacked as an explanation of economic phenomena, however, it supplied in ideology, for Locke's dismissal of the extrinsic value of money was simultaneously a rejection of an economic model that incorporated all the variables of rising demand, imaginary wants, and cavalier acts of sovereign authority. His natural law of money turned economic reasoning back to its basic foundation in substantial values and moved speculation away from the consideration of the behavioral imperatives of the market. If he ascribed the source of money's worth to an imaginary value, at least he grounded that value on "the universal consent of mankind." Moreover, Locke's emphasis upon the exclusive wealth-producing capacity of foreign trade suppressed again the centrifugal forces of the market economy, where each man in pursuit of his own gain was a law unto himself. Denouncing artificial reductions of the interest rates because they merely altered the distribution of wealth at home, Locke wrote, we "endeavour with noise, and weapons of Law, to drive the Wolf from our [own], to one anothers

[93] William Cobbett, ed., *The Parliamentary History of England*, vol. 5, London, 1806-20, p. 997. See also *Reflections upon a scandalous libel*, 1697, K 2045. *An account* is frequently attributed to another nonjuror, Thomas Wagstaffe, but the efforts to prosecute Grascome for the libel are detailed in Narcissus Luttrell, *A Brief Historical Relation of State Affairs*, vol. 4, Oxford, 1857, pp. 154, 483, 534. Despite the proscription, *An Account* was republished in *A choice collection of papers*, 1703, and *A collection of scarce and valuable papers*, 1712, Ks 2575.

doors . . . For Want, brought in by ill management, and nursed up by expensive Vanity, will make the Nation Poor, and spare no body . . . 'Tis with a Kingdom, as with a Family. Spending less than our own Commodities will pay for, is the sure and only way for the Nation to grow Rich."[94] At a time when half the English population was not yet participating regularly in the nation's economic life, the balance-of-trade model of a corporate national effort was not without its appeal.

[94] *Some considerations*, p. 118.

Nine

An Ideological Triumph

IN THE MIDDLE OF A LENGTHY TREATISE ON
England's waning economic power, Roger Coke paused to
underscore a personal affirmation. "I will never believe," he
wrote, "that any man or Nation ever will attain their ends
by forceable means, against the Nature and Order of
things."[1] The forceable means in this instance was the
legislative prohibition of the export of money. But what was
"the Nature and Order of things" against which the coercive
power of the state was unavailing? For Coke, as for the
dozens of other writers whose publications we have analyzed, the "Nature and Order of things" was the inexorable
flow of goods and payments through the intricate lanes of a
world commerce. No more powerful notion came out of the
seventeenth century than that of a natural order of economic relations impervious to social engineering and political interference. As William Letwin has observed, "It
was difficult enough to make chemistry and physics into
sciences . . . It was exceedingly difficult to treat economics in
a scientific fashion, since every economic act, being the action of a human being, is necessarily also a moral act."[2]
And being the action of a human being, every economic act
is also a social act deriving its utility and meaning from the
economic organization and intellectual traditions of a particular society. Yet despite these obstacles to economics
being treated in the scientific mode, early in the seventeenth
century writers chose to ignore what was fortuitous, capri-
cious, or socially conditioned about commercial transactions
and to fix instead upon the regularities in the buying and
selling patterns they observed. Responding to the intellectual challenge to explain how prices were set and pay-

[1] *England's improvements*, 1675, p. 57, K 1380.
[2] *The Origins of Scientific Economics*, London, 1963, p. 148.

ments made, they created an abstract model of their subject. In their model, the pattern of exchanging was consistent, therefore it was lawful. The behavior of people engaged in market transactions was predictable, therefore market behavior inhered in human nature. The flow of goods and payments continued without human interference, therefore it was automatic. No men—not even monarchs—could control its workings, therefore its processes were inexorable. This model, subject to elaboration and modification, became a reference point for all subsequent thinking about economic relations in modern society.

The actual round of economic activities in seventeenth-century England was composed of richly varied parts not at all suggestive of uniformities. Raising and marketing food and fibers involved a thousand variations of soil, seed, stock, technique, and lore. The number of kinds of ownership and tenantry were narrowing, but there were still many and they colored by local usage. Climatic conditions changed from day to day, season to season, year to year, cycle to cycle. What happened in any given market was conditioned by customs, prescribed by law and shaped by events throughout the commercial sphere. Bargains were influenced by the wits, information, leverage, and moral latitude of those involved. Every decade in the century saw the introduction of new raw materials, new industrial processes, new imports, and new points of contact between England and the expanding trade world. To reduce the multifarious details of these economic activities to a system of general laws represented an imaginative leap of great consequence. The creation of this economic model was not, however, done in a vacuum. Adopting the scientific mode of analysis for the study of the market was a selective act, but the kind of scientific thinking evident in the writings of the century owed much to the larger intellectual currents of the period.

"The Nature and Order of things" Coke believed in was not a sixteenth-century order of ultimate purpose, but a seventeenth-century order of cause-and-effect relationships. The peculiar qualities of observations and model building found in seventeenth-century economic reasoning were not unique to the writings on trade. When Misselden and Mun self-consciously confined themselves to explaining the way in which the exchange operated, they were reasoning in the spirit of their contemporary, Francis Bacon, who urged his contemporaries to abandon the search for primary causes in the material world in order better to pursue inquiries about how things worked. Knowledge would be advanced, Bacon claimed, if the initiators of new information would stop asking such questions as what purposes eyelashes served and asked instead how the composition of the pores at the end of the eyelid facilitated the growth of hair. This approach involved limiting the scope of the inquiry and isolating the subject under investigation. What became real to scientific investigators was not ultimate purpose or design but the instrumentation of that purpose. When this method of building knowledge about complex systems through isolating the interaction of their parts was applied to economic reasoning, it meant separating the discrete acts of producing and exchanging from the social organization in which they took place. Just as Galileo had to imagine a situation in which falling bodies were unaffected by air resistance in order to deduce certain generalizations about their behavior, so Mun and Misselden posited the movement of money as if the debasement and devaluations of particular currencies did not exist to impede the inexorable flow of money in payment of goods. The "as if" theorizing, however crude, of the early economic theorists involved the extraction of commercial transactions from their social context. This, of course, is how the human mind creates its own world of objects, but wrenching economic relations from their social setting decisively changed the activities themselves. To reason as if society did not control the production and distribution of its material resources was to deny the very composition of society. At the same time such reasoning created the possibility of disentangling economic relations from overt social control.

The direction of economic reasoning owed much to the actual changes in the English economy. The abolition of feudal tenures—confirmed in 1660—emancipated the principal landowners of the country from most forms of external control in the use of their property. This meant that decisions affecting the renting and working of land were made by private individuals in response to their own goals rather than by the king through policies for the public. More and more, the terms of tenantry were set in a free competition for leases and farmers. Changes in agriculture also led to larger holdings in fewer hands, and men and women who had once been tenants or cottagers became wage earners. Through this process, land and labor—the fundamental components of the society—were brought into the commercial system. The centralization of purchasing power in the London area extended the standardizing influence of the market throughout England and promoted regional specialization. Middlemen formalized the sale of government loans and company shares so that people with wealth could easily invest. The competition for capital introduced a uniformity in the rate of returns for different ventures. As men and women sold their labor instead of the product of their labor, the principle of competitive pricing spread to every element in the economy, replacing custom or authoritarian direction with the market's aggregation of individual choices.

The market, of course, did not impose itself upon unwilling subjects. In fact the buying and selling of land, labor, goods, even coin, became a more attractive alternative to the old ways of distributing society's material resources to those in a position to make the relevant choices. Clearly, the dramatic reorganization of social priorities around production for private profit required a change of consciousness. Central to this change was the ability to calculate equivalencies. As long as a piece of gently undulating meadow land bordering a copse of birch adjacent to a family homesite retained its unique identity, finding an exchange equivalent was difficult. Similarly, the individuality of a landlord's relation with his tenant, a husbandman's with his servant, or a clothier's with his spinner impeded the operation of a free exchange of labor. The extension of the market was absolutely dependent upon the extension of a consensus on equivalent values. Regular market dealings in land and labor required that the perception of the uniqueness of persons and things be replaced by the peculiar cognitive processes of market calculations. Thus, evaluation replaced appreciation as a fundamental attitude, and the depersonalization, the calculations, and the uniformities introduced by this change of consciousness helped prepare for the imagining and accepting of the scientific model of economic relations.[3]

The extension of the market through individual initiative also worked to activate the participants' imaginative powers. The capacity to plan new ways of exploiting possibilities for profit preceded the advance of the market into new areas. At the same time successful exploitation of potential commercial opportunities put new demands upon the participants' understanding of economic relations. As long as custom or authority prescribed the form and defined the range of markets, the act of exchanging could be carefully institutionalized. Those who produced and exchanged goods could learn their tasks without ever understanding the system as a whole. They participated in economic life as carriers of a cultural tradition. When, however, individual initiative and ingenuity were drawn into the commercial process, the person's intellectual grasp of the pertinent economic factors contributed to success in market dealings. The understanding of the market, moreover, involved an understanding of other market participants. Motives had

[3] On this subject, see S. C. Humphreys, "History, Economics, and Anthropology: The Work of Karl Polanyi," *History and Theory* 8 (1969).

to be imputed, responses predicted, circumstances assessed, and norms surmised. While the exchanges of the free market required a detachment from specific objects and people, it demanded at the same time an awareness of the market process itself. The tactile and the sentimental aspects of human activity were suppressed, but the capacity to manipulate the elements in an abstract model was greatly enhanced. The subsequent conceptualizations of economic relations reinforced this tendency.

Treating economic relations as part of a natural order involved the assumption of certain basic regularities which made possible explanations and predictions. As a social activity, economics offered only one source of predictability: a consistent pattern of human behavior. As long as human beings appeared, as they did in Shakespearean literature, as creatures riven by reason and passion or, as in Reformation writings, as struggling between their "fallen" and "redeemable" natures, they offered no firm basis for constructing a natural social order.[4] But if, in certain areas, observers found a behavior so consistent as to be predictable, that social area would lend itself to scientific investigation. Thus, the conception of human nature embedded in discussions of economic behavior became crucial to the adoption of the scientific mode of analysis. All the theorizing about economic life that imputed lawfulness to market relations rested upon the assumption of the invariable desire of market participants to seek their profit when reaching a bargain. In the seventeenth-century analysis, the whole elaborate construction of the natural rates of interest and exchange, the automatic pricing mechanism, the interchangeability of investments rested upon the presumed de-

[4] E.M.W. Tillyard, *The Elizabethan World Picture*, New York, 1943, pp. 73-76; and William Haller, *The Rise of Puritanism*, New York, 1938, pp. 3-48. For the seventeenth-century exploration of the problem of passions see Albert O. Hirschman, *The Passions and the Interests*, Princeton, 1977, pp. 15ff. By looking at philosophers rather than economic writers, Hirschman overlooks the earliest writings on the dependability of the passion of self-interest.

pendability of human beings to seek actively to maximize gain in the market. Because self-interest was construed as dependable and constructive, economics had acquired that rationality which, as William Petty put it, made it worthwhile for a man "to imploy his thoughts about."[5]

This conception of human nature had underlain economic reasoning since the 1620s, but it did not become apparent until the 1690s, when implicit assumptions became explicit assertions. With this exposure the political and social implications stood forth. In the debates over East Indian imports and recoinage, the conceptualization of the free market economy reached a new level of sophistication. Dozens of publications declared the goal of favorable balances outmoded, argued for free trade as a sure way to prosperity, and dismissed the idea that gold and silver had any peculiar value. Yet political decisions made between 1696 and 1713 turned England toward a different course of economic development, and the moribund balance-of-trade theory was called into service as a defense. This check to the expression of liberal economic thought at the end of the seventeenth century has not been thoroughly explored, and the intellectual responses to capitalism remain tangled in the ideological origins of classical economic theory.

Between 1696 and 1713 a new economic policy took shape which subordinated the interests of English merchants to those of English manufacturers. Through a series of laws designed to restrict continental imports, protect English industry and bind the economy of English colonies to the mother country, Parliament redirected growth away from England's old trades in northwestern Europe in favor of commerce with the Baltic, the Mediterranean, and the New World.[6] At the same time the war that had broken out at the accession of William and Mary was seriously disrupting English foreign traffic. French privateers wreaked havoc on

[5] *A treatise of taxes & contributions*, 1662, p. 33, K 1098.
[6] Ralph Davis, "English Foreign Trade, 1700-1774," *Economic History Review* 2nd ser. 15 (1962), 288ff.

English shipping, merchants were withdrawing their capital from trade, speculation grew as investors sought other, safer outlets, and public finances were severely strained by war-incurred debts.[7] There is hardly an economic event of the eighteenth century that cannot be traced to these dislocations, but the war does not explain either the form of these new policies or the theories used to justify them. In the 1690s William secured across-the-board increases in custom duties, which subsequently were refined through a process of selective retention. What began as a fiscal measure became very quickly a new policy of industrial protection.[8] Prohibitive duties on French goods were kept in force for nearly a century. The campaign launched earlier by the clothiers against East Indian imports was crowned with success in 1701 when the special duties of the 1690s were converted into a complete prohibition. The African trade interlopers were successful in securing an open trade for English slavers in 1698, but the navigation system was reorganized with the legislation of 1696, which produced the Board of Trade, a fitting symbol of the rejection of free trade.[9] In 1713 Queen Anne's ministers negotiated a commercial treaty with France that would have eliminated the wartime duties. When Parliament refused to liberalize Anglo-French trade the door was slammed on England's most promising continental trade partner. The subsequent

[7] D. W. Jones, "London Merchants and the Crisis of the 1690s," in Peter Clark and Paul Slack, eds., *Crisis and Order in English Towns 1500-1700*, London, 1972, pp. 334-38; P.G.M. Dickson, *The Financial Revolution in England*, New York, 1967, pp. 348ff. A contemporary pamphlet, *Some thoughts concerning the better security of our trade and navigation*, 1695, p. 5, Ks 1905, lists nine reasons why trade was more hazardous in this particular war period.

[8] Ralph Davis, "The Rise of Protection in England, 1689-1786," *Economic History Review* 2nd ser. 19 (1966), pp. 306-10.

[9] *Ibid.*; G. L. Cherry, "The Development of the English Free-Trade Movement in Parliament, 1689-1702," *Journal of Modern History* 24 (1953), 113ff; Peter Laslett, "John Locke, the Great Recoinage, and the Origins of the Board of Trade: 1695-1698," *William and Mary Quarterly* 24 (1957).

erection of tariff walls throughout Europe rang in a new era of domestic protection and international rivalry.[10]

While Parliament recharted the course of English economic development in the early eighteenth century, economic theory stagnated. As Ralph Davis has pointed out, the eighteenth-century system of protective duties did not grow out of seventeenth-century precepts.[11] In fact it was formed during a period when the virtues of free trade were being widely celebrated. The preface to Dudley North's *Discourses upon trade* had exuded a confidence that the "Vulgar Errors" evoked to defend trade restraints would soon be corrected.[12] Writers of broadsides spoke disparagingly of those who "puzzle the Country with the Balance of Trade" and Locke's critics had condescendingly attributed his fallacious arguments to a want of practical experience.[13] Yet the vulgar errors persisted. Locke defended recoining at the old standard by asserting that gold and silver had only intrinsic value, that they represented true wealth, and that England could only acquire them through war or trade.[14] The balance-of-trade theory was similarly evoked by the clothiers.[15] The exploration of self-interest that had played so seminal a role in economic analysis earlier ceased, giving way to platitudinous references to national interests.[16] Thus, the first appearance in England of anything that could be called mercantilism—that is, a body of public law directed

10 Davis, "Rise of Protection"; G. N. Clark, *Guide to English Commercial Statistics, 1696-1782*, London, 1938, p. 23.

11 Davis, "Rise of Protection," p. 306.

12 [North], 1691, pp. v-vii, K 1767.

13 *A further essay for the amendment of the gold and silver coins*, 1695, p. 6; *A letter humbly offered*, 1696, p. 22, K 1978.

14 [Locke], *Some considerations of the consequences of the lowering of interest*, 1692, pp. 15-16, K 1792; *Further considerations concerning raising the value of money*, 1695, pp. 1ff, K 1905.

15 E.g. [Simon, Clement], *The interest of England*, 1698, K 2074; *The great necessity and advantage of preserving our own manufacturies*, 1697, pp. 20-21, K 2019.

16 P. J. Thomas, *Mercantilism and the East India Trade*, London, 1963, pp. 72-73.

toward state economic goals—emerged at the beginning of the eighteenth century under the sponsorship of landlords and manufacturers rather than that of the merchants from whom its name is derived. Writing some years ago, Jacob Viner added the goal of plenty to the mercantilists' more widely advertised concern with power.[17] A far more accurate depiction of the sequence of economic concerns in England would be: first plenty, and later, power. Restoration writers concerned themselves with the prosperity of the individual Englishman. Even during the war period, pamphleteers defended taxes by referring to the importance of government to the enjoyment of one's property.[18] Only in the eighteenth century was national power regularly evoked as a central benefit of the growth of trade.

This puzzle of a torrent of liberal economic writings followed by a long dry spell in economic speculation has been noted before, but historians, looking at only a small proportion of the total writing on economic topics, have depicted the early free trade enthusiasts as lonely path breakers. John Ramsay McCulloch named North "an Achilles without a heel" and celebrated Henry Martyn for his remarkable grasp of true economic principles.[19] Sir

[17] "Power versus Plenty as Objectives of Foreign Policy in the Seventeenth and Eighteenth Centuries," *World Politics* 1 (1948).

[18] "Peace and Security are the Nurses of Plenty, Wealth and Honour; but an obstruction of Trade as naturally impoverishes a Nation, as an Atrophy leads to a Phthisis. And therefore though we may be forced to buy our Peace and Security at such a rate, as seems now dear and high, yet when we come to have our ends served by it, we shall find and see the reembursements will make an ample amends, and pay us the best interest for our mony" is a typical statement from *Short reflections upon the present state of affairs in England*, 1691, p. 21. See also *A discourse on the nature, use and advantages of trade*, 1694, p. 25, K 1842; [John Briscoe], *A discourse of money*, 1696, pp. 18-23, K 1936; [Henry Layton], *Observations concerning money and coin*, 1697, p. 34, K 2031; Sir William Temple, *Observations upon the United Provinces*, 1673, pp. 189-90, K 1349; and Robert Murray, *A proposal for the advancement of trade*, 1676, "to the reader."

[19] *A Select Collection of Early English Tracts on Commerce*, London, 1856, pp. xii-xiv.

William Ashley drew attention to the liberal economic writings of the late seventeenth century but explained away their significance by asserting that "they secured no appreciable notice from contemporaries."[20] This conclusion has been repeated up to the present. Charles Wilson called North a swallow who did not produce a summer.[21] Viner looked at many more publications, but he, too, concluded that Barbon and North were exceptions. In fact, Viner made explicit what others had suggested: that had there been Barbons and Norths to defend free trade when the 1713 treaty was debated, the result might have been different.[22]

The Great Depression of the 1930s and the Keynesian critique of classical economic models made possible a new line of inquiry about seventeenth-century economic writings. By calling attention to the limited applicability of classical economic theories, Keynes restored the historical dimension to the investigation of economic change. His work encouraged historians to examine the specific characteristics of early modern England to discover if there were a rapport between economic descriptions and the prevailing problems in the economy.[23] Examination of the actual way in which international accounts were settled lent some credibility to the seventeenth-century preoccupation with favorable balances, but more recently scholars have concluded that by 1688 the use of a multilateral exchange system "made mercantilist doctrine in defence of a constant favour-

[20] *Surveys Historic and Economic*, London, 1900, p. 292.

[21] *England's Apprenticeship, 1603-1763*, New York, 1965, p. 184. See also J. D. Gould, *Economic Growth in History*, London, 1972, p. 224. Gould's reference is [Henry Martyn], *Considerations upon the East-India trade*, 1701, K 2310.

[22] *Studies in the Theory of International Trade*, New York, 1937, pp. 52-57, 90, 117-18.

[23] See particularly Charles Wilson, "Treasure and Trade Balances: The Mercantilist Problem," *Economic History Review*, 2nd ser. 2 (1949) and R.W.K. Hinton, "The Mercantile System in the time of Thomas Mun," *ibid.* 7 (1955); and J. D. Gould, "The Trade Crisis of the early 1620s and English Economic Thought," *Journal of Economic History* 15 (1955).

able balance of payments increasingly unacceptable."[24] From this point of view, Mun's grasp of economic realities was sound, but continued obsession with the need to obtain a favorable balance of trade was reactionary. Another group of scholars investigating the mercantilists' ideas has stressed that their principal concern was with employing the poor and that the balance-of-trade idea was more a euphemism for encouraging those enterprises that provided employment.[25] This tack led to an examination of the social structure of preindustrial England and revealed how large the problem of unemployment loomed during the transition from an agrarian to an industrial economic order. Both bodies of scholarship have drawn attention to changes in the nature of the market economy over time.[26] However, the tendency to rehabilitate the reputation of the mercantilists by making the balance-of-trade concept appear reasonable has obscured the more important fact that many seventeenth-century writers had rejected the theory as an inadequate description of market relations. Without this knowledge, historians have depicted the course of economic reasoning as a slow process of enlightenment instead of a problematical intellectual development that was brought to an abrupt halt.[27]

[24] J. Sperling, "The International Payments Mechanism in the Seventeenth and Eighteenth Centuries," *Economic History Review*, 2nd ser. 14 (1962), p. 446. See also Jacob Price, "Multilateralism and Bilateralism: The Settlement of British Trade Balances with the North," *ibid.*

[25] D. C. Coleman, "Labour in the English Economy of the Seventeenth Century," *ibid.* 8 (1956); Richard C. Wiles, "The Theory of Wages in Later English Mercantilism," *ibid.* 21 (1968); and N. G. Pauling, "The Employment Problem in Pre-Classical English Economic Thought," *The Economic Record* 27 (1951).

[26] For explorations of this point see Ronald Meek, *Economics and Ideology*, London, 1967, pp. 179-95 and Fritz Redlich, "Towards the Understanding of an Unfortunate Legacy," *KYLOS* 19 (1966).

[27] Charles Wilson, "Trade, Society and the State," *The Cambridge Economic History of Europe*, vol. 4, Cambridge, 1967, p. 503; see also Letwin, *Origins of Scientific Economics,* pp. 176-81; Jelle C. Riemersma,

Viewed through the filter of classical economic theory, the free trade advocates and their opponents present a curious muddling of opinions. Locke, who defended revaluation of the shilling because of the unique and unalterable value of specie, dogmatically denied that the government could affect the real monetary system but advised government regulation to secure favorable trade balances.[28] His opponents dismissed the idea that international trade balances were necessarily settled in specie, recommended that government leave economic life free, but recognized the central role of the political authority in establishing legal tender currency.[29] It is important to sort out these positions, for Locke has frequently been claimed as a critic of mercantilism where in truth, if English mercantilistic policies date from 1696, he must be considered their principal architect.[30] His candidacy as critic rests upon his belief in a natural economic order. In *Some considerations of the consequences of the lowering of interest* he argued that statutory limits on interest rates were of no avail because the price of borrow-

---

"Usury Restrictions in a Mercantile Economy," *Canadian Journal of Economics and Political Science* 18 (1952), 17; and Hirschman, *Passions and the Interest*, pp. 9-15, for similar emphases on the gradual development of ideas.

[28] [Henry Layton], *Observations concerning money and coin*, 1697, p. 37, K 2031, snidely joins Locke's assertions that "Parliament must take care of Trade, and provide that the Ballance of it may be in favour of ourselves" with his appointment as a member of the Board of Trade who will set things right by an "extraordinary, and yet unrevealed Knowledge in Trade."

[29] [John Law], *Money and trade consider'd*, Edinburgh 1705, pp. 20ff, K 2463, developed this idea the most fully by pointing out the foolishness of Great Britain's using a commodity as money whose supply was controlled by Spain. He also noted that Spain benefited by increasing the supply of silver since that country would get all the initial advantage of the addition and share proportionally in the loss of value.

[30] Charles Wilson, "The Growth of Overseas Commerce and European Manufacture," in J. O. Lindsay, ed., *The New Cambridge Modern History*, vol. 7, Cambridge, 1966, p. 48.

ing money was set through free bargaining and laws could not deter men from pursuing their profit. This position drew criticism from moralists, but it cannot distinguish him from other seventeenth-century economic writers.[31] Since the 1620s, when Mun conjured up a "Necessity beyond all resistance" to explain the flow of trade and treasure, all economic writers had found compelling the idea of a natural order of things. Even a rigid balance-of-trade thinker like John Pollexfen spoke of trade as being ordained by providence and "govern'd by the Laws of the Creation, Cause and Consequence," while Charles Davenant in the same spirit declared that "Trade is in its Nature, free . . . and best directeth its own Course."[32] What is central to the division between liberals and conservatives at the end of the seventeenth century was what constituted that natural order invoked by both groups.

Conservatives who recommended industrial protection and the channeling of trade through navigation laws believed in a natural order of cause and effect in the market, but reasoned that men and women could pursue private interests inimicable to the public weal. Positive laws working with the natural order could prevent this from happening. What was missing from their conception of economics was the nineteenth-century belief in a natural tendency toward equilibrium. Adam Smith had joined natural law to laissez faire policies by demonstrating that the actions of self-seeking individuals balanced one another to produce a natural harmony and a momentum toward the maximization of productivity. Instead of the restraint of government, what was required to control the self-interested market participant was freedom for the real natural laws of economic life to operate.[33] The conservatives had more faith in gov-

[31] See chapter 8, n. 49.

[32] *England's treasure by forraign trade*, 1664, p. 219, K 1139; [John Pollexfen], *A discourse of trade, coyn, and paper credit*, 1697, Preface, K 2041; and [Charles Davenant], *An essay on the East-India-trade*, 1696, p. 25, K 1954.

[33] Letwin, *The Origins of Scientific Economics*, pp. 176-81.

ernment control than in the automatic checking of economic competitors when it came to wealth-producing activities, but they would not let government define wealth itself. Specie, as Feavearyear pointed out, acquired a new sanctity from the recoinage of 1696, and it was a sanctity conferred by a new interpretation of nature, not by government decree.[34]

What proved provocative about the free trade thinkers of the 1690s was their unabashed acceptance of the intangible forces in the market economy. In their thinking the government could add an extrinsic value to gold and silver, and specie substitutes could serve for money because the order they espied had psychological roots. Security made a medium of exchange useful and hence valuable, and security was a human judgment. Without working out all the equilibrating mechanisms of classical economics, they endorsed economic freedom for its more salient advantage of enlisting individual initiative in the commercial process. Exploring the psychological determinants of market participation—desire, emulation, ambition, competition, entrepreneurial knowhow—they uncovered natural forces far different from the fixed portions of wealth and natural surpluses of their balance-of-trade critics. As students of market behavior, Houghton, Thomas, Martyn, Gardiner, Barbon, and North were optimists. Living at a time when the human passions were being given a searching examination, the economists pursued the more modest task of understanding the cause-and-effect relations of a commercial economy.[35] A new range of human activity came under their systematic observation. Neither moralists nor philosophers, they observed a

[34] Sir Albert Feavearyear, *The Pound Sterling*, Oxford, 1963 (originally published in 1931), pp. 148-49. See also Karl Polanyi, *The Great Transformation*, New York, 1944, pp. 3ff, for a discussion of the critical role specie standards played in the nineteenth century.

[35] Eric Vogelin, *From Enlightenment to Revolution*, Durham, North Carolina, 1975, p. 56; and Albert Hirschman, *The Passions and the Interests*, pp. 14-66.

system in which they were deeply involved. Watching their fellow human beings work and invest, buy and sell, allocate resources and reap the rewards of accurate planning, they detected a happy rapport between self-interest and rational calculation. Unruly passions did not mar their optimism, for the passions they observed were disciplined by the desire to gain through an orderly system. The economic freedom of the seventeenth century—the negative laissez faire policy of a disordered political body—had permitted material ambitions to escape supervision, and the economic pattern of the unplanned appeared. Or at least one was described: so long as men applied their wits to enhancing their wealth-creating capacities, there was a natural dynamic toward growth and swift circulation of vital information. Cheap Indian silk imports bettered the trade of the silk weavers, Gardiner said, "by whetting their Industry and Invention."[36] Competing individuals, not knowing each other's plans, overproduced for known markets and were forced to pioneer new ones, Houghton related, and Child explained that legislating good trade patterns was not necessary because shopkeepers and merchants "will do it without forcing" under the profit motive.[37]

Unlike Bernard Mandeville, whose *Fable of the bees* created a furor in 1714 by suggesting that the private vice of indulging in luxury was a public virtue, the liberals of the 1690s had an egalitarian conception of economic ambition. It was the pervasive and universal capacity of demand to grow from the desires of ordinary men and women that made it a natural and powerful stimulant to productivity. No such leveling tendencies emerged from Mandeville who stressed that, since "all hard and dirty work in a well-govern'd Nation" falls to the poor, ignorance and necessity must be enlisted to keep them to their task.[38] It was exactly

[36] [Gardiner], *Some reflections on a pamphlet*, 1697, p. 24, K 1968.

[37] [Houghton], *England's great happiness*, 1677, pp. 10-13, K 1431; and Child, *A new discourse of trade*, 1693, p. 86, K 1811.

[38] 1714, 3rd ed., pp. 472-73 (originally published as *The grumbling hive*, 1706).

the opposite conclusion—that is, that competition and envy can drive the poor to work and the country as a whole to higher levels of productivity—that the economic liberals came to. Where Mandeville merely advertised the hypocrisy of the eighteenth-century moralists' praise of contentment and frugality, they proposed an open competition for material rewards. Theirs was a radicalism distinguished by its detachment from the sensibilities of a hierarchical society and the inviolability of property, once acquired.

Assessing the origins of scientific economics, William Letwin has drawn a different dividing line among the seventeenth-century economists, with Child and Barbon representing an old style distinguished from the new of John Collins, Petty, Locke, and North. Critical to the new style, Letwin has argued, is the sundering of the moral aspect of a subject from its technical aspect. "Economic theory," he writes, "owes its present development to the fact that some men . . . were willing to consider the economy as nothing more than an intricate mechanism, refraining for the while from asking whether the mechanism worked for good or evil."[39] In this view, economists were able to perceive the workings of their subject by creating that impoverished reality of the ideal model. However, both the liberals and the conservatives sundered the moral from the technical aspects of the market economy, but the model each group created was not the impoverished reality of the scientists but the selective reality of men deeply involved in the system they were attempting to explain and justify. The economic model of Locke and the landed Whig magnates who made the critical decisions for English economic development rested upon the sanctity of the silver standard and the notion of balancing trade accounts, ideas replete with political meaning. The liberals conceived of a commercial society built upon an economic meritocracy and uniform market responses, a competitive model rendered safe to

[39] *Origins of Scientific Economics*, pp. 147-48.

(258)

them by their own commercial aptitude. Both groups built upon Coke's idea of the "Nature and Order of things." It wound its way through all discussions on trade. If we are to explain why one prevailed and the other did not—or indeed why they held the views that they did—it will be necessary to look at the ideological implications rather than the technical virtues of their respective conceptions of the market economy.

To discuss the eighteenth-century triumph of the balance-of-trade explanation of economic growth in ideological terms is to give preeminent place to the theory's importance as a rationale for statutory definition of national trading areas and as a justification for directing the labor of the poor. It was also significant for providing a fund of rhetorical images useful in extolling restraint, frugality, and co-operation in economic life. The alternative explanation of economic growth—that put forward by the advocates of free trade and the devaluation of the shilling—drew different conclusions in its train. Its theoretical propositions supported the extension of economic freedoms in internal as well as foreign trade and minimized the tension between private gain and public good. Both theories rested upon a common fund of observation, but diverged through different constructions put on competition, wealth, trade balances, money, and domestic commerce. In these differences lie their respective ideological import. Ideologies appear, Norman Birnbaum has said, "wherever systematic factual assertions about society contain (usually by implication) evaluations of the distribution of power in the societies in which these assertions are developed and propagated."[40] The power attached to commercial success had grown enormously during the course of the seventeenth century, and the theories created to explain this new force had an irreducible ideo-

[40] "The Sociological Study of Ideology (1940-1960): A Trend Report and Bibliography," *Current Sociology* 9 (1960), 91. See also Clifford Geertz, "Ideology as a Cultural System," in David Apter, ed., *Ideology and Discontent*, Glencoe, Illinois, 1964, pp. 164-71.

logical component. Moreover, because market participants were also members of a political body and a social structure as well as transmitters of values, any analysis of market relations carried with it corollaries about the political, social, and moral order. It is from this perspective that the failure of the late seventeenth-century liberals can best be appreciated.

During the critical decades preceding the decisions of 1696 several long-term developments clouded the economic future of England. There was first of all the persistent underemployment of England's able-bodied, laboring men and women. Since no one envisioned a return to the old economic order that had provided a place for their forebears, writers emphasized the need to find work for the poor. Their idleness was rarely attributed to their moral defects, but rather to the want of employment. At the same time, contemporaries realized that farming would be absorbing fewer hands. Food surpluses after the Restoration had relieved England from fear of famine. With the possibility of exporting grain regularly, landlords and tenants came in closer contact with world trade. While the production of food increased, the population of England stabilized, and the earlier high prices that had stimulated agricultural investments dropped. The lower return on farming investments hastened the disappearance of the English peasantry while among landlords it heightened a concern with national economic policies.[41] Practically, this abundance of food removed grain growers from the application of the Tudor patrimonial statutes that subordinated private interests to public needs while intellectually it encouraged writers to treat food, and the labor and land that produced it, as abstractions to be manipulated as any other economic

[41] A. H. John, "Aspects of English Economic Growth," *Economica* 28 (1961) and "Agricultural Productivity and Economic Growth in England, 1700-1760," *Journal of Economic History* 25 (1965); and E. L. Jones, "Agriculture and Economic Growth in England, 1660-1750: Agriculture Change," *ibid*.

unit of interchangeable value.[42] During these same years the merchants and manufacturers who engaged in the processing and marketing of calicoes, silks, sugar, and tobacco to an expanding group of European and English consumers prospered.[43] Commercial growth in the Restoration depended upon these new avenues of economic development but, like agriculture, these trades employed relatively few new workers, so the unemployment problem persisted despite real advances in capital accumulation and productivity.

The outbreak of King William's war in 1689 increased the gravity of the long-term problems in the English economy. Specie shipped to Europe to pay for England's participation in the general war against France exacerbated the coin shortage. The fighting itself interrupted England's most profitable trades. Aggressive French privateering wiped out much of the capital created in the previous period of commercial prosperity. Showing a decided liquidity preference, many merchants withdrew their investments from trade, a response that left their suppliers without customers and workers bereft of support. This cashing-in of trading assets created a pool of capital that was later drawn upon to finance the lengthy war, but it also demonstrated the tenuousness of the merchants' connection with the productive sector of the economy. The city scramble for company shares contrasted vividly with the restriction of choices the war brought to manufacturers, landlords, and the laboring poor. While the successful floating of the Bank of England owed much to this speculative fever, the inflation accompanying

[42] Thomas, *Mercantilism and the East India Trade*, pp. 5, 60-61. It is interesting in this connection to find the spirit behind Tudor economic legislation revived in the late eighteenth century when population again began to press upon the food supply, as described in E. P. Thompson, "The Moral Economy of the English Crowd in the Eighteenth Century," *Past and Present* 50 (1971). See also C. R. Fay, "The Miller and the Baker: A Note on Commercial Transition, 1770-1837," *Cambridge Historical Journal* 1 (1923).

[43] Wilson, *England's Apprenticeship*, pp. 160-84.

the bank's funding only added to the impression of insta-bility.[44] A run of bad harvests intensified the dislocations in the wartime economy.[45] The pamphlet controversies over the theoretical merits of banning calico imports and revalu-ing the shilling thus came at a time when the sense of na-tional crisis strengthened the appeal of conservative ar-guments.

It is no accident that the men who wished to widen the ambit of economic freedom were merchants, bank pro-moters, stock jobbers, and projectors: Henry Martyn and Francis Gardiner, who were outspoken defenders of the East India Company; Dalby Thomas, an investor with West Indian and African interests in addition to his banking schemes; Dudley North, a prominent Turkey merchant; John Houghton, a commercial publicist; and Nicholas Barbon, a real estate developer, builder, and insurance pro-moter. They were not involved, like the manufacturers, in the mobilization of labor. The important variables in their affairs were markets, prices, shipping costs, interest rates, and the return on stock. The lower class loomed larger to them as likely customers than potential workers, and the ideas they propagated revealed little concern with the distress of the clothiers, the intractability of the employ-ment problem, or the decay of rents lamented by the land-lords. Instead they stressed that free rein be given to the acquisitive urge, which would create the effective demand to absorb the product of England's land and industries. When they introduced a theory of economic growth that endorsed competition and acclaimed vanity, ambition, and

[44] Jones, "London Merchants and the Crisis of the 1690s," pp. 334-38; Feavearyear, *Pound Sterling*, p. 130; and K. G. Davies, "Joint Stock In-vestment in the Later Seventeenth Century," *Economic History Review* 2nd ser. 4 (1952). For contemporary comments on stock-jobbing see [Daniel Defoe], *An essay upon projects*, 1697, p. 36, K 2024; and *The linnen and woollen manufactory discoursed*, 1691, p. 14, Ks 1734.

[45] W. G. Hoskins, "Harvest Fluctuations and English Economic His-tory, 1620-1759," *Agricultural History Review* 16 (1968).

emulation as part of a new market dynamic, they were taking a tack that cut deeper than the superficial clash of interests. They were revealing the socially radical force of the free market. Close on the heels of the circulation of these ideas was the vivid demonstration during the war crisis years that the men who held them had only a superficial interest in the society they were addressing. The economic freedom they endorsed held little promise of employing the poor, maintaining the price of corn and wool, or helping those English industries that did utilize the nation's labor and material. Their example gave no proof that the men of new wealth would commit their resources to the task of transforming the displaced English peasantry into a population of productive workers attuned to the integrating forces of a liberal society. Nothing in the recommendations of North, Barbon, Houghton, Thomas, or Martyn revealed an awareness of the difficulty of preparing traditionally oriented people for new and demanding tasks. The problem of providing direction for coherent social action did not exist for them. Instead they advanced a criticism that implied there was a natural progression in economic development. They faulted the balance-of-trade theory for its inadequacy in accounting for commercial realities, unmindful of the social values imbedded in the theory. Having located the dynamic of economic growth in the desire of individuals to possess material goods—with the hint that this desire was perhaps unlimited—these writers in varying degrees endorsed a freeing of the individual without apparently realizing that those men and women who had no capital must depend upon the capitalists for an opportunity to pursue their new ambitions.

Extrapolating from the narrow sample of energetic self-made men they saw about them, they assumed that "the wants of the Mind . . . causeth Trade" instead of discontent, aversion to work, and a churlish want of respect for betters.[46]

[46] [Nicholas Barbon], *A discourse of trade*, 1690, p. 73, K 1720. See

They failed to demonstrate how the majority of men, women, and children without skills or modern work habits would acquire a new consciousness and a new capacity to harness desire to long-range plans for increased productivity. Their own incentives and priorities formed the basis for theorizing about market mechanisms, while their depiction of the naturally active, profit-seeking person was an attribution of the behavior of their group to the species as a whole. The sensibilities of the entrepreneur were projected onto the human race, and the characteristics of men active in trade and finance became the norm for society as a whole. The egocentricity so long stigmatized as selfishness appeared to them in a new and acceptable guise as legitimate self-interest in a society run by the pervasive pursuit of profit. Between the clothiers' world of workers so surly they would often mar their work and the merchants' image of ambitious social climbers "spurr'd up" by the rich "to imitate their industry" there was an unbridgeable conceptual gulf.[47]

The merchants of England had prospered during the Restoration and had acquired, in the process, a sharp sense of how the market operated. Their political power, however, had not grown commensurately, and their self-interest had permitted them to stray far from the propertied Englishman's traditional preoccupation with controlling the lower class.[48] England's striking economic development had also dramatically reshaped the outlook of the nobility and gentry.[49] Through the course of the seventeenth century

---

also [Sir Dalby Thomas], *An historical account of the rise and growth of the West-India collonies*, 1690, p. 6, K 1749.

[47] [William Carter], *The ancient trades decayed*, 1678, p. 8, Ks 1464; and North, *Discourses*, p. 15.

[48] See the Introduction to Clark and Slack, eds., *Crisis and Order in English Towns*, for a discussion of the failure of the city corporation to maintain political control over economic developments; and T. H. Marshall, "Capitalism and the Decline of the English Guilds," *Cambridge Historical Journal* 3 (1929).

[49] Lawrence Stone, *The Crisis of the Aristocracy, 1558-1641*, Oxford,

they had taken an active part in enhancing the productivity of England's landed resources and were important investors in commercial and banking ventures as well. They had acquired a modern mentality that made them receptive to the idea of viewing the market as a part of a natural order of things. As leaders of the century-long struggle against the claims of prerogative power from a succession of Stuart kings, moreover, they had become attuned to those parts of a natural rights philosophy that would justify their repeated rebellions.[50] What the crisis of the war period brought to a head was not the divergence of interest between a progressive and a backward part of the upper class, but rather between the manufacturers and the landlords as employers in a modernizing economy and the merchants whose speculative ideas moved as freely as their capital.

Two institutional ties in England strengthened the association of the manufacturers and landlords with the entire economy: the Poor Laws, which mandated tax support for the unemployed in need, and the land tax. While the poor did not escape the indirect taxation from excises and customs duties, English property owners made the lion's share of contributions to the king's revenue. The initial cost of paying for the war fell most heavily on them, and poor rates soared as well during the last decade of the century.[51]

1965, pp. 335-84. For a discussion of innovations in property law undertaken by landowners at the end of the seventeenth century see R. S. Neale, "The Bourgeoisie, Historically, Has Played a Most Revolutionary Part," in Eugene Kamenka and Neale, eds., *Feudalism, Capitalism and Beyond*, London, 1975, pp. 95-102.

[50] W. H. Greenleaf, *Order, Empiricism and Politics*, London, 1964, pp. 271-79; Quentin Skinner, "History and Ideology in the English Revolution," *Historical Journal* 12 (1969); C. B. Macpherson, *The Political Theory of Possessive Individualism*, Oxford, 1962, pp. 194-251; and J. R. Western, *Monarchy and Revolution*, Totowa, New Jersey, 1972, pp. 19-31.

[51] Wilson, *England's Apprenticeship*, pp. 234-35; Dickson, *Financial Revolution*, pp. 17-29; and J. H. Plumb, *The Growth of Political Stability in England 1675-1725*, London, 1967, p. 142.

The sudden withdrawal of merchant capital from the productive sector of the economy drew attention to the fluidity of the new wealth and, by inference, the relative freedom of merchants, stock jobbers and financiers from concerns with the persistent problems of unemployment and fluctuating levels of investments in an unregulated economy.[52] At the very time that an argument for expanding economic freedoms was being most widely made, the limitations of the profit motive as a guide stood revealed in the retreat of the merchants from those concerns to which the well-being of the manufacturers and landlords was tied. Apparent as well was the indeterminacy of the free market's employment patterns. Worse yet, the theoretical analysis offered by the economic liberals robbed the control of wage and investment policies of a supporting rationale.

The expansion of economic freedom in the last half of the seventeenth century had brought prosperity to England, but a prosperity with an uncertain future. The liberties so widely enjoyed had served to advertise the critical shift of power away from government toward the individual market participant. As economic power grew, the centrifugal force of the market could not be ignored. The liquidity preferences of commercial investors revealed the vulnerability of others to their choices. Representatives of the landed class fought back. As P.G.M. Dickson noted, with an appropriate touch of sarcasm: "True to its tradition of frowning on new forms of economic enterprise—unless practised by landowners at the expense of tenants—Parliament made repeated attempts between the 1690s and the 1770s to check the growth of Exchange Alley, and the activities of its denizens."[53] For men who wanted plenty and power, however, the market had the characteristics of the goose that laid the golden egg. James Hodges nicely captured the dilemma of trying to control a commercial economy. The

[52] Gould, *Economic Growth*, pp. 152-62; Jones, "London Merchants and the Crisis of the 1690s."
[53] Dickson, *Financial Revolution*, p. 516.

government, he said, could not force credit because credit came from a belief that one would be repaid, nor could it force exchanges because they were made to achieve satisfaction, which also depended upon opinion.[54] The balance-of-trade logic, however, went beyond justifying legislative forays; it offered theoretical support for economic development without profound social change.

England's swift conversion to protectionist legislation and balance-of-trade thinking after such a vigorous assertion of liberal sentiments has suggested to some that the free traders were actually silenced. Sir William Ashley called attention to the fact that four prominent free trade advocates—Davenant, Child, Barbon, and North—were all Tories, which indicated to him that their politics explained their opinions. Ashley assumed that the opposite persuasion could likewise be attributed to association with the Whigs. "No one," he wrote, "would accuse Locke of intellectual dishonesty," and then proceeded to describe a series of events that amounted to just such a charge.[55] P. J. Thomas, questioning Henry Martyn's switch from the advocacy of free trade in the closing years of the century to opposition in the fight against the liberalization of Anglo-French commerce in 1713, concluded that England had become so thoroughly protectionist that any ambitious man had to hide his free trade views.[56] The biographer of William Paterson, one of the founders of the Bank of England, also pondered the fate of the free trade advocates in the first two decades of the eighteenth century.[57] Evidence does not abound, but at least in the public condemnation of Samuel

[54] [Hodges], *A supplement to the present state of England*, 1697, pp. 11-15, K 2030.

[55] *Surveys Historical and Economic*, London, 1900, pp. 298, 294-96. Ashley's discussion is marred by the fact that he did not realize how widespread free trade ideas were and does not perceive the relation between revaluation of the currency and the balance-of-trade theory.

[56] *Mercantilism and the East India Trade*, pp. 172-73.

[57] S. Bannister, *William Paterson, the Merchant Statesman, Founder of the Bank of England*, Edinburgh, 1858, pp. 407-11.

Grascome's attack on Parliament's recoinage scheme we have an act attesting to the gravity of the issue in the eyes of the majority in the Commons.[58]

A more persuasive argument would place economic freedom and the sovereign right to adjust the mint ratio in the same category as frequent elections and a wide suffrage. All were spurned by the Whig oligarchy in the last years of the century. As J. H. Plumb has shown, while Whig rhetoric celebrated the preservation of Englishmen's constitutional liberties, the number of elections and the size of electorates were reduced to figures manageable by corruption.[59] Similarly, J. R. Western has stressed that, after the destruction of libertarian forces before the Glorious Revolution, central authority was left stronger than ever in 1689. Only the pursuit of a costly continental war, Western argues, compromised the independence of the monarchy because financing the war created that engine of corruption, the funded debt, which the Whig magnates used to their advantage in the consolidation of power.[60] If more representative government was the political casualty of Whig dominance, commercial freedom was the economic sacrifice. With political stability at last achieved, England's era of negative laissez faire could be brought to an end. Like the effusion of republican sentiments, the endorsement of economic freedom can be seen in retrospect as part of the "world turned upside down," which had to be turned right-side up again.[61]

[58] See chapter 8, n. 93 above.

[59] J. H. Plumb, "The Growth of the Electorate in England from 1600 to 1715," *Past and Present* 45 (1969), 111.

[60] Western, *Monarchy and Revolution*, pp. 342ff.

[61] Christopher Hill, *The World Turned Upside Down*, New York, 1972, pp. 308-13, and J.G.A. Pocock, *The Machiavellian Moment*, Princeton, 1975, pp. 423-61, offer assessments of the reactionary ideas of the period. By slighting the economic writings of the seventeenth century, Pocock (p. 460) claims for the Augustan period an undeserved priority in the discussion of market economics and political power. See also Margaret C. Jacob, *The Newtonians and the English Revolution, 1689-1720*, Ithaca, New York, 1976. According to an anonymous pam-

The fascinating and instructive epilogue to the adoption of a mercantilistic system at this late date in the career of English capitalism concerns the fate of economic reasoning. Why was there a resort to the balance-of-trade model of economic well-being? Using political authority to mobilize the economic resources of the country was eminently reasonable? So, too, could revaluation of the coinage be justified on practical grounds. Why then were the official measures to protect English manufacturing couched in terms of producing a favorable balance of trade? Why were ideas already repudiated as explanations of economic data dragged in to defend policies that were highly defensible in terms of social realities? The answer lies in the connection the English ruling class had forged between its claim to power and the philosophy of political liberalism. The notion of a natural order in human affairs was one of the most powerful ideas of the seventeenth century and one that had served its turn in 1688 to explain and justify the move to block the resurgence of Stuart pretentions in James's brief rule. To reassert the preeminence of social concerns as a justification for checking economic freedoms would certainly have evoked echoes from the century-long struggle over monarchical authority. What the balance-of-trade theory then offered was a competing description of the nature of the market economy. By clinging to a defense marred only by a dispute over particular facts, the parliamentary majority was able to avoid the more perilous course of challenging the liberal assumptions about natural rights. The first decade of the eighteenth century was too close to 1688 for England's ruling class to say with Burke that they loved their constitution because it had been theirs for time out of mind. Far

---

phleteer, author of *Some short considerations* [1697], p. 10, K 2051: "We are intirely unsettled, as to the Government. The King's Title and Legality of it, are as publickly disputed, and with as little Fear of Punishment, as any Point of Natural Philosophy in the Schools at Oxford."

better to maintain the connection between property rights and the natural order of things and confine dissent to conflicting interpretations of the data. To ideological, not intellectual, causes should be attributed that triumph of balance-of-trade thinking that made the expression of free trade sentiment a form of political heresy in the early eighteenth century.

Left alone, the predominating forces in a market economy are both centrifugal and psychological; prices are set by increments of demand at diverse points of sale and the elasticity in demand comes from individual choices. Both qualities had become salient by the end of the seventeenth century, and a group of writers had advertised their advantages. With an intellectual freedom verging on abandon, they had called attention to the fact that the amount of money in circulation was a reflection of demand not policy, and that silver would become a shilling rather than a goblet because, as one anonymous commentator said, it "is per Ounce more valuable to me than uncoin'd."[62] The recognition that money, too, was a commodity—desired because it was useful as a measure of value—even suggested freeing domestic economic life from reliance upon silver. Since money's value came from a feeling of security rather than the substance of the coins, England might stop using a product of Spain for its currency. Locke's conflicting assertion that commercial prosperity depended upon the possession of silver was more than an argument for preserving the old denomination of the shilling; it was a reinvestment of meaning in the favorable balance concept, which in turn provided a justification for centralizing economic direction. One anonymous broadside writer admitted bafflement at why "Landed Men who are not Members of Parliament, [are] so violently hot for the old Standard."[63] He failed to see that in the validity of "old standards" the landed men

[62] *A method proposed for the regulating the coin* [1696], p. 1, Ks 1960.

[63] *A letter to two members* [1696], p. 1, Ks 1957.

of England had found a stabilizing force. Moreover, the immutability of silver as a measure of commerce was a double-edged sword for Locke: it created the necessity of protecting English industry and with it confining English patterns of consumption; at the same time it explained why the distribution of wealth was a reflection of the order of things and therefore not amenable to government interference. In this, the debates of the 1690s carry with them a faint echo of Mun and Misselden's dispute with Malynes in the 1620s. The difference is that, where Malynes had urged a return to a royal standard, Locke's economic reasoning strengthened a new sovereign, the class of landed and industrial employers who seized the initiative in 1696 and replaced the invisible hand of the market with the official hand of mercantilist regulation.

If the history of economic reasoning is approached as the study of successive opinions held by contemporaries instead of as a progressive development in itself, this first sustained inquiry into the market economy during the seventeenth century holds some important clues about the origins of capitalism. A canvass of the full range of economic speculation makes it impossible to characterize two centuries of thought as minimal variations on a solitary theme. Instead, we see the balance-of-trade ideas changing as contending groups within English society changed. Initially appearing as part of an analysis of money flows, the real career of the balance-of-trade theory began almost a century later when it was pitted against a subtle and sophisticated concept of market behavior. As an explanation for economic growth in 1696, it became what it had never been before: an ideological force capable of distributing power, justifying policies, and prescribing a new form of social solidarity. In this guise the theory offered Adam Smith his straw man in 1776. As theory it had long been moribund; as ideology it was no longer relevant. Smith said the architects of the mercantile system had confused wealth with specie, and he criticized them for chasing the chimera of the favorable balance when in fact international trade patterns would frustrate all contrived efforts to achieve permanent surpluses of exports. Smith's famous articulation of the workings of a free economy was suffused with a faith in the automatic harmony of market relations. Convinced of the uniformity and constancy of the "desire of bettering our condition," Smith assumed what earlier had to be proved: that the tendencies to truck and barter, to work and improve were natural rather than socially acquired traits. While Smith recognized the leisure preferences of working-class men and women, he failed to incorporate them into his model, thereby perpetuating the belief that economic development was a matter of impersonal factors like the widening of markets and the accumulation of capital.[64] Nineteenth-century liberals could scorn the help of government because those investments that promoted employment had already been protected and the poor trained up to the disciplined labor required of them.

Nothing written in the seventeenth century can match the analytical rigor or comprehensiveness of the *Wealth of Nations*, but Smith's system was not just a more elaborate version of his precursors' ideas. There are significant differences in these two liberal programs, and a comparison shows the debt Smith owed to the mercantilists he demolished. Where North, Barbon, Thomas, Gardiner, Houghton, and Martyn probed the dynamic elements in economic life, Smith created a model with balances and mechanical adjustments. The earlier writers were concerned with how appetites were whetted, new goods marketed, and levels of spending raised. Smith defined the end of economic activity as consumption, but he bestowed his approval upon the

[64] *Wealth of Nations*, book 4, chapter 1; book 1, chapter 8; book 3, chapters 1, 2. For a discussion of the inappropriateness of classical economic assumptions about human nature see Solo, *Economic Organizations and Social Systems*, pp. 432-37; and Dean C. Tipps, "Modernization Theory and the Comparative Study of Societies: A Critical Perspective," *Comparative Studies in Society and History*, 15 (1973), 206-10.

savers who automatically became investors.[65] The seventeenth-century liberals celebrated the accomplishments of the projector and merchant, whereas Smith, as Fritz Redlich has pointed out, ascribed no positive functions to the entrepreneur beyond the accumulation of capital.[66] There was, moreover, no hypostasizing of nature in the earlier writers. They insisted that official authority, like the aggregate decisions of men in the market, could affect the terms of trade. They did not extol economic freedom because of a belief in automatic equilibrating mechanisms, but rather because it created an environment favorable to the release of energy and the prompting of ingenuity. Such observations are inhospitable to mathematical modeling, but it would be to confound precision with accuracy to say that their descriptions provided a less adequate account than Smith's of the market phenomena under their observation. When Smith explained the setting of price, he returned to the quantitative analysis of Petty and Locke, not to the exploration of imaginary wants of Locke's critics. By assuming that market behavior was natural and uniform, he could avoid the subjective determinants of price and wash from economic theory the shaping role of society.

An economic theory that excludes social influences has little light to shed on the crossroads of English economic development at the end of the seventeenth century. Capital accumulation did not necessarily lead to greater productivity. The attractiveness of becoming a creditor to the king impaired the flow of capital to agriculture, and free trade tended to employ more Indians than English.[67] The commercialization of agriculture turned men and women into wage earners, but the quantity and quality of their labor depended upon the number of jobs, the acquisition of skills, the wage rate, and the administration of outdoor relief. A

[65] *Wealth of Nations*, book 2, chapter 3.
[66] "Towards the Understanding of an Unfortunate Legacy," pp. 709-15.
[67] Dickson, *Financial Revolution*, p. 29.

society undergoing transformation, England was also a dual society, with people from the old agrarian order living at the same time as those who had already been absorbed in the new commercial system. The liberal writers of the 1690s evidently looked at the prospering tradesmen and shopkeepers of London's burgeoning population and conceived of economic freedom as a way to accelerate the movement from the old to the new society. Clothiers and landlords looked instead at the displaced persons of the old order: the pauper, the poor, and the underemployed laborers forced in bad times to rely on the parish for assistance. Free trade ideas had pushed to the fore the problem of social control in a liberal society. Through the seventeenth century upper-class Englishmen had disentangled themselves from the cohesive ties of a corporate society. Slowly the individual's right to be free of inherited social obligations had gained precedence over the older notion of society's primary claim upon its members. Outside the purview of moralists, economic writers had domesticated passion, defined away the solidity of wealth and questioned the utility of frugality.[68] While liberal ethics freed property owners from traditional restraints, it also undermined the justification for some people's being invested with permanent authority over others. In arguing for personal liberties, upper-class leaders had delivered the propertyless to a new master: the market through which they sold their labor and bought their bread. The unseen market replaced the visible and personal authority of the master. Contemporaries recognized the coercive power inherent in the market, but its efficacy as an implement of control depended upon whether it was a buyer's or a seller's market. This was the principal danger of extending economic freedom: it left to chance the advance of manufacturing and the preparation of an industrial labor force.

In the Marxist analysis of economic change, social power

[68] [Gardiner], *Some reflections*, p. 24, and Layton, *Observations*, p. 29, express weariness with praise of Dutch frugality.

is given its due place, but it is the exercise of power by a new class of men that Marx pointed to in explaining the rise of capitalism.[69] The English experience at the end of the seventeenth century suggests a different story. The new men of banking and commerce did not triumph, even though they waged a vigorous campaign in defense of devaluation and free trade and used empiricism in a socially radical way. They cut through the penumbra of conceits about wealth and virtue to make room for the free manipulation of the elements in the market. Their intellectual daring only advertised the social dangers of their program. In opposing these ideas, however, the landowning leaders of England revealed just how progressive they had become for it was not tradition or state authority they summoned to their cause, but a different theory about the market economy with the same presumed basis in nature, the same regularities, and the same expectation of human profit seeking.[70] In the balance-of-trade concept they found an ideology that welded together the interests of employers, the politics of liberalism, the patriotism of Whiggery, and the economic virtues of the Puritans.

Eric Hobsbawm has argued that private enterprise is blind, conjuring up a mindless system of organisms responding to the stimuli of profit.[71] If private enterprise is blind, entrepreneurs are not, and their function as profit seekers does not exhaust the many roles they play in society.

[69] For a discussion of this point, see Neale, "The Bourgeoisie, Historically, Has Played a Most Revolutionary Part." Challenging his opponents on all fronts, Gardiner, *Some reflections*, pp. 22-23, even "discovers" the era of finance capital when he notes that the Dutch, by sending money to England "at excessive Interest, will bring a considerable addition to the Riches of their State without the Exporting their Product for it, or the Labour of their People."

[70] The modern bias of the Whig oligarchy can best be appreciated in comparison to that of the opposition of the early eighteenth century as discussed by Isaac Kramnick, *Bolingbroke and his Circle*, Cambridge, 1968, pp. 56-83, and Pocock, *Machiavellian Moment*, pp. 423-61.

[71] "The Seventeenth Century in the Development of Capitalism," *Science and Society* 25 (1960).

In the case of the English landowners, their vested interests created a complementary responsibility, which was not true of the merchants. They were unavoidably concerned with the fate of the poor. Mindful of the financial burden of trade depressions, they identified the expansion of employment as the critical need of the time. As the traditional carriers of status in English society, they were also more likely to take offense at the merchants' approval of social climbing through economic success. The dangerous leveling tendencies lurking behind the idea of personal improvement through imitative buying no doubt were more conspicuous to those who benefited from the prevailing patterns of deference. Their response calls to mind Karl Polanyi's observation that the fate of classes is much more often determined by the needs of society than the fate of society by the needs of classes. The desire for power cannot explain change, Polanyi maintained, for "the chances of classes in a struggle will depend upon their ability to win support from outside their own membership, which again will depend upon their fulfillment of tasks set by interests wider than their own."[72]

In meeting this need, the parliamentary leadership endorsed a secular ethic as well as a theoretical rationale for economic legislation. The cluster of social values Max Weber associated with the spread of Calvinism—economic rationalism, zeal in one's calling, disciplined working, and spending habits—survived into the Restoration but lost its religious provenance. Frugality and industry, like the charging of interest and the enclosing of land, were recommended for their utilitarian merits. The disappearance of religious references in the writings on trade after 1660 indicates that economic virtues could be defended on purely economic grounds. Thus, there were no religious obstacles to arguing, as the free trade advocates did, that frugality and restraint impeded economic development. The win-

[72] *The Great Transformation*, New York, 1944, pp. 152-53.

ners of England's commercial meritocracy of the Restoration had no difficulty living with the morals of the market, just as they had no difficulty grasping the nature of economic changes around them. But the supplanting of their sophisticated analysis by the truisms and pieties of the balance-of-trade theory suggests that Weber was correct in insisting that economic development was as much a matter of ideas as of material change.

Behind the balance-of-trade theory there lay a model of the national economy linking all classes in England to a common goal. Since the theory stipulated that wealth accrued from the net gain from foreign trade, the whole economy could be viewed of as of a kind of national joint stock trading company. In this concept, the members of society did not compete with each other but rather participated jointly in England's collective enterprise of selling goods abroad. Emphasis fell exclusively upon mobilizing labor and exploiting new resources and for markets outside the kingdom. This joint stock enterprise was a powerful image for it provided symbolic cohesion to a society being atomized by the market. Tying wealth to power, the balance-of-trade theory offered a justification for protectionist legislation firmly grounded on national security. To entertain the idea that "the whole World as to Trade, is but as one Nation or People" as Dudley North's pamphlet announced, was to bring into question the entire navigation system as well as the wisdom of England's calculatedly aggressive national posture. The English ruling class swiftly closed ranks behind a program to create employment, protect English industry, capture lost European markets in North and South America, and coerce the lower class through the work provisions of the Poor Laws which suggests that merchants recognized that their social interests lay with this policy even if their economic interests were better served with more freedom.

The consumption-oriented theories of economic growth had depicted the market economy as an aggregation of separate, self-interested, producer-consumers whose aims were often mutually exclusive. The only social values adducible to this particular view were the freedom to aspire and act in one's own interest and an affirmation of the pleasure of consuming and possessing. The liberals had produced an ideological fragment. Attached to a new concept of political power or a redefinition of human purpose, their conclusion that self-interest was a propelling force toward economic progress might have provided the basis for constructing a new social reality. As it was, the clarity they achieved in discussing coin and the source of market value only advertised the dangers of their intellectual freedom. Publicly they had appropriated a set of images and words with which to discuss economic relations and over time they had changed the meaning of wealth, money, gain, consumption, and commerce by placing them in contexts shaped by their observations of the novelties in seventeenth-century economic life. Economic writers had created the terms for subsequent discussions of the market economy, but they did not control the use of those terms.

All historical writing carries with it a theory about human society. The historian who sets out to explore ideology is saying that the past cannot be understood without reconstructing the system of ideas through which the consciousness of men and women was organized. Implicit in this approach is the assertion that people do not choose their ideas freely but rather share in a socially constructed reality. In their infancy they learn a way to perceive the material world and acquire a set of concepts that explains their society's invisible world of values and truths. As adults, they partake in the reshaping of this ideology through their intellectual response to new experiences. People behave according to the ideas they hold, and these ideas are continuously exposed to reworking. It is in reference to this complex and elusive process that J.G.A. Pocock has written that "men cannot do what they have no means of saying they have done; and what they do must in part be what they can say and conceive that it is."[73]

Men in the seventeenth century found a way of conceiving of economic life as part of the natural order of things. The global dimensions of seventeenth-century trade and the rapid diffusion of certain commercial arrangements encouraged a long line of observers to conclude that common responses in the marketplace reflected innate human qualities. Anxious to understand the new sources of wealth, they took the market's transcendence of political boundaries as evidence of a natural force. The appeal of this concept, however, was inseparable from the attractiveness of the deductions to be drawn out of it. From Mun's prediction that the flow of treasure behind trade "must come to pass by a Necessity beyond all resistance" to Locke's disavowal of the extrinsic value of money, the belief in natural economic laws served as a solvent of political authority based upon will or sovereignty. In rejecting the rationalization for complete economic freedom, however, English leaders found a way of preserving natural economic laws without sacrificing political direction. The triumph of the balance-of-trade theory affirms the presence of choice in the forming of social truths. To reverse Pocock's sequential linkage of language and behavior we can say that men and women cannot long conceive of ideas that suggest actions they do not want performed. Which is another way of saying that in studying ideology we are looking at the vital point where the sensibilities of the past, the power distribution of the present, and the hopes for the future come together and shape the compelling ideas of an age.

[73] "Virtue and Commerce in the Eighteenth Century," *Journal of Interdisciplinary History* 3 (1972), 122.

Index

Abstract of the grievances of trade which oppress our poor, 162n
Account of the French usurpation, 112
Advancement of merchandize, 96n
Africa, 249
Aglionby, William, 76n
agriculture, 25ff, 36, 57ff, 84, 86ff, 100f, 124, 129ff, 151, 178, 233, 245, 273
Aldergate, 141
Allan, D. G., 58n
Amsterdam, 85, 228
Ananias and saphira discovered, 166
Anderson, Perry, 3n
Appleby, Andrew B., 28n
Appleby, Joyce Oldham, 221n
Apter, David E., 6
Aristotle, 24
Art of good husbandry, 133
Ashley, Maurice, 102n
Ashley, Sir William, 252, 267
Ashton, Robert, 32n, 103n
Ashton, T. S., 7n
Axtell, James, 190n
Aylmer, G. E., 54n

Bacon, Sir Francis, 34, 69, 115, 133, 244
balance-of-trade theory, 38-44, 81, 95, 125, 158ff, 167, 170, 174ff, 181, 198, 202ff, 231ff, 248ff, 259, 267ff, 269-71, 277
Baltic, 73, 248
Bank of England, 261, 267
Bannister, S., 267n
Barbon, Nicholas, 137, 166n, 168f, 172-83, 196f, 225, 229, 231, 234n, 252, 256, 258, 263, 267, 272
Barrow, Humphrey, 139
Battie, John, 119f
Beales, H. L., 131n
Bellers, John, 143f
Beloff, Max, 138, 236n
Bentham, Joseph, 69n

Berger, Peter L., 6n
Bethel, Slingsby, 133, 181n
Birmingham, 130
Birnbaum, Norman, 6n, 9n, 10n, 13n, 259
Birquet, J., 186n
Blanch, John, 192
Bland, John, 117
Blaug, Mark, 8n
Blaxton, John, 67f
Blith, William, 86
Blitz, R. C., 202n
Board of Trade, 249
Bodin, Jean, 49
Bolton, Robert, 67f
Bowley, Marian, 182n
Boyle, Robert, 188n
Brenner, Robert, 17n, 53, 55n, 102n, 105n
Brewster, Sir Francis, 135n, 142, 147, 163n, 197
Brief observations of J. C. concerning trade and interest of money, 90f, 215n
Briscoe, John, 118, 189, 237f, 251n
Bristol, 130

Calvinism, *see* religious attitudes
Canning, W., 186n
Canterbury, 76
Carter, William, 124f, 146, 148, 163f, 166n, 264n
Cary, John, 155, 163n, 170, 197, 208, 226
Certain considerations relating to the Royal African company, 161n, 163n
Chamberlayne, Edward, 134, 166, 215n
Chamberlen, Hugh, 211
Chamberlen, Peter, 110, 139f, 140n, 144
Chambers, J. D., 17n, 129n
Chaudhuri, K. N., 212n
Cherry, G. L., 249n

(281)

Child, Sir Josiah, 88-95, 113, 147, 149, 190f, 215, 257f, 267

Clark, G. N., 80n, 250n

Clark, Peter, 53, 130n, 218n, 262, 264

class, 10ff, 276ff

classical economic theory, 7-8, 12, 18-20, 80, 93, 248, 252, 254-57, 272

Clement, Simon, 196n, 250n

clothiers, 36ff, 100, 117, 123ff, 162, 194ff, 262, 274

Clothiers complaint, 167nn

Cobbett, William, 33n, 240n

Cocks, Sir Richard, 178

coinage, 20, 35, 37, 43ff, 102, 159, 199-241, 250

Coke, Roger, 77, 109, 113, 116, 119f, 135, 168, 172, 216, 242f, 255

Colchester, 76

Coleman, D. C., 153, 202n, 253n

Collins, John, 147, 258

Considerations requiring greater care for trade in England, 96n

Cook, John, 56f, 139f, 151

Cook, Moses, 86

Cooley, Charles Horton, 16n

Cooper, J. P., 17n, 54n, 101nn, 102n, 103n, 113n, 117, 133n

Cotton, Sir Robert, 49, 159

Coventry, Sir William, 188

Cradocke, Francis, 213

Cromwell, Oliver, 101

Culpeper, Sir Thomas, Jr., 83, 88-91, 122, 125, 143, 147f, 163n, 181n

Culpeper, Sir Thomas, Sr., 88, 94, 192n

Cypress, 121

Dalton, George, 14n, 182n

Davenant, Charles, 148, 164f, 167, 180n, 187, 191f, 255, 267

Davies, Godfrey, 57n, 163n

Davies, K. G., 164n, 165n, 262n

Davies, Margaret Gay, 27n, 29n

Davis, Ralph, 3n, 55n, 248n, 249n, 250n

Decker, Matthew, 158

Decus and tutamen, 233n, 234

Defoe, Daniel, 134, 144, 165, 172, 182, 197, 210, 262n

Derbyshire miners, 236

Dering, Sir Edward, 149

de Roover, Raymond, 65n, 180n, 223n

Dickson, P.G.M., 219n, 249n, 266, 273n

Digges, Sir Dudley, 106

Discourse consisting of motives, 109f, 113

Discourse of the commonweal of this realm of England, 38, 158

Discourse of the duties on merchandize, 185n

Discourse of the nature, use and advantages of trade, 184n, 192, 215n, 251n

Discourse of the necessity of encouraging mechanick industry, 156n

Dumont, Louis, 182n

Dunning, Richard, 131n

Dutch Republic, 73-98, 102f, 110, 120f, 125ff, 137, 140f, 161f, 185, 197, 203, 213, 215, 226, 228, 275n

Dymock, Cressy, 213n

East Anglia, 27

East India Company, 40f, 102ff, 125, 166ff, 195, 216

enclosures, 17, 58ff, 69

England's exchequer, 120n

Englands vanity, 134

Evelyn, John, 76

Everitt, Alan, 130, 152,

Eversley, D.E.C., 17n

Exeter, 130

Farnell, J. E., 103n, 120n

Fay, C. R., 219n, 236n, 261n

Feavearyear, Sir Albert, 102n, 218n, 228n, 235n, 239, 256, 262n

Fenton, Roger, 66f, 71f

Ferguson, Robert, 108f, 216

Filmer, Sir Robert, 24, 68

Firmin, Thomas, 125, 140f

Firth, C. H., 222n

Fisher, F. J., 141n

food production, *see* agriculture

INDEX

Ford, Edward, 213
Fortrey, Samuel, 83, 86f, 108, 122f, 136f, 161, 163, 207f, 216n
Foster, William, 106n
France, 8, 93, 109, 112, 121ff, 161, 171f, 180, 197, 205, 228, 248f, 261
Fromm, Erich, 9n
Further essay for the amendment of the gold and silver coins, 235n, 250n

Gardiner, Alderman Francis, 145, 168, 170-83, 227, 230, 234n, 256f, 272, 274n
Gardiner, S. R., 34n
Gaskell, Philip, 5n
Gay, E. F., 58n
Geertz, Clifford, 6n, 259n
Gentleman, Tobias, 74
Germany, 8f, 102, 167
Gerschenkron, Alexander, 8n
Gervaize, Lewis, 219, 233
Gilbert, Sir John, 95n
Glass, David Victor, 17n, 131n
Goffe, William, 76, 139f
Gonner, E.C.K., 57n
Goode, William J., 19n
Gould, J. D., 27n, 35n, 51n, 58n, 159n
Grand concern of England explained, 146n, 189n, 215n
Grascome, Samuel, 170n, 237, 239, 240n, 268
Graunt, John, 82f, 138, 164
Great necessity and advantage of preserving our own manufacturing, 166n, 195
Greenleaf, W. H., 265n
Gregory, T. E., 125

Haines, Richard, 87n, 126f, 140f, 142, 163, 209, 234
Hale, Sir Matthew, 143, 147, 149
Halhead, Henry, 69, 70n, 139
Halifax, 130, 236
Haller, William, 247n
Harrington, James, 24, 116
Hartlib, Samuel, 86, 101, 139f, 212f
Hartwell, R. M., 165n

Heaton, Herbert, 26n, 202n
Heckscher, Eli, 26n, 172n
Helleiner, Karl, 27n
Hexter, J. H., 10n
Hill, Christopher, 33, 268n
Hinton, R.W.K., 78, 115n, 159n, 202n, 212, 252n
Hirschman, Albert O., 247n, 254, 256n
Hobbes, Thomas, 24, 190f
Hobsbawm, Eric, 114, 275
Hodges, James, 138, 224, 229, 231, 234n, 266
Hodges, Sir William, 228
Holmes, G. S., 138n
Holmes, Nathaniel, 67f
Horsefield, J. Keith, 170n, 220n
Hoselitz, Bert F., 9n
Hoskins, W. G., 57n, 262n
Houghton, John, 86, 119, 146, 168, 175-79, 196, 227, 256f, 263, 272
Hull, 130
Humphreys, S. C., 62n, 246n

ideology, 5ff, 41, 46, 96ff, 217, 237, 259, 270, 278
Interest of money mistaken, 90, 112
Ireland, 119, 197
Is not the hand of Joab in all this?, 117, 189n
Italy, 8

Jacob, J. R., 188n
Jacob, Margaret C., 268n
John, A. H., 260n
Johnson, Edgar Augustus, 28n, 65n
Johnson, Thomas, 107
Jones, D. W., 218n, 249n
Jones, E. L., 17n, 260n, 262n
Jordan, W. K., 102n, 106n

Kayll, John, 75, 106
Kendal, 236
Kerridge, Eric, 101n
Keymer, John, 74f, 83, 111, 116, 160
Keynes, John Maynard, 8, 252
King, Gregory, 138, 165, 179f

INDEX

Kramnick, Isaac, 275n
Kuhn, Thomas, 41

labor, 15ff, 82, 126ff, 132ff, 144,
    152, 177, 182, 227, 245, 248
Lambert, James, 86
landlords, 11, 28, 31ff, 54f, 101,
    177, 215, 235, 246, 251, 260,
    264ff, 270, 276
Laslett, Peter, 19, 30n, 68n, 220n,
    236n, 249n
Law, John, 230n, 254n
Layton, Henry, 229-35, 237, 251n,
    254n, 274n
Lee, Joseph, 59f, 71, 87
Lee, Leonard, 139
Leeds, 130
Leicestershire, 60, 63
Leigh, Edward, 200
Leonard, E. M., 68n
L'Estrange, Sir Roger, 140n
*Letter from an English merchant
    at Amsterdam*, 234
Letter humbly offer'd, 225n, 231n,
    234n
Letter of advice, 235
*Letter to two members of Parlia-
    ment*, 234nn, 270n
Letwin, William, 109n, 171n,
    174n, 216n, 239n, 242, 253n,
    255n, 258
Levant, 104
Lewis, Mark, 214
Lichtheim, George, 6n
Lilburne, John, 107, 139
*Linnen and woollen manufactory
    discoursed*, 111, 146, 162
Little, David, 13n, 30n
Littleton, Edward, 154, 186n
Locke, John, 24, 113n, 170n, 184,
    188, 192, 203, 210, 220-41, 250,
    254, 258, 267, 270f, 273, 279
London, 4, 31, 46, 104, 117, 121,
    130, 137, 142, 147f, 165, 195, 245
Lowndes, William, 219ff, 231, 233,
    236
Luckmann, Thomas, 6n
Lukács, George, 12n
Luttrell, Narcissus, 240n

Macaulay, T. B., 222n

McCulloch, John Ramsay, 202n,
    251
McKendrick, N., 156n
McKinley, Erskine, 9n
Mackworth, Sir Humphrey, 138,
    211, 213
Macpherson, C. B., 14n, 15, 265n
Malthus, Thomas, 154
Malynes, Gerald de, 41-48, 50, 70,
    80, 94, 108, 191
Manchester, 121, 122n, 130
Mandeville, Bernard, 182n, 257
Manley, Thomas, 76, 91f, 125,
    142, 146, 148, 163
Mannheim, Karl, 6n
manufacturing, 58f, 81, 99ff, 104,
    113, 120ff, 135, 146ff, 159, 167ff,
    195ff, 233, 246, 261, 269, 271
Markham, Gervaise, 86
Marshall, T. H., 264n
Martyn, Henry, 167f, 171ff, 177,
    181f, 196, 216, 251f, 256, 263,
    267, 272
Marx, Karl, 7ff, 274f
May, John, 53n, 122n
Mediterranean, 36, 100, 248
Meek, Ronald, 8n, 12n, 253n
mercantile system, *see* balance-of-
    trade theory
Merchant Adventurers, 102, 104ff,
    110, 127
*Method proposed for the regu-
    lating the coin*, 230n, 231n,
    234n, 270n
Milles, Thomas, 117n
Misselden, Edward, 41-48, 50, 52,
    70, 80, 94, 118, 191, 198, 229,
    244, 271
Moir, T. L., 34n
Moore, Adam, 139, 141
Moore, John, 59ff, 139
Mun, Thomas, 37-41, 48f, 52, 69n,
    70, 76, 80, 91, 109, 115n, 116f,
    136, 152, 158f, 160f, 184, 191,
    198, 202n, 203f, 215n, 223, 229,
    244, 253, 255, 271, 279
Murray, Robert, 225n, 251

Nalson, John, 210n
Navigation Acts, 103, 120, 249
Neale, R. S., 265n, 275n

Nelson, Benjamin, 64n, 65n
Newcastle, 130
Norfolk, 196
North America, 105, 119
North, Sir Dudley, Jr., 134, 168f, 172f, 174n, 183, 196f, 226, 250f, 252, 256, 258, 263, 267, 272, 277
North, Sir Dudley, Sr., 134
Norwich, 130, 141, 195, 227

Only way to have the rents of England well paid, 219n

Parker, Henry, 107f, 142
Parliament, 5, 31ff, 58, 101, 103f, 225, 233, 235, 237, 239f, 249f, 266, 268, 270
Parsons, Talcott, 13n
Paterson, William, 267
patrimonialism, 30ff, 46f, 159, 198
Pauling, N. G., 153n, 172n, 253n
Peacham, Henry, 200
Pepys, Samuel, 218n
Petty, Sir William, 77, 81f, 92, 96, 122, 134, 138, 144, 147f, 152f, 164, 172n, 178, 180, 182n, 183n, 185, 204, 207f, 248, 258
Petyt, William, 125f, 136, 138, 147, 207
Philips, Fabian, 215n
Plumb, J. H., 265n, 268
Pocock, J.G.A., 34n, 268n, 275n, 278f
Poland, 42
Polanyi, Karl, 15f, 132n, 246n, 256n, 276
Pollexfen, John, 163, 166, 168, 173, 184, 197, 207, 255
Poor Laws, 3, 29, 53ff, 101, 131, 138ff, 143, 149, 163, 265, 277
Portugal, 85, 104, 119, 273
Postlewayt, Malachy, 158
Potter, William, 119, 207
Powell, Robert, 56f
Prat, Samuel, 234
press, public, 4f, 35, 48, 71, 186, 190n, 193, 201, 217
Price, Jacob, 253n
Priestly, Margaret, 123n
Primatt, Stephen, 165n
Privy Council, 35f, 219, 227

Profit and loss of the East-India-trade, 163, 167, 195
Proposals for the better management of the affairs of the poor, 155n
Proposals for the raising of the silver coin of England, 233n
Proposals to the Parliament, 234n
Puckle, James, 75, 138, 142, 149, 154
Pullberg, Stanley, 6n

Rabb, Theodore K., 32n, 102n
Raleigh, Sir Walter, 111, 160, 234
Ramsay, G. D., 53n, 100n
Reasons for a limited exportation of wooll, 148
Reasons humbly offered for the passing of a bill, 167, 194n
Redlich, Fritz, 253n, 273
Reflections upon a scandalous libel, 240n
religious attitudes, 13-19, 24, 47, 52ff, 95, 165f, 247, 276f
Reynell, Carew, 113, 136, 163
Rich, E. E., 158n
Riemersma, Jelle C., 253n
Right way to make money more plentiful, 234n
Roberts, Lewes, 106, 121, 122n, 160, 216
Robinson, Henry, 69n, 76f, 83, 87, 91, 95, 107, 119, 222n
Robinson, Joan, 8n
Roe, Sir Thomas, 49n, 160n
Russia, 104

Sandys, Sir Edwin, 76
Scarlett, John, 135n
Schumpeter, Joseph A., 8n
Scott, William Robert, 36n, 165n
Select observations of the incomparable Sir Walter Raleigh, 234n
self-interest, 93ff, 108, 115, 118, 183f, 187ff, 191ff, 247ff, 264ff
Shaw, William A., 95n, 222n
Sheffield, 130
Sheppard, William, 134
Sheridan, Thomas, 122, 126, 137, 186n, 188

Short reflections upon the present state of affairs in England, 251n

Siebert, Frederick, 5n, 190n

Slack, Paul, 53, 130n, 218, 262, 264

Skinner, Quentin, 190n, 265n

Smart, John, 186n

Smelzer, Neil, 14n

Smith, Adam, 7, 26, 94, 172, 182, 194, 202, 227n, 255, 271ff

Smith, Captain John, 86

Smith, W., 117n, 151n

Smyrna, 122

Solo, Robert, 18

Some seasonable memorandums, 219n

Some short considerations, 269n

Some thoughts concerning the better security of our trade, 177n, 249n

Spain, 74, 104, 119f, 124, 270

Sperling, J., 253n

Spitalfield silk throwers, 167

Spotswood, James, 68n

Sprinzak, Ehud, 13n

Standish, Arthur, 86

Stanleyes remedy, 139

Stone, Lawrence, 11n, 32n, 55, 103n, 264n

Suffolk, 196

Supple, Barry, 20n, 27n, 30n, 35n, 37n, 38n, 49n, 99, 199n, 202n, 204n, 229

Suviranta, Bruno, 38n, 158n, 166n, 199n, 202n, 206n, 216n

Sydenham, William, 186n

Sydney, Algernon, 24

Tawney, R. H., 8

taxation, 32ff, 134, 138ff, 150, 184ff, 210

Taylor, A.J.P., 189n

Taylor, James Stephen, 132n

Taylor, Silvanus, 69

Temple, Sir Richard, 224

Temple, Sir William, 75, 83, 137, 189, 198, 231, 234n, 251n

Thomas, Keith, 3n, 156n

Thomas, P. J., 167n, 250n, 261n, 267

Thomas, Sir Dalby, 133, 168, 171, 173, 177n, 181, 191, 211, 227, 256, 263, 272

Thompson, E. P., 27n, 53, 54n, 146n, 156n, 261n

Tillyard, E.M.W., 247n

Tipps, Dean C., 272n

Trevers, Joseph, 124

True Cess, 186n

True relation of the rise and progress of the East India company, 167n

Tucker, Josiah, 158

Turkey, 91, 104

Use and abuses of money, 85n, 210, 214

Usher, Abbott Payson, 187n

usury, 34, 39, 51, 63ff, 70, 87ff

Usury araigned, 69

Vaughan, Rowland, 86

Vaughn, Rice, 49, 94, 119, 179, 200, 204

Verney, Robert, 211

Vickaris, A., 231, 233f

Viner, Jacob, 150, 158n, 202n, 251f

Violet, Thomas, 92, 95, 121

Vogelin, Eric, 256

Waddell, D., 220n

Wagstaffe, Thomas, 219n, 240n

Wallerstein, Immanuel, 3n, 18n, 206n

Walter, John, 54n, 100n

Weber, Max, 12ff, 30, 276f

Webster, Charles, 86n, 101n, 213n

West Country, 27

Western, J. R., 265n, 268

Weston, Sir Richard, 86

Wheeler, John, 94, 105f, 116

Wiles, Richard C., 145, 202n, 253n

Williams, Dale Edward, 54n

Willson, David H., 34n

Wilson, Charles, 38n, 74n, 103n, 133n, 158, 165, 202n, 252ff, 261, 265n

Wilson, Thomas, 141

Winstanley, Gerald, 139
Word in season, 219n, 234n, 235n
Worsley, Benjamin, 77f, 81, 120
Wrightson, Keith, 54n, 100n

Wrigley, E. A., 130n, 165n

Yarranton, Andrew, 215f
Yorkshire, 27

Library of Congress Cataloging in Publication Data

Appleby, Joyce Oldham.
    Economic thought and ideology in seventeenth-
century England.

    Includes index.
    1.   Economics—England—History.   I.   Title.
HB103.A2A6   330'.0942   77-85527
ISBN 0-691-05265-4